SOLUTION FOCUSED ANXIETY MANAGEMENT

A Treatment and Training Manual

SOLUTION FOCUSED ANXIETY MANAGEMENT

A Treatment and Training Manual

ELLEN K. QUICK

Kaiser Permanente, San Diego

ELSEVIER

AMSTERDAM • BOSTON • HEIDELBERG • LONDON
NEW YORK • OXFORD • PARIS • SAN DIEGO
SAN FRANCISCO • SINGAPORE • SYDNEY • TOKYO

Academic Press is an imprint of Elsevier

Academic Press is an imprint of Elsevier
32 Jamestown Road, London NW1 7BY, UK
225 Wyman Street, Waltham, MA 02451, USA
525 B Street, Suite 1800, San Diego, CA 92101-4495, USA

First edition 2013

British Library Cataloguing-in-Publication Data
A catalogue record for this book is available from the British Library

Library of Congress Cataloging-in-Publication Data
A catalog record for this book is available from the Library of Congress

ISBN: 978-0-12-394421-4

For information on all Academic Press publications visit our website at elsevierdirect.com

Typeset by TNQ Books and Journals Pvt Ltd.
www.tnq.co.in

Printed and bound by CPI Group (UK) Ltd, Croydon, CR0 4YY
Transferred to digital print 2012

CONTENTS

PREFACE

I have had the privilege of seeing clients build their courage and coping skills for a very long time. During the early years of my practice (initially in the Pittsburgh, Pennsylvania area), I certainly did not view myself as having any more expertise with anxiety treatment than any other therapist. But I was a psychologist, and my non-psychologist colleagues assumed that anyone who had recently completed a psychology graduate program knew more about "the new behavior therapy for anxiety" than they did. Certainly, I wasn't doing solution-focused therapy at the time. Solution-focused therapy was just beginning to develop, and I had not yet heard of it.

An interesting exercise sometimes conducted in solution-focused training workshops asks therapists to do the following "sentence completion" exercise: "I first knew I was solution-focused when..." During the preparation of this book, I reflected on when the "anxiety management" I was conducting first became solution-focused. I think it happened long before "solution-focused" was a term that meant anything to me. In the early 1980s, during a presentation on phobia management to primary care physicians, I was talking about building "fear ladders" (the term we used, at that time, for *in vivo desensitization*), and a member of the audience asked, "Why don't you call it a courage ladder?" I did not know then, and I do not know now, the name of that physician. I probably did not thank him for his direction-changing question. I doubt that this physician realized that he was "solution-focused" or that his question was setting the tone for a wonderful new direction in anxiety management. As solution-focused therapists know, language and creative ideas make a tremendous difference and sometimes emerge in unexpected places.

This book presents the conceptual foundation, methods, and attitudes of a solution focused (and strategic solution focused) approach to anxiety management. It includes all the materials needed to teach the program in a four-session psychoeducational class (complete instructor guide and learner readings). It also covers how to use the approach in individual therapy. For readers interested in using the approach in their own lives, the book offers methods that can be used on one's own and/or in combination with consultation with healthcare providers.

The focus is on anxiety management, not "elimination." The idea is that people do not have to wait to fully eliminate their anxiety to experience it differently and to notice that it is not such a problem in their lives. The book demonstrates how solution focused anxiety management transforms anxiety to courage, coping, appropriate caution, and choice.

The primary audience for this book is the behavioral healthcare professional who treats anxiety disorders in adults. This audience includes psychologists, social workers, psychiatrists, marriage and family counselors, college health service personnel, psychiatric nurses, pastoral counselors, and trainees in those fields. Physicians and nurses who work in primary care and program developers and administrators in behavioral and integrated healthcare will also be interested in an evidence-based and cost-effective program that has a track record of service delivery in a large staff health maintenance organization.

The secondary audience for this work is people who are experiencing anxiety and their significant others. This group includes those who might be attending a solution focused anxiety management class. These readers will be particularly interested in the learner readings; they may be interested in the other materials as well. Some readers may be receiving other treatment for anxiety or other concerns, whereas other readers may be considering seeking treatment. Other readers may be exploring the self-help literature. These people want to learn about the topic and discover solutions in their own way and are an ideal audience for an approach that emphasizes doing what works for one's unique situation.

COMPANION WEBSITE AND MATERIALS THAT CAN BE DUPLICATED FREELY

A special feature of this book is its companion website, http://booksite.elsevier.com/9780123944214, accessible to anyone who purchases the book. This website includes the full text of the instructor notes (Chapters 3–6) and the learner readings (Appendices A–D). This hands-on resource makes this book user friendly to readers who prefer to use the material online.

In addition, the publisher has kindly agreed that the following forms used during the class may be duplicated freely: the Solution Focused Anxiety Management Class Description, (p. 27 in Chapter 2), the End of Session Form (p. 22 in Chapter 2 and at the end of each appendix), and Worksheets C.1, C.2, D.1, D.2, and D.3 in the appendices.

OVERVIEW OF THE BOOK

Chapter 1 introduces the conceptual foundation, attitudes, and methods of solution-focused practice and the author's strategic solution focused perspective. It discusses the concept of anxiety management and how it differs from an "anxiety elimination" paradigm. The chapter covers how the class began and evolved over the years. There is discussion of the "common and specific" components of evidence-based treatment and how this approach is similar to and different from cognitive behavioral therapy, Acceptance and Commitment Therapy, and process group therapy. Throughout, there is an assumption that people already have significant strengths and that they can discover and build on what works for them.

The practical details of planning and facilitating a solution focused anxiety management class are reviewed in Chapter 2. There is discussion of how to describe the program, with a handout that can be given to potential participants. The chapter covers how the book might best be used by different readers, including therapists teaching the program, therapists using it with individual clients, class participants, and people who are interested in learning the solution-focused philosophy, principles, and tools on their own. Common challenges encountered when teaching solution focused anxiety management—and solution-focused ways of managing them—are also addressed in this chapter.

Chapter 3 provides complete instructor notes for teaching Topic One. This session describes how normal physical reactions sometimes scare us, especially if we are "body reactors," an important concept introduced here. The material teaches how even scary sensations diminish on their own when you "just leave them alone." This session also introduces and invites the class to experience five physical coping techniques: "belly button" breathing, Claire Weekes' "wave" (great for panic), Autogenic Training, "Just Because" (also useful for anger and when one needs to be alert), and mindfulness. Participants are invited to sample and use what works for them.

The instructor notes for Topic Two are presented in Chapter 4. This chapter introduces exposure and habituation and the view that anxiety management is a fascinating combination of "the commonsense and the counterintuitive." This session covers building and using a "courage ladder." When exposure in "real life" is impractical, participants are invited to imagine encountering difficult scenarios—and coping with them. The session introduces the "Write, read and shred" exercise. People are encouraged to tap what they already know about learning new things and coping with discomfort and to notice what that tells them about "being anxious and doing it anyway."

Chapter 5 contains the instructor notes for Topic Three. Participants are invited to recognize thoughts that already support their courage and coping. The session presents some tools for transforming thoughts that increase anxiety. It emphasizes that acceptance—of uncertainty, danger, and existential realities—helps to remind us that having frightening thoughts does not mean that one is "crazy." Participants are encouraged to recognize supportive messages received in the past, along with those that they already give to others. They are invited to discover perspectives that resonate with personal images and experience and to notice how doing so makes a difference.

The instructor notes for Topic Four are presented in Chapter 6. This session addresses the interface between life issues and anxiety. It invites labeling "pros and cons" of decreasing anxiety, including openly acknowledging challenges that "being less anxious" might bring—and possible solutions. The presentation covers changing "I can't" to "I don't want to," the normalcy of ambivalence, and how assertiveness interfaces with anxiety management. Because people sometimes forget that life always includes challenges, the class invites reflection about areas where one already has healthy, appropriate caution. Participants are encouraged to recognize how "normal" anxiety (not "no anxiety") supports "the four Cs": courage, coping, appropriate caution, and choice.

Solution focused anxiety management works in individual therapy, and how to use the approach in individual sessions is the topic of Chapter 7. Using solution-focused methods and conveying solution-focused attitudes, the therapist collaborates with the client to discover and amplify what happens when anxiety is not a problem. Tools from the program are then introduced as appropriate, and they are adapted to the client's style and preferences. In addition, people often use individual sessions to extend what they have taken from the program. Case examples illustrate the process in brief therapy, single session therapy, and intermittent therapy over a number of years.

Chapter 8 elaborates on the perspective that appropriate caution is often a valuable component of solution focused anxiety management. There is discussion of the concept of defensive pessimism and its relationship to this program. Acceptance of a preference for routine and the predictable can be viewed as a personal style rather than as "psychopathology" that needs to be eliminated. Case examples illustrate these principles in individual solution focused anxiety management with clients who have received diagnoses of obsessive compulsive disorder and generalized anxiety disorder. The chapter provides some examples of how these ideas may emerge both in individual sessions and in discussion in the class.

Chapter 9 shares the wisdom of eleven solution-focused therapists. Through interview or written comments, these therapists describe how they have seen clients transform anxiety to courage, coping, appropriate caution, and choice. They discuss how they use and trust the basic solution-focused process. The therapists note whether they add other tools to the treatment; some do so, whereas others do not. They also comment on strengths their clients have shown and what these clients have taught them. The chapter summarizes the common themes and the diversity that emerged in the respondents' comments.

Chapter 10 looks at factors that may account for change in solution focused anxiety management. It describes a pilot qualitative analysis of what stood out to people from the program. Acceptance of discomfort and mixed feelings, "doing it even in the presence of anxiety," "baby steps," and a recognition that one is not alone were among the recurring themes. This chapter also discusses two factors that may explain why different components all work. First, there are the "common factors" that emerge in meta-analyses of psychotherapy outcome research: client variables, the therapeutic relationship, and expectancy of change. Second, the chapter discusses Fraser and Solovey's concept of "second-order change" as the "golden thread" that runs through interventions that "work" in psychotherapy. When people are anxious, their first reaction is often to take what Fraser and Solovey would call a "first-order change" approach that does not work well enough. Although they do so in different ways, the different components of this program all shift perspectives or invite the unexpected—all things that create second-order change. Finally, this chapter looks at some ways that solution focused anxiety management is an example of the continuing evolution of solution-focused practice, and it considers how readers can extend the approach and build on what works in multiple ways.

The book includes four appendices. They present the four learner readings, one for each session. All of the readings include ideas for practice on one's own. They invite learners to adapt and use the ideas in ways that work for them. Some of this material deliberately repeats sections of the instructor notes so that learners who do not wish to read the longer instructor notes may have the most important information, including all worksheets and end of-session suggestions. Like the instructor notes in Chapters 3–6, the learner readings (the four appendices) are on the companion website, as noted previously.

ACKNOWLEDGMENTS

The support and ideas of many, many people made this book possible. First, I am grateful to the mentors who contributed to my thinking about solution-focused practice over many years. The ideas developed by Steve de Shazer and Insoo Kim Berg and their colleagues at the Brief Family Therapy Center in Milwaukee have had an important role in the development of solution focused anxiety management. My work at the Mental Research Institute at Palo Alto (and with Richard Fisch in particular) was another important influence. Study with Milton Erickson also was the source of important ideas. Reid Wilson's ideas and creative strategic methods shaped my thinking as well. Colleagues from the San Diego Strategic Solution Focused Interest Group provided valuable support and wisdom and contributed to the development of the strategic solution focused perspective.

My passion for including multiple "tools in the toolbox" has led me to the work of many other scholars and therapists. Colleagues at the Sharp Rehabilitation Center Chronic Pain Management Program introduced me to the notion of "management, not elimination." I very much appreciate the ideas and methods described by Aaron Beck, Albert Ellis, Erik Erickson, Steven Hayes, Bill O'Hanlon, Claire Weekes, Joseph Wolpe, and many others.

I would like to thank Nikki Levy, Barbara Makinster, Chuck Hutchinson, and Caroline Johnson at Elsevier. Their support throughout the preparation of this book has been invaluable.

Several managers in the Department of Psychiatry and Addiction Medicine at Kaiser Permanente, San Diego, provided the opportunity to experiment with the program development that led to the initial creation of classes for people who wanted help with anxiety. In particular, Gary Wolfe, Marcia Kagnoff, John Blasi, Beverly Bernard, and Denise Costa provided valuable administrative support. My colleague Janice Brookes also taught some of the early classes, and I appreciate the ideas she has shared with me over the years. I am grateful for the opportunity I have had to collaborate with Dan Gizzo on research on solution-focused group therapy.

I appreciate the support, friendship, and clinical wisdom of my many friends and colleagues at Kaiser Permanente, at the SFBTA [Solution Focused

Brief Therapy Association], and the EBTA [European Brief Therapy Association]. I particularly want to thank the therapists who graciously agreed that their comments could be shared in this book: Elliott Connie, Yvonne Dolan, Heather Fiske, Adam Froerer, Bruce Gorden, Ross Kremsdorf, Jay McKeel, Linda Metcalf, Joel Simon, Frank Thomas, and Terry Willey.

I have had the privilege of working with so many incredibly courageous clients over the years. I have seen you transform fear into courage, coping, appropriate caution, and choice in multiple ways. You have tapped strengths, within you and in your worlds, in creative ways that I could never have imagined. I learned from you that I did not have to be afraid to suggest ideas, even if they seemed strange, because you knew what would and would not work for you. If something didn't fit, you let me know, and you did something different. You continue to demonstrate that anxiety does not prevent you from doing amazing things.

Finally, I want to acknowledge my husband, Frank, and my daughter, Melissa. Your support and love are so special to me.

My heartfelt thanks to all of you!

CHAPTER 1

What Is Solution Focused Anxiety Management, and How Is It Different from Other Approaches?

Solution focused anxiety management is a class—and a philosophy. This chapter introduces the conceptual foundation, attitudes, and methods of both the class and the overall perspective. The *class* is a four-session psychoeducational program for adults. It blends psychoeducation about anxiety and other concepts, some acceptance-based, with solution-focused, strategic, and cognitive behavioral components. It also utilizes group process. The material is presented from a solution-focused perspective, with a style designed to invite members to tap into and utilize individual strengths and ways of learning. The therapist trusts that class members will use the material and the experience in ways that work for them. The content can also be used in individual therapy, a topic discussed in more detail in Chapter 7.

In this approach, the focus is on anxiety *management*. This is different from an anxiety *elimination* paradigm. The idea is that people do not have to wait to fully eliminate their anxiety to be able to experience it differently and to notice that it is not such a problem in their lives. People can discover that they do not have to wait for their anxiety to disappear to do both ordinary and extraordinary things.

THE SOLUTION-FOCUSED PERSPECTIVE

Solution-focused therapy is a strength-based model, developed by Steve de Shazer, Insoo Kim Berg, and their colleagues at the Brief Family Therapy Center (BFTC) in the 1980s (de Shazer, 1985). Solution-focused therapy minimizes emphasis on past failings and problems. Instead, it focuses on clients' strengths and previous successes. It works from the client's understanding of the situation and what the client wants to be different. It also assumes that no problem happens all the time. There are exceptions: times when the problem *could have* happened but for some reason *did not* happen. The therapist attempts to discover what was different when the "exception" to the problem occurred. What was the difference that made a difference?

Solution Focused Anxiety Management
http://dx.doi.org/10.1016/B978-0-12-394421-4.00001-2

Once that is known, the goal is to amplify those differences, creating more and more occasions when the problem is not a problem.

METHODS IN SOLUTION-FOCUSED THERAPY

Solution-focused therapy often uses future-focused conversation, inviting people to describe a future time when the desired changes are already happening. The "miracle question" is sometimes considered to be solution-focused therapy's best-known method and "signature" technique.

However, solution-focused therapy is far more than miracle questions. In fact, a recent book is titled *More Than Miracles: The State of the Art of Solution-focused Therapy* (de Shazer & Dolan, 2007). Nonetheless, miracle question inquiry continues to be a valuable and versatile technique in solution-focused practice.

The basic miracle question says something like this: "Imagine that after you and I get done talking and you do whatever you're going to do today, eventually you go home, and go to bed, and fall asleep. And while you're sleeping, a miracle happens. And the miracle is that the problem you just told me about is resolved. It isn't a problem any more. What will be the first thing that will be different, that lets you know: 'This isn't a problem any more'?"

After the therapist asks this question and hears the response, it is important to conduct detailed follow-up inquiry. This important component frequently includes two kinds of questions: *difference* questions and *relationship* questions. Difference questions ask things like this: "What will be different?" Building on the last change described, the therapist invites specific detail. "What else?" "And as a result of what you've just described, what else will be different?" "And when *X* happens, what will be different about how you respond?" "And how will that make a difference?"

Relationship questions ask questions similar to the following: "Who will notice your change (using the language of whatever the person has just described)?" "And how will he/she be different, as a result of your changes?" "And how will that make a difference?" "Who else will notice?" "What will he/she notice about you?" "Really! And how might he/she respond?" "How will that make a difference?"

The therapist continues with this kind of inquiry, amplifying and inviting detail about multiple situations and relationships in the person's life. "And that other problem you were telling me about, what will be different about that, as a result of those other changes?" As the inquiry continues, more and more specific detail will be elicited, and it becomes increasingly likely that the person is describing some things that are already happening.

Then the therapist asks what is sometimes called an *exception* question: "This scenario you are describing—are there any pieces of it that are already happening?" It is extremely likely by now that the answer is "Yes." The therapist is then able to say, "Really? Tell me about it." Again, specifics are invited and highlighted. It often becomes evident quite quickly that the person did not have to wait for the full "miracle" to be able to experience important parts of it.

When it is clear that pieces of the solution are already happening, it follows that the person can do these things again. This is evident even if the therapist does not directly suggest it. (And some solution-focused therapists would say that the therapist does not have to suggest anything. Simply as a result of having elaborated this detail, people recognize what they want to do again.) Often, however, the therapist will directly (or indirectly) invite continuing pieces of the solution that are already present. Or there may be an invitation to observe or be curious about where and when these pieces will happen next.

In solution-focused therapy, it is of critical importance to use this detailed follow-up to the miracle question (or to any of its variations, discussed in more detail later). *This fact cannot be overemphasized.* Therapists who ask the miracle question, just get an answer or two, and move on to something else are often the ones who say, "I tried that solution-focused stuff, and it didn't work." The follow-up inquiry may be the most important—and clinically elegant—method in solution-focused therapy.

Another solution-focused tool is the *scaling question*. Scaling questions are by no means unique to solution-focused practice. They may be seen as similar to SUDS [Subjective Units of Discomfort Scales] and other rating scales. Here is how solution-focused therapists tend to use scaling questions. They often ask, "On a zero to ten scale, where zero is when the problem was at its worst and ten is when it isn't a problem any more, where are you now?" The next question might be, "How did you do get up to a three?" Then the therapist inquires, "And what will be different when you're at a four?"

What happens when the client describes a miracle that is "impossible" (something that could never really happen)? Here is an example from Steve de Shazer in a session with a man who had been seriously depressed since an accident in which he lost his arm. de Shazer asked the miracle question, and the man said he would have his arm back. de Shazer nodded and said, "Sure"—and he waited. After a long silence, the man said, "I guess you mean something that could happen." de Shazer nodded. The man then described how he would get up and make breakfast with his one arm. There was no further discussion about getting the arm back (de Shazer & Dolan, 2007, p. 40, as described in Quick, 2012, p. 105).

There are many different variations of the miracle question. It is absolutely not a requirement to use the word "miracle." In fact, sometimes the word "miracle" is deliberately omitted, because inquiry is always tailored to individual client variables and preferences.

The following are some examples of variations on the miracle question: "What are your best hopes from coming here? What will let you know those hopes have been met?" (George et al., 2009). "If we're having our next conversation and I'm asking you what's better or different, and you're telling me that you're feeling really good about how you're handling things, what might you be telling me?" "What will let you know you are on track to a solution?" "When you are going in the right direction, how will your email conversations (texts, tweets) be different?" "What will your Facebook friends notice about you?"

Variations used in the solution-focused Doing What Works Group (Quick & Gizzo, 2007; Quick, 2008) invite people to imagine "that this group helped you just as you hoped it would." In other sessions, participants envision "writing the next act" in the drama of their lives and "looking through a crystal ball" to a better time. At another session, they imagine what they will be describing at a "one-year group reunion." Some future-focused questions invite anticipation of "slips and recovery" (Quick, 2012).

One extremely important variation on the miracle question is often described as "the coping question." If a person has just been through something horrendous, a miracle question that makes it sound as though the problem is "gone" can come across as disrespectful, as if the therapist didn't "get it," as if the magnitude of the pain or fear had not been heard or appreciated. Expert solution-focused therapists often use a different kind of future-focused inquiry. Their coping questions ask something like this: "Given what you've been through, how *do* you get through the day?" One of the most common responses is this: "I don't know. I just do it."

As Quick (2008) has pointed out, sometimes simple behaviors include strength and courage. The wording of the coping question communicates a coping choice, even in simple behaviors. "How did you manage to keep going?" implies that it was not just by chance that the person got through.

Even if the coping behavior did not seem particularly remarkable at the time, the therapist is gently pointing out that the person did have a choice.

Sometimes the author asks class members if they know the answer to the following question: "When you're depressed, what's the reason to get up in the morning?" The answer is: "To go to the bathroom." People laugh—and they understand: The person who got up to go to bathroom could have lain there and wet the bed. There was an active choice, a coping choice, reflected in that seemingly simple decision.

What does solution-focused therapy do at the end of a session? Generally, solution-focused therapists give input to their clients. Sometimes they call it homework; often they talk about it as an experiment or a project. It might include noticing pieces of the miracle or doing more of what works, or it might invite doing something different. It might be noticing examples of coping, such as "how you do it when you have discomfort and get through it," or "when you slip, noticing how you get back on track." One tool, called the first session formula task, invites people to notice things in their life or family that they want to continue to have happen. The best solution-focused suggestions often include the client's own language and metaphors.

It might be noted that it is usually hard to predict at the beginning of a session of solution-focused therapy what suggestion will be given at the end, because that task is likely to be co-constructed, growing from shared language during the session. One of the interesting differences between homework in solution-focused therapy and homework in positive psychology/positive psychotherapy is the following: Positive psychotherapy (Seligman, Rashid, & Parks, 2006) more frequently suggests standard tasks, such as "List five things you're grateful for," whereas solution-focused therapy might not necessarily talk with a client about a concept such as gratitude unless it was already part of the client's language.

The same is true for how solution-focused therapists approach asking people to use journaling, writing, and record keeping. The therapist checks out whether writing is a useful tool for this person. If writing is useful, or if the person is interested in experimenting with it, it can become part of the therapy. If writing is experienced as a burden, irrelevant, or simply not helpful, it will not be required. This is part of a solution-focused attitude: The therapist assumes that people know the modalities that work best for them.

Solution-focused therapists use language in specific ways. As Trepper et al. (2010) pointed out,

> *[T]he signature questions used in solution-focused interviews are intended to set up a therapeutic process wherein practitioners listen for and absorb clients' words and meanings (regarding what is important to clients, what they want, and related successes), then formulate and ask the next question by connecting to clients' key words and phrases. Therapists then continue to listen and absorb as clients again answer from their frames of reference, and once again formulate and ask the next question by similarly connecting to the client's responses. It is through this continuing process of listening, absorbing, connecting, and client responding that practitioners and clients together co-construct new and altered meanings that build toward solutions.*

Some fascinating process research on microanalysis of solution-focused therapy sessions has recently indicated that solution-focused conversations do differ from conversations in other kinds of therapy. When they are compared with conversations in sessions of cognitive behavioral therapy, motivational interviewing, and client centered therapy, the following differences emerge. Solution-focused therapists tend to ask more questions, with less of a "teaching" or psychoeducational component. They tend to make more positive utterances. When they paraphrase or repeat client language, they tend to preserve positive language or coping statements rather than pain or pathology (De Jong & Bavelas, 2010).

ATTITUDES IN SOLUTION-FOCUSED THERAPY

Solution-focused practice involves much more than applying a set of methods. Being solution-focused is also an attitude (Quick, 2012). That attitude includes multiple components. There is an absolute refusal to pathologize people for their complaints. There is little discussion of pathology or formal psychiatric diagnosis. In some situations, there may be a sense that diagnostic labeling has the potential to make things worse. That is the case even when there appears to be a biological component and when medicine is part of the solution. At the same time, there is an important exception: When the *client* (or someone else who is in the client's world) thinks that those things are important, the therapist is ready to actively address them. The attitudinal components of "speaking the client's language" and respecting what the client thinks is important take priority over the attitudinal components that focus away from discussion of diagnosis or symptoms!

The same thing is true for the past and the history. The therapist does not need to understand every detail about the history or *even the problem* to be able to facilitate solution-building now. However, if it is important to the *client* for the therapist to hear something about the problem or the past, the therapist listens attentively. What the client chooses to emphasize probably holds clues about the solution.

As described previously, there is an assumption that clients have strengths and resources, both within themselves and in their worlds, and that those strengths frequently become the foundation for individualized solutions. It is assumed that when one can label one positive thing, that leads to another, and then another. Small positive changes can be amplified, leading to bigger changes. There is an expectation that therapy will be brief—"except when it's not." The length of the treatment will be tailored to the situation. But the therapist's initial assumption is likely to be an expectation that solutions can emerge quickly. Any change suggested might be small and seemingly insignificant, but its effects might be far reaching. A tiny change can be like tossing a stone into a pond: It sends out ever-widening circles. And the "solution" of "coming for treatment" should not become a burden or add to the problem.

Another component of a solution-focused attitude is openness to the unexpected. Solution-focused therapists value careful listening to the client. Sometimes this is described as "leading from behind." There is an expectation that "extreme listening" (Bliss, 2010) or being a "solution detective" (Sharry, Madden, & Darmody, 2003) can provide "clues" (de Shazer, 1988) toward the solution. The assumption is that the client, not the therapist, is the true expert on this situation. As noted previously, the best ideas for practice frequently come from the client, or they may be co-created.

Solution-focused therapy conveys an attitude of respect, in which clients are valued and supported. Insoo Kim Berg often said "Wow!" in response to something a client said. The therapist certainly does not have to say "Wow!" all the time—in fact, each therapist needs to discover and utilize what is most special about his or her personal style—but the "Wow!" exclamation reflects a core attitude. It captures the flavor of solution-focused admiration, often mixed with surprise and excitement, about something the client said or recognized.

STRATEGIC SOLUTION FOCUSED THERAPY

In addition to relatively "pure" solution-focused therapy, there are "blended" approaches. As Trepper et al. (2010) pointed out,

> *[S]olution-focused therapy can easily be used as an addendum to other therapies. One of the original and primary tenets of SFBT [Solution Focused Brief Therapy]—"If something is working, do more of it"—suggests that therapists should encourage their clients to continue with other therapies and approaches that are helpful... SFBT could be used in addition to or as a component of a comprehensive treatment program.*

One blended model, strategic solution focused therapy (Quick, 2008), sometimes called "the doing what works approach solution-focused therapy" (Quick, 2010), combines solution-focused methods with those from brief strategic therapy. Brief strategic therapy was developed at the Mental Research Institute (MRI) in Palo Alto in the 1970s by John Weakand, Richard Fisch, Paul Watzlawick, and their colleagues (Fisch, Weakland, & Segal, 1982). It should be noted that de Shazer and Berg initially used the MRI model, eventually changing it in some important ways.

The strategic solution focused approach retains the MRI emphasis on precise clarification of the client's complaint, combining this with the solution-focused emphasis on detailed elaboration of the solution. In addition, strategic solution focused therapy retains the MRI idea that sometimes people's best attempts to solve problems unwittingly result in the maintenance of those problems, and sometimes well-meaning efforts make things worse. Changing what does *not* work complements amplifying what *does* work in strategic solution focused therapy.

Like solution-focused therapy, strategic solution focused therapy is far more than technique. Many of the same attitudes described previously are part of strategic solution focused practice. Like solution-focused therapists, strategic solution focused therapists deemphasize pathology. They assume that multiple "ingredients of solution" are already present and can be amplified. As Quick (2012) pointed out, strategic solution focused therapists also assume that clients can learn, understand, and apply the philosophy of "doing what works and changing what does not," as well as other psychoeducational material. As a result, strategic solution focused therapists may do somewhat more "teaching" than "pure" solution-focused therapists. Strategic solution focused therapists assume that ambivalence and "slips and recovery" are normal phenomena, and they believe that it can be useful to openly discuss them. As Quick (2012, p. 26) noted, "flexibility is valued in the strategic solution focused approach. There is an expectation that different things will work for different people—and for the same person at different times."

THE EVOLUTION OF SOLUTION FOCUSED ANXIETY MANAGEMENT

The content and format of the solution focused anxiety management program have evolved over more than 30 years. During that time, the author practiced in an outpatient psychiatric setting in a large staff model health maintenance organization. Working with adults, she and her colleagues noticed that they were seeing many people who struggled with anxiety. They began to consider how psychoeducational groups or classes might be helpful to these people.

The first class the author developed and facilitated was a two-session Phobia Management Class. Referrals came immediately, and the class was always filled. It soon became apparent that many of the people who came to the class described concerns other than phobias. Even without specific instruction on how to apply the material to other anxiety complaints, they spontaneously did so. It was becoming clear that the class was not simply "phobia management" any more. Soon the class grew to four sessions and expanded to cover other anxiety disorders as well.

Solution-focused therapy was just beginning to develop in 1982, and it was not well known. The author did not know much about it at that time. Some of the other approaches that are included in this program, such as the acceptance/mindfulness component, were not very well known, either. Relaxation techniques, behavior therapy, and cognitive therapy were the treatments of choice. Dr. Claire Weekes, an Australian psychiatrist, had written about "riding through" panic attacks, and this concept was tremendously helpful to people (Weekes, 1978). "Riding the wave" is very much like mindfulness. It was clear that people who struggled with anxiety also experienced concerns in other areas of their lives, and it seemed important to address the interface between anxiety and other life issues.

Before working at the health maintenance organization, the author worked briefly in a physical rehabilitation setting and was involved in the development of some pain management programs. The philosophy there emphasized "management, not elimination." This approach made sense with anxiety as well. Just as people did not have to wait for all of their medical problems to heal to have a vastly improved quality of life, they did not have to wait for every symptom of anxiety to disappear in order to feel and function much, much better.

Another influence on the anxiety management program was the author's experience of spending some time training with Dr. Milton Erickson in the late 1970s. A psychiatrist and hypnotist who himself had polio—and nevertheless did amazing things—Erickson used an indirect approach that emphasized "utilization." Utilizing the qualities and characteristics unique to the individual, Erickson created trance states that built on strengths and knowledge that a person already had. No *formal* hypnosis was used in the original anxiety management programs (or in the variations that evolved later), but a flavor of inviting people to utilize strengths has been present in this approach since the very beginning.

Over the years, the author became interested in the strategic and solution-focused approaches and increasingly incorporated them into her clinical practice. "You can—and you don't have to," a message adapted from Bill O'Hanlon's ideas about "inclusive" therapy (O'Hanlon, 2003), also became part of the strategic solution focused approach. In the cognitive behavioral arena, more became known about the techniques of "interoceptive exposure" for panic (Craske, Rowe, Lewin, & Noriega-Dimitri, 1997) and "exposure and response prevention" for obsessions and compulsions (Huppert & Roth, 2003). This information could be seamlessly included in the class. As more became known about stages of change (Prochaska & DiClemente, 1992) and motivational interviewing (Miller & Rollick, 2002), ideas about respecting client readiness for change were introduced as well. And as Acceptance and Commitment Therapy and mindfulness-based cognitive therapy became better known, ideas from those perspectives felt tremendously consistent with what the author believed and was teaching about anxiety management.

The instructor notes used for the class and shared with colleagues evolved over the years, as did the handouts given at every session. As the author's style became more solution-focused, there was a change in the language used. Earlier versions, both of the instructor notes and the learner readings, seem more rigid and absolute, as the author looks back on them now. The current versions are softer, more often inviting people to notice what works for them, with fewer "prescriptions" and implications that certain homework tasks will work for everyone. And as research on evidence-based treatment increasingly pointed to the importance of "common factors," described in more detail later in this chapter, there was an increasing emphasis on encouraging people to use those pieces of the class that fit for them and to discard what did not fit.

HOW IS SOLUTION FOCUSED ANXIETY MANAGEMENT SIMILAR TO AND DIFFERENT FROM COGNITIVE BEHAVIORAL THERAPY FOR ANXIETY?

This program clearly includes a cognitive behavioral component, with a strong mindfulness and acceptance-based flavor. The variation of mindfulness based cognitive therapy, discussed later in this chapter, is particularly similar to solution focused anxiety management in many ways. Many readers of this book probably have some familiarity with a basic cognitive behavioral perspective. That approach is briefly summarized here.

As its name suggests, cognitive behavioral therapy (sometimes called CBT) includes two components: the cognitive and the behavioral. The behavioral part came first chronologically. "Behavior therapy," as it was called, included systematic desensitization, or graduated exposure to feared stimuli. This could be done "in vivo" (in real life), or when that was not possible or practical, in one's imagination. The latter technique is sometimes done in combination with physical relaxation and/or guided imagery. The idea is that relaxation and comfort are incompatible with anxious arousal. Gradually, the client learns to relax in the once-feared situation.

Another behavioral principle is that behaviors that are followed by positive reinforcement are likely to increase in frequency. As people engage in the once-feared behaviors and discover that anticipated negative consequences do not follow, they often discover something else as well: Positive things frequently begin to happen. As the new "approach" behaviors are "reinforced," the "habit strength" of those new behaviors increases. Wolpe and Lazarus (1966) described many details of behavior therapy.

The "cognitive" aspect, sometimes referred to as the "second wave" of CBT, says something like this: Thoughts, assumptions, and beliefs exert a tremendous influence on how people feel and on what they do. Often without realizing it, people have "cognitive distortions" that result in subjective distress and maladaptive behavior. In anxiety, the feeling is most frequently fear, and the behavior is often avoidance. Treatment involves identifying and challenging the maladaptive thoughts. It sometimes also includes looking at *patterns* of thoughts, or consistent ways of viewing the world, sometimes called core "schemas," that may appear across different situations. Therapists teach clients alternate ways of looking at things, and they encourage identification of triggers, automatic thoughts, and alternate thoughts. Often clients are asked to keep written "thought records." Ellis (2003), who used the term "Rational Emotive Therapy" to describe his approach, and Beck (1993) were among the therapists who introduced the notion of reducing distress by changing one's thoughts. In therapy that is "cognitive behavioral," changing one's thoughts is combined with gradually changing one's behavior.

What is sometimes called the "third wave" of CBT adds this view: If "first wave" treatment attempted to change behavior, and the "second wave" emphasized changing thoughts, the "third wave" adds the idea of changing one's *relationship* to one's thoughts (Hayes, Follette, & Linehan, 2004). Mindfulness based cognitive therapy (Segal, Williams, & Teasdale, 2002) and

Acceptance and Commitment Therapy, described in more detail in the next section, are examples of "third wave" approaches.

Although CBT is clearly part of the program presented in this book, solution focused anxiety management includes additional components and perspectives that are not present in most cognitive behavioral treatments for anxiety. The psychoeducation/information about the developmental stages of adulthood, "ambivalence training," and the discussion of "the commonsense and the counterintuitive" go beyond what is included in most cognitive behavioral approaches for anxiety. And the solution-focused flavor, with its invitation to discover and tap resources and ways of learning not directly connected to one's anxiety concerns, is somewhat different. The permission to discard certain tools—including changing one's thoughts, if doing so is not particularly helpful—would not typically be found in cognitive behavioral therapy.

HOW IS SOLUTION FOCUSED ANXIETY MANAGEMENT SIMILAR TO AND DIFFERENT FROM ACCEPTANCE AND COMMITMENT THERAPY FOR ANXIETY?

Solution focused anxiety management is also similar in many ways to Acceptance and Commitment Therapy (ACT, pronounced like the word "act," not like the letters "a-c-t"). Eifert and Forsyth (2005) described ACT in the following way:

> *In a nutshell, ACT is about helping clients to do three things: accept themselves and others with compassion, choose valued directions for their lives, and commit to action that leads them in those directions. ACT teaches clients that it is okay to have whatever unwanted thoughts and feelings their minds and bodies come up with. Rather than struggling with those thoughts and feelings, clients learn new ways of relating to them as experiences to be had. (pp. 6–7)*

In a review of Eifert and Forsyth's work, Saavedra (2006) pointed out that although CBT and ACT may appear to use similar procedures, there are important differences. He wrote

> *[W]hile CBT focuses on symptom management and reduction, ACT focuses on symptom acceptance and doing, in spite of all the inner stuff that may show up, for purposes of living a chosen, valued life. ACT claims convincingly that the road to a good life and mental health is not trying to feel good, but to become able to do what is required (i.e., act) to live a meaningful life, guided by a person's valued directions.*
>
> *Maybe exposure work, perhaps the main contribution of the behavioral tradition to psychotherapy, best illustrates the contrast between ACT and CBT: while in CBT exposure is undertaken with the purpose of reducing symptomatology, in*

> *ACT it is undertaken with the purpose of increasing behavioral flexibility, i.e., expanding the behavioral repertoire of the person in the presence of anxiety provoking stimuli, and ultimately actualiz[ing] willingness to move in the direction of the person's values.*

Addressing an audience of therapists, Walser (2011) recently commented that many ACT therapists believe that the fields of psychology and psychiatry may have done the public a disservice by being very quick to assign labels of psychopathology to common undesired experiences and feelings such as anxiety. People assume that "normalcy" means no anxiety. When they feel anxious, they compare themselves with that ideal and feel that something is terribly wrong with them. Walser (2011) pointed out that some people who have objectively minor psychological (and medical) conditions stay home from school, work, and other life activities, whereas others who have significant psychological and medical challenges nonetheless manage to "show up for life." According to ACT, anxiety is simply part of life. Therefore, the goal for the anxious person does not have to be—and probably should not be—an anxiety-free existence. Rather, the challenge is to label what is meaningful and to "show up" for those activities that are important and consistent with one's values, even when anxiety is present.

As indicated previously, acceptance and mindfulness are critical ingredients in both ACT and solution focused anxiety management. Dr. Steven Hayes's image of "holding your discomfort gently in your hand, like a delicate flower, as you walk forward toward a life worth living" (Hayes, 2006) is a beautiful and poignant perspective, one that often resonates well with anxious people. This is highly consistent with a solution-focused perspective, because solution-focused therapists know that even in the presence of significant distress, including significant anxiety, people do some pretty amazing things.

The author has found it useful to share this perspective directly with many anxious people, both in classes and in individual sessions. The balance between acceptance and change is addressed extensively in strategic solution focused therapy in particular, and the concept appears in multiple ways in solution focused anxiety management. However, solution focused anxiety management is also different from ACT in some important ways. Solution-focused therapy has somewhat less direct emphasis on identification of core values and commitment to action than Acceptance and Commitment Therapy does. In addition, the solution-focused flavor of this class and some of the exercises have a different "feel" from some ACT techniques and exercises. The "You can—and you don't have to" perspective is given more emphasis in the approach emphasized in this book. Sometimes people discover that "not acting" is an important ingredient of the solution.

THE STRATEGIC COMPONENT

As noted earlier, the author typically uses a strategic solution focused approach, and the strategic component is very much a part of solution focused anxiety management. Strategic therapists describe how "attempted solutions," things done in an attempt to solve a problem, too often have the opposite effect. Not only do they not solve the problem, but they may contribute to the maintenance of that problem. For example, telling oneself to "relax" sometimes is ineffective and even makes anxiety worse. One strategic therapist, Reid Wilson, described ways of disrupting patterns and helping clients recognize that sometimes "you actually have to go toward distress to get better instead of being relaxed" (Wilson, in Yapko, 2011). This is absolutely the opposite of what most people expect! Solution focused anxiety management introduces the notion of "the commonsense and the counterintuitive" as an ingredient of the solution, with the idea that sometimes doing what works includes things which may seem to be paradoxical but which nevertheless "work."

WHAT MAKES THIS PROGRAM "SOLUTION-FOCUSED"?

This program is solution-focused because it repeatedly invites discovery-based learning and assumes that many "ingredients of solution" are already present in a person's life and can be amplified. There is a deep assumption that clients can discover and build on what works for them. "Coping questions," described earlier, emerge throughout the class. Even when tools and information from other modalities are presented, the solution-focused attitudes are predominant.

One might ask the following two questions: First, if this is "solution-focused therapy," why doesn't it start with or emphasize the miracle question? Second, why would a program that claims to be "solution-focused" include so much didactic information? Those questions are addressed next.

The miracle question is a powerful and versatile technique, one that the author regularly uses in both individual therapy and in process groups. (How to use the miracle question in a group setting, in the solution-focused "Doing What Works Group," is described elsewhere [Quick, 2008].) The author regularly uses variations of miracle questioning with many, many people who complain of anxiety. But miracle question inquiry (the original version, using the word "miracle") is *not* a core component of the class.

Why not? When people are feeling anxious, their most common initial response to the miracle question is "I won't feel anxious any more." In individual therapy, and, to some extent, in a process group, there is an immediate opportunity to elaborate what "not feeling anxious any more" will look like. The therapist invites a detailed description of how the person will cope with unusual sensations and intrusive thoughts when anxiety is not so much of a problem. But in a class, especially a class where many participants may not be speaking aloud, there is far less opportunity for individual elaboration of the solution scenario. Far too often, the anxious person takes from this exercise an "anxiety elimination" perspective—and then feels disillusioned when "anxiety elimination" does not happen. As emphasized throughout this book, solution focused anxiety management classes emphasize anxiety *management*, in contrast to anxiety elimination. The "management" perspective is, in itself, a solution-focused philosophy. In this program, techniques other than the miracle question are used to invite participants to envision a future where anxiety is not so much a problem.

Traditional solution-focused therapy includes far less didactic information than this program. As noted previously, one might reasonably ask: Is it consistent with solution-focused practice to add the kind of information presented here? The author believes that it is, and she believes that the therapists who developed solution-focused therapy thought so, too. Dr. Terry Trepper has described a conversation he had with Insoo Kim Berg about this in regard to presenting specific techniques in sex therapy. Berg said, "Just because you're solution focused doesn't mean you get stupid" (Trepper, Treyger, & Yalowitzh, 2007). It is fully consistent with a larger theme of building on what works to use techniques that are available and have been demonstrated to make a difference with particular concerns.

WHY IS THIS PROGRAM PRESENTED AS A CLASS?

The initial reason for offering a class was the recognition that many therapists in the clinic were providing the same information about managing anxiety to many clients. Many individual sessions were spent teaching the same principles. There were several reasons to experiment with the class format. It would be a cost-effective way of presenting the material, and clients might benefit from the experience of being in the same room with other people who had similar concerns. Many people who experience panic or other anxiety symptoms have never met anyone else who acknowledged symptoms like theirs. They are afraid that they are terribly abnormal—sick, dying, or going crazy. The experience of being in a room with other people with similar concerns could be tremendously therapeutic, even if class members did not interact with each other very much.

The experience of running the class immediately confirmed the author's hunch that the class setting would be useful for many people. (As with any approach, nothing works for everyone. Some people simply don't like classes, and they shouldn't be required to attend them.)

HOW DOES THIS APPROACH FIT WITH EVIDENCE-BASED TREATMENT?

Readers of this book probably recognize the importance of providing evidence-based treatment in behavioral healthcare. But exactly what "counts" as evidence-based treatment? There is a lively debate going on in the field about that. On one hand, some professionals take "the specific treatments position." These people assert that specific methods and treatments should be used for specific conditions (e.g., "cognitive therapy for depression" or "exposure therapy for phobias").

There is also "the common factors position." Lambert (1992) found that careful examination of meta-analyses of psychotherapy outcome research provided the following interesting information: 40% of the variance could be accounted for by client factors—things like personal strengths, resources, social networks, values, motivation. All of these are things that a person brings to the treatment *before he or she ever gets into the therapist's office!* Another 30% was explained by relationship factors—the warmth, caring, and empathy in the therapeutic alliance. It is important to emphasize that this refers to the therapeutic alliance as the *client* perceives it. "Hope," or positive expectancy or anticipation of change, accounted for another 15%. *Only 15%* was accounted for by "the model" or specific techniques. That percentage is significantly smaller than many therapists might predict.

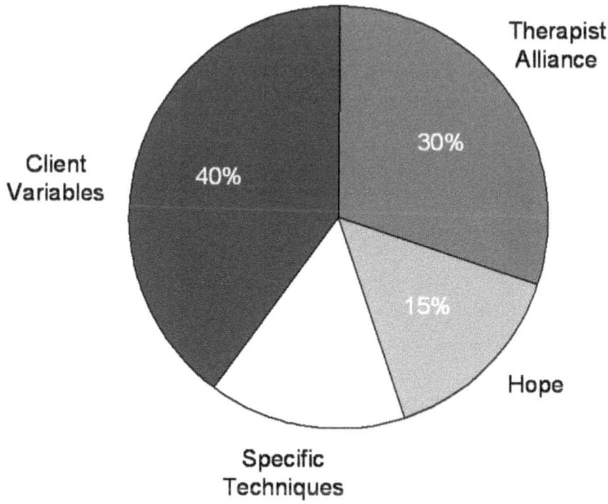

Figure 1.1 Common factors "pie chart."

Solution focused anxiety management attempts to tap the "common factors." To utilize that essential "client variables" component, the program repeatedly invites participants to use the information and tools presented in the class in ways that work for them. Participants are encouraged to use strengths and ways of learning that are already in their repertoires.

The "relationship" component is also present. In any group or class, group members have a relationship with the facilitator. They also have relationships with each other and with the material. A "same boat phenomenon" occurs when people recognize that they are not alone with their concerns.

An expectancy of positive change develops when people join a class, see a curriculum, and learn that this was designed for people with concerns "just like theirs." And when they experience and discover that they already have skills and abilities to cope with their discomfort, "hope" grows.

In all of these ways, solution-focused practice in general and solution focused anxiety management in particular create and enhance the common factors. The following pie chart illustrates this phenomenon.

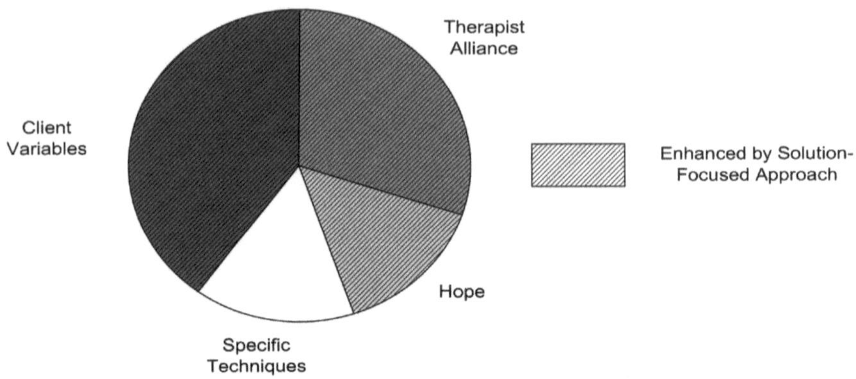

Figure 1.2 Factors enhanced by solution-focused approach.

What about the specific techniques? They may account for only 15% of the variance, but that 15% can be of huge importance. In the solution focused anxiety management class, there is often discussion about how solutions, like recipes, have multiple ingredients. The dried cranberries and sun-dried tomatoes in the author's favorite risotto recipe may comprise less than 15% of the volume, but they clearly contribute to the distinctive flavor. In the same way, cognitive behavioral techniques, acceptance, and mindfulness have been demonstrated in multiple studies to be associated with successful treatment of anxiety.

Does this combination of techniques, presented in this kind of class setting, "work"? Informal studies, conducted over the years, suggest that the answer is "Yes." On a number of occasions over the years, people who have come to the class have completed anxiety rating scales at each session, and ratings of anxiety have decreased after participation in the class (Quick, 1983; Quick, 1996). A recent pilot study also collected some written comments about what participants wanted to remember from the program, and informal qualitative research on that information is presented in Chapter 10. People "take" from the class what resonates for them, that which fits with their readiness for change. Those who are ready for action take action, whereas those who are still contemplating change take a new perspective and "permission" to change at their own pace. More formal research on this program would clearly be desirable—and may be conducted by some readers of this book in the future.

CHAPTER 2

Conducting a Solution Focused Anxiety Management Class: "The Nuts and the Bolts"

This chapter covers the details of conducting a four-session solution focused anxiety management class, a program that is inclusive and user-friendly for both the leader and the participants. The message "You can—and you don't have to" is conveyed in multiple ways. For professionals teaching the class, the instructor notes can be used exactly as they are, or they can be adapted. For participants, this is a class, not a group. Self-disclosure is not required, so it is "safe" for people who are anxious about being in a setting where they would "have to talk." Significant others are welcome (but not required) to attend. The chapter covers how people may begin any week and how anyone who is interested is welcome to attend. The chapter also describes what people can expect to happen at a solution focused anxiety management class.

As described in Chapter 1, the focus in this program is on anxiety management, not "elimination." Throughout, the program reminds participants that people do not have to wait to fully eliminate their anxiety to be able to experience it differently and to notice that it is not such a problem in their lives.

Anyone who is interested in learning about managing anxiety is welcome to attend this program. It is not necessary for someone to have a formal "diagnosis" of an anxiety disorder. Some people who come to the class do have such a diagnosis and have struggled with feelings of panic, phobia, worry, shyness, obsessive thoughts, compulsive behaviors, or post traumatic stress disorder for many years. Some describe depression and other unwanted feelings in addition to their concerns about anxiety. Other class members have just recently begun to experience feelings of panic, whereas others are feeling anxious about some specific life situation. Some may have been diagnosed with a condition other than anxiety, but "anxiety" is the name they give to their subjective experience. All are welcome.

http://dx.doi.org/10.1016/B978-0-12-394421-4.00002-4

People do need sufficient cognitive functioning to understand and participate in the process, and they need to be able to sit in a classroom for about an hour and a half. Severe and acute medical symptoms (e.g., severe pain) or acute behavioral symptoms (e.g., constant speech, active hallucinations) or active substance use (e.g., coming to class drunk or high) can interfere with learning and the process. However, the same people who might not be able to benefit from the process when symptoms such as those described here are acute often benefit immensely at some later time. Comorbid diagnoses of depression, personality disorder, substance abuse, and medical conditions are not automatic contraindications for inclusion.

Significant others are welcome, and encouraged to attend, but it is perfectly fine for people to come alone—consistent with the idea that people will do what works for them. Sometimes people come alone and then decide to repeat the class accompanied by a significant other. At times they may hope that the people they bring will use the tools too. Some people who come to the class also take medicine, and some also see individual therapists. Sometimes that individual therapist is the class facilitator, and sometimes it is someone else. For some members, the class is the only service or treatment for anxiety they need or want. For others, it is a first step in care. After completing the class, some people request individual (or couple or family) sessions. Those who have found the group process component especially helpful may join another group or class.

The material is organized so that it can be presented in a class format, in four weekly sessions. Sessions typically last one and a half to two hours. Members may begin any week, and the topics keep repeating. It should be noted that the program is described to members as a "class," not a "group." The idea is that the instructor will be doing most of the talking (giving information), assuring members that no one is ever put on the spot to say "what I am anxious about" or why he or she is there.

The only things people are asked to share, if they are comfortable doing so, are their first names, at the beginning of each session, and their responses to the "What do you want to remember?" question at the end. There are opportunities for discussion and participation in exercises, but those are entirely optional. Some people learn best by talking, whereas for others, "freedom from any pressure to talk" is essential for comfort and safety. When there is absolutely no pressure to talk, people often decide that they wish to do so!

Usually, chairs are arranged in a circle so that class participants can see one another. The instructor sits near a blackboard (or white board or flip chart). Each session begins with a general orientation to the solution focused anxiety management program. Following this, the instructor often suggests going around the room and sharing first names. Whether to include this "introduction component" may depend a bit on the size of the class. When the class is small, everyone may feel more comfortable when first names are shared. *Not* inviting introductions may feel impolite, impersonal, or awkward for people who will be spending more than an hour together. When the class is larger, however, it may feel more appropriate to skip the introductions. Hearing far more names than one can possibly remember may not be helpful and in fact can increase anxiety for some people. Whether or not to invite the sharing of first names is really up to the instructor.

Then the session's information is presented, with exercises, some written, as described in the instructor notes. Readings are suggested at the end of every session. They are included in the four appendices of this book and on the accompanying online website. Each session ends with an opportunity for discussion and some ideas for practice.

At the end of the session, the instructor also distributes the End of Session Form. This short form includes a scaling question. Participants are asked to select a number on a zero to ten scale, where zero is "When you first called for help with your anxiety" and ten is "Your level of concern or caution is appropriate, not excessive. Anxiety is not so much a problem any more." There are also three open-ended questions:

- What do you want to remember from today?
- What helps you to cope with discomfort, uncertainty, worry, and stress?
- What else do you want to continue, because you know it works for you?

If possible, this form is duplicated so that participants and the instructor can each keep a copy.

The End of Session Form, printed here, may be reproduced. For the convenience of learners, it is also included as the final page in each of the four learner readings, which, as noted, are in Appendices A–D and also in the online companion website that accompanies this book.

Finally, the instructor invites members to go around the room and briefly share what each most wants to remember from today.

SOLUTION FOCUSED ANXIETY MANAGEMENT

END OF SESSION FORM

Name ______________________________ Date______________________

When you first called for help with your anxiety	Your level of concern or caution is appropriate, not excessive. Anxiety is not so much a problem any more

0 1 2 3 4 5 6 7 8 9 10

What do you want to remember from today?

What helps you to cope with discomfort, uncertainty, worry, and stress?

What else do you want to continue, because you know it works for you?

HOW IS THIS PROGRAM SIMILAR TO AND DIFFERENT FROM GROUP THERAPY?

As described in the preceding chapter, this program initially began as a way of providing information to multiple people at the same time, with the hope that it would be helpful for people to recognize that their concerns were not unique. It quickly became clear that participants very much appreciated the opportunity to simply be in the same room with other people who had concerns similar to their own. Even knowing that concerns were so common that an "anxiety management class" existed was reassuring for some people.

This is a "class" and not a "group" for two reasons. First, there is a great deal of material to cover. Second, many people who experience anxiety are anxious about being around other people and "having to talk." "Group therapy," where people generally anticipate sharing and discussing personal concerns, can feel threatening to some people when they are anxious. A "class," on the other hand, is a setting that most people have been in on multiple occasions, and it is one that is often acceptable to them.

The author's experience has been that when self-disclosure is not required, many people comfortably ask questions and participate in exercises. Some go further, choosing to share information about their lives or concerns. In response, other class members sometimes volunteer their experiences, and a kind of group process emerges, even though this is a "class" and not a "group." In practice, most sessions include some people who talk more and some who talk less. That provides an opportunity to introduce the "You can—and you don't have to" perspective that is valuable to so many people.

This program offers members the opportunity to begin any week. This provides immediate access to the class. There is also the opportunity for new members to hear other people describe positive changes they have made, and this builds hope, one of the common factors associated with change. For many people, hope is a critical ingredient of the solution. It has not seemed to make any difference which topic someone hears first, and members have expressed appreciation for the opportunity to start the class right away.

It certainly would be possible to present this information in a slightly different format, with a new class beginning every four weeks. In this variation, all members would begin with Topic One and learn together for four weeks. This could contribute to group cohesiveness. However, many people would probably have to wait almost a month to begin the program. In the author's practice, this has not been the preferred option. But it certainly could be tried elsewhere, if that seemed to be a useful variation for a particular setting.

Therapists who facilitate process groups may wonder if there is a way to use solution focused anxiety management in groups they are currently running. This definitely can be done, at any time that anxiety emerges as a theme during a session. If it is consistent with the therapist's style to offer a comment or to suggest an exercise or group experience, he or she can seamlessly add any part of this program. Because of how common anxiety is, it is highly likely that multiple group members will indicate that the therapist's input resonates for them. Those participant responses provide an opportunity for the group therapist to process similarities and differences.

The therapist might mention that the "Four Cs"—courage, coping, appropriate caution, and choice—are sometimes described as "ingredients of solution" for anxiety. He or she might ask group members to notice where these are already happening. Group members are frequently tolerating discomfort, taking interpersonal risks, and accepting input from others as part of the group process. When this occurs, the therapist can comment on it, pointing out that the "Four Cs" are happening right here in the group, as well as in people's daily lives.

WHAT ABOUT MEDICATION?

Some people who come to classes like these are already taking medicine for their anxiety, sometimes for many years. Others begin taking medication around the same time they start this program. Many other people who come to the class use no medicine at all. Summarizing what the literature says about medicine in anxiety disorders, Dr. Alisa Duclos-Robinson (2009) recently stated that for panic, non-medication treatments, including those included in this program, are recommended as a first-line approach. However, as described throughout this book, treatment works best when it is tailored to individual needs and preferences. As with so many things, medication is sometimes—but not always—an "ingredient of the solution."

HOW TO USE THIS INFORMATION IF YOU ARE TEACHING OR PREPARING TO TEACH A SOLUTION FOCUSED ANXIETY MANAGEMENT CLASS

Chapters 3–6 present detailed instructions for facilitating this program. As noted previously, an introduction to the program begins each session, since new members may join the class any week. For the convenience of the instructor, this introduction is included in each of the four "scripts." As noted earlier, Appendices A–D of this book include the learner readings, one for each of the four sessions. Both the instructor notes and the learner readings are also available on the companion website that accompanies this book.

The reader might be wondering: Do I have to memorize the "script" as outlined in this book to be able to teach this program? No! An underlying tenet of the solution-focused approach is the belief that people will do what works for them. It would be presumptuous and hypocritical for this book to say that this applies to our clients—but not to us as therapists or class facilitators. This book came to be because multiple therapists have asked the author to share the program as she ran it. The reader is welcome to use the examples, style, and language presented here if it is helpful to do. In addition, readers who will be facilitating solution focused anxiety management are actively encouraged to adapt the program so that it works for them. Every facilitator has a unique style, with individual language and ways of presenting material. Integral parts of being solution-focused are recognizing and using one's unique resources and special strengths, so therapists are enthusiastically encouraged to let their personal styles as facilitators shine through!

The one exception to this might be if one is using this program as part of clinical research on the solution focused anxiety management program. "Fidelity to the model" is sometimes discussed in the research literature as an important component of clinical research. If one is conducting research on this program, having the full "script" and readings makes it very easy to administer the program exactly as described in this book.

If this kind of research is being conducted, one can seamlessly weave a program evaluation component into the clinical work by doing the following two things. First, intake paperwork in the treatment setting can be designed to include the same scaling question included in the End of Session Form. ("Please circle a number on a zero to ten scale, where zero is 'When you first called for help with your anxiety' and ten is 'Your level of concern or caution is appropriate, not excessive. Anxiety is not so much a problem any more.'") Second, the instructor (or a research associate) can compile the numerical data (scaling question responses) from the intake paperwork and End of Session Forms. Since the same question is being asked on multiple occasions, with numerical ratings each time, various repeated measures research designs are possible. In addition, the narrative comments from the End of Session Forms provide a rich source of data.

Qualitative analyses, both formal and informal, could categorize themes that emerge. More sophisticated research designs could further examine whether particular clusters or patterns in the narrative data are associated with improvement on the numerical scaling question ratings. This kind of clinical research is very much needed in the field. In addition, it can easily turn into a dissertation, thesis, or publication, becoming something that "works" on multiple levels: for the investigator, for the client, and for development of an even more robust evidence base on the efficacy of solution-focused practice.

HOW TO DESCRIBE THE PROGRAM AND INVITE PARTICIPANTS

All of the information described in this chapter can be shared with prospective participants and referral sources (therapists, psychiatrists, physicians and other healthcare providers in primary care and other specialties, clergy, teachers, school counselors, etc.). During intake appointments in psychotherapy settings, therapists can describe the program as "an item on the menu." When clients are requesting tools for managing their anxiety, it can be particularly valuable to let people know that solution focused anxiety management exists and is available immediately—or at any time in the future. The form on the next page (which may be reproduced freely, and which can easily be adapted to include details about time and location) describes the format and content of the class.

If this program is offered over time in a particular treatment setting, both providers and consumers may come to expect that this is the "default first step" when someone expresses concerns about anxiety. That is, all other things being equal, coming to the class will be seen as the first step in treatment. Of course, all treatment plans need to be tailored to individual client preferences and needs. Some people feel more comfortable beginning the class after they have had a few sessions with an individual therapist. If the therapist who is facilitating the class also sees people individually, it is easy for him or her to invite clients to attend as an adjunct to individual therapy. Clients can also be told that they are welcome to repeat the class if they wish. As noted previously, some people choose to come alone and then repeat the class, sometimes immediately and sometimes many months or even years later, with a significant other accompanying them. The solution-focused attitudes of flexibility and "one size does not fit all" emerge clearly here.

SOLUTION FOCUSED ANXIETY MANAGEMENT

Description of Class

- A class for courage, coping, appropriate caution, and choice
- Four weekly sessions
- Participants may begin any week
- Significant others welcome (but not required) to attend
- This is a class, mostly instructor presentation. Participant questions, comments, and discussion welcome, mostly at the end of each session.

1. **Physical Sensations and Coping Techniques**
   Normal physical reactions to stressors: how they sometimes scare us (the panic cycle)
   Discovering how sensations diminish on their own
   "Body reactors" (and "mind reactors")
   Smorgasbord of coping tools: belly button breathing, "the wave" (for panic), Autogenic Training, "Just Because," and mindfulness
   Sampling and discovering what works for you

2. **Behavioral Techniques**
   The commonsense and the counterintuitive
   Exposure and habituation
   "Courage ladder" (for phobias and many other things)
   Exposure to sensations (for panic)
   Variations for obsessive compulsive disorder and generalized anxiety disorder
   Discovering what you already know about "having discomfort and doing it anyway"

3. **Thinking Techniques**
   The "cognitive perspective": recognizing how thoughts make a difference
   Accepting (reality *and* your reaction to it) and
   Changing (your thoughts *and* "your relationship to your thoughts")—the "third wave cognitive behavioral perspective"

4. **Life Issues and Anxiety**
   Pros and cons of managing anxiety—and discovering strategies for coping with "the cons"
   "Ambivalence 101": Mixed feelings are normal
   How assertiveness enhances courage, coping, appropriate caution, and choice
   Issues on "the road of life" (independent of anxiety)
   Appropriate caution (not "*no* anxiety")
   Envisioning travel on the "road of life" from this perspective

CHALLENGES ENCOUNTERED AND MANAGING THEM

Sometimes people who are experiencing frequent or severe panic attacks are concerned that they will panic during the class. Other people who have felt panic for the first time share that fear. When people voice these concerns, it is valuable to validate and empathize with those feelings. Of course! It can be pretty scary to think about being in an unfamiliar room, usually with the door closed, with a bunch of strangers! The instructor may be a total stranger, and even if one has been told about the class, one does not really know what it will be like—or how one's body will react in a new setting. People who are afraid that they will become panicky during the class can be reminded that it is fine to leave the room at any time, for a restroom break or any other reason, with no questions asked. They may also be invited to select a chair near the door. One can leave and come back, and if, for any reason, one decides to leave and not return, the sessions "just keep repeating," and it is fine to come back the next week, or at a later time.

The number of people who worry about having a panic attack during a class is far greater than the number of those who actually have one. But sometimes this does happen. What happens when this occurs? Especially when reassured ahead of time that they may do so, participants occasionally leave briefly. Most do not leave the building. Almost always they return. Some comment at the end of the session that they had sensations of panic at some time during the class—and that the sensations diminished on their own. When this occurs, there is an opportunity for the class facilitator to highlight (to that participant and everyone else) the strength demonstrated just a few minutes ago! Occasionally someone says, "I'm panicking right now!" Again, this provides an opportunity to normalize the experience. The facilitator might point out that this was a here-and-now example of courage and "riding through" uncomfortable sensations. After sensations have subsided, the therapist might ask this solution-focused question: "How did you get through that just now?" This question elicits details of courage and coping.

Some prospective members worry that they will "pass out" or faint in a room full of people. In the author's experience, this did happen exactly once, years ago. The reader might wonder: Was the person who fainted someone who had severe panic attacks? No. Was it someone who had worried about fainting? No. The person who fainted was someone without any known anxiety or severe medical conditions: a therapist trainee who was observing the class and who had not eaten breakfast that morning! Here is what happened after she fainted. Class members expressed concern. The trainee "came to" on her own. She was embarrassed and apologetic. Clinic support staff escorted her to Primary Care (in an adjacent building) to be medically cleared. The next week she returned to observe again and to let the members know that she was fine. Several participants commented that it had actually been helpful to observe the process. If the "worst happened" and they fainted, they now knew what would happen.

Some participants expect something different from what actually occurs in the class. They may think they are coming to an unstructured process group, a medication evaluation, an assessment for psychiatric disability or time off work, or an individual therapy session. This may occur either because the class was not accurately explained or because someone misunderstood what was presented. More often, the latter is the case, since it is not uncommon for all of us to sometimes "hear" what we hope to hear. Occasionally someone wants to ventilate at length about a personal situation, to give emphatic advice that is not being requested, or to push quieter members to talk more than they want to. The instructor does need to use his or her clinical skills and knowledge of group process on these occasions.

In spite of an instructor's best efforts to clarify to referring providers and prospective members that attendees need to be able to sit in a room and make use of the process, occasionally someone comes who is not in a position to do so. In addition to the situations described previously, occasionally a participant is experiencing cognitive impairment, acute medical symptoms (such as severe pain), acute behavioral symptoms (such as manic speech, active hallucinations), or active substance use (coming to class drunk or high). What happens when there is someone whose issues interfere with understanding and participating in the process? The therapist manages the situation and may talk with the member (and/or the referring provider) after the class about the fact that this may not be the best time for this person to attend. But in the author's experience, this situation does not really happen very often.

What about people who come once or twice and then do not return? Depending on the setting, the facilitator or the referring provider may want to contact the person. Maybe the person got what was needed. Maybe something else became more urgent. Maybe the timing was not right. People are welcome to return later to complete the class. The author has had the experience of clients calling more than a year later to ask "Which week is the topic on *X*?" Or, maybe the class was simply not a good fit. After all, as Norcross (2005) pointed out, nothing works for everyone!

HOW TO USE THIS INFORMATION IF YOU ARE A THERAPIST WHO SEES PEOPLE INDIVIDUALLY

This program has been designed for and is used primarily in a class format, but the information can certainly be presented in individual sessions as well. It can be used by therapists of any theoretical orientation. When the client wants tools for anxiety management, the therapist can offer this material—in its entirety or specific pieces—and invite the client to use it in a way that fits for him or her. Chapters 7 and 8 describe this in more detail, with particular emphasis on how the program fits with solution-focused or strategic solution focused individual therapy, including some case examples.

HOW TO USE THIS INFORMATION IF YOU ARE TAKING A SOLUTION FOCUSED ANXIETY MANAGEMENT CLASS

For readers who are currently enrolled in this program, the learner readings in Appendices A–D (and the online companion website) may be the section of this book that is of greatest interest. The class instructor may recommend particular sections after specific topics have been presented. Class participants are welcome to read the instructor notes (and any other parts of the book that are of interest) as well. Some of the case examples may remind participants of experiences other class members have described. Other sections of the book may stimulate thinking about new ways of creating solutions and building courage. Reflecting about the many different ways people cope and make choices might lead to a question to ask or a topic to bring up during the discussion section of the class.

The reader may notice that the instructor and learner versions have considerable overlap. That is intentional: The idea is for the readings to include much of what is presented in class so that no one feels pressure to take notes or capture ideas before they "get away."

One might ask: Does it interfere with the learning process for the learner to have access to the instructor information, maybe even before material has been presented? Definitely not! Learning often increases with repetition, and there are no "secrets" hidden in the instructor version. The more the learner understands about the program and the thinking on which it is based, the better.

HOW TO USE THIS INFORMATION IF YOU ARE NOT TAKING A SOLUTION FOCUSED ANXIETY MANAGEMENT CLASS AND WOULD LIKE TO LEARN THIS MATERIAL ON YOUR OWN

People learn on their own for a variety of reasons. Some prefer not to consult with therapists, doctors, or counselors. Others don't know where to go, or they don't have insurance or money to pay for care. Some don't have transportation. Some don't go anywhere very often, either because of anxiety or for some other reason. Some may be concerned that a doctor will give them a diagnosis they don't want or tell them they should take medicine that they don't want to take. Some have gone for care in the past and have not found it helpful. Some might be considering seeing a counselor at some point in the future, but not just yet. And some people just prefer to do things on their own. If, for whatever reason, you are using this program on your own, you might find the following thoughts useful.

Readers of this book who are not currently taking a solution focused anxiety management class but who are interested in learning the material are invited to read the instructor notes in Chapters 3–6. You might want to imagine that you are actually taking a solution focused anxiety management class. The instructor might be this author, or a therapist or counselor that you have worked with in the past, or it might be someone completely different. The reader might imagine that the instructor is extending an invitation to you in the following way.

The instructor begins the class with a warm welcome. You hear that this is going to be a class about courage and strength, and that your being here today is a good thing that you are doing for yourself.

Next there is discussion of what happens during the class. Following introductions, there will be a presentation of some information. This will last through most of the time in the class. After the information part, there will be time for discussion and questions. The instructor explains that no one is ever "required to talk" in this class. As far as participating in discussions goes, the philosophy is "You can—and you don't have to." The instructor also notes that the concept of "You can—and you don't have to" will appear multiple times during the class, because it applies to so many things.

The instructor explains that at the conclusion of the class, people fill out a short form. This form will invite you to rate your own progress and to write down what you most want to remember, or your individual "take home message" from the day. There will be an opportunity to share this aloud, if you wish.

You will hear that there are four different information presentations and that the topics just keep repeating. So it is fine to begin any week during the cycle. You will learn that there are readings for each topic and that parts of that material repeat what is presented at the class. The instructor will mention that after people have been to all four classes, they are welcome to go through the series again, either right away, or at a later time, if they ever want to.

The instructor will also encourage you to bring a significant other to the class, if you would like to. For many people, the more that someone in their lives understands about anxiety management, the better. Of course, it's also perfectly okay to come to this class alone. You will hear encouragement to use this program and all of the material in it in whatever way works best for you. The instructor will tell you that "discovering and building on what works for you" is a message you will hear over and over again in this program.

A really important thing you will hear from the instructor is the name of the class, Solution Focused Anxiety Management. You will learn that the program is *not* called "solution focused anxiety *elimination*" (even though "anxiety elimination" is what people typically want)! The instructor will explain that this program won't claim to teach you how to make all of your anxiety disappear, but it *will* teach you how to be stubborn enough not to let anxiety get in the way of things you want to do. You will hear that you don't have to wait for anxiety to totally go away in order to do things, both the tasks of daily living and some wonderful, amazing things.

You might imagine the other people in the room. Some don't say very much, whereas a few make lots of comments. Someone smiles at you. One person asks several questions about panic attacks, so you conclude that this person must be struggling with those sensations. For many of the people, you have absolutely no idea what they might be anxious about. In fact, sometimes it's hard to tell who is there as a significant other and who is there for him or herself.

In the class, you will hear a variety of ideas. The instructor may describe "the Four Cs" (courage, coping, appropriate caution, and choice). Some of these ideas may be new to you, while others may remind you of things you already know but may not have associated with the growth of courage. At the end of the session, as other members say aloud what they want to remember, you may hear some reactions very similar to your own. Other reactions may be very different.

Later, as you review the learner readings, you may remember more details from the class. You might do some of the experiments suggested, and you might find yourself just naturally modifying them in a way that fits for you. And you might remember: That is exactly what the instructor said might happen!

The following week, you will see some familiar faces, along with some new ones, since members join and graduate at every session. The class will seem more familiar. You might find yourself adding more thoughts when there is an invitation for class input.

After you have completed all four sessions, you will probably notice that your courage and coping skills continue to develop over time. You may occasionally decide that you want to review the learner readings again. Now that you have been practicing, different parts of the program may stand out to you. And you may discover your courage growing in multiple ways, including some that you hadn't anticipated. Positive changes often appear in unexpected places long after attending a solution focused anxiety management class.

If you are having symptoms that concern you or your family, you may decide to consult a therapist, physician, or clergy, in addition to participating in this program. You might also want to share this information with the support people in your life, so that they can know about the good things you are doing for yourself by using the information in this book. By understanding what you are learning, they may be able to support your journey toward courage in multiple ways.

CHAPTER 3

Instructor Notes for Topic One: Physical Reactions and Coping Techniques

WELCOME AND INTRODUCTION

(Instructor may want to bring copies of the End of Session Form to this session. This form is p. 22 , in Chapter 2; it is also the final page of the learner readings for this session [Appendix A]. Or the instructor may use an equivalent form, tailored to the specifics of the practice setting.)

Welcome to Solution Focused Anxiety Management! I'm delighted you're all here today! We are going to be celebrating and building courage, and this is an awesome thing you're doing for yourself, being here today. Just being here takes courage and is a step in the right direction!

For those of you who are here today for the first time, I want to go over what we do in here. We go around and share first names, although if our class is so big that we will never remember them, we may decide to skip our introductions. Then I present some information about managing anxiety. That part is mostly me talking, for two reasons. First, there are a lot of things I want to be sure to have enough time to tell you. Second, in a class on anxiety, there are sometimes people who wouldn't feel comfortable if they felt as though they "had to talk." So, as far as talking out loud in here goes, "You can—and you don't have to." By the way, "You can—and you don't have to" is a phrase that you're going to hear again and again in this class because it applies to so many things!

Anyway, after the information part, we take some time for discussion, questions, whatever people want to talk about and that we have time to talk about. Then we end with a short form for you to fill out, and by going around and everyone having a chance to say aloud, if you want to, what you want to remember or take with you from today. We do the same thing every week. There are four different information presentations. Every time you'll be encouraged to do some reading, and parts of that material repeat exactly what I'm presenting. We do that because some people have requested it in the past, so you don't have to feel like you have to take notes. After people

Solution Focused Anxiety Management
http://dx.doi.org/10.1016/B978-0-12-394421-4.00003-6

have been to all four classes, they're welcome to go through the series again, either right away, or at a later time, if they ever want to.

Significant others are welcome and encouraged to come with you to the class, too, if you would like them to do so. Many people find that the more that someone in their lives understands about anxiety management, the better! If someone in your life isn't here today, it's fine to repeat a session to bring him or her along. And, of course, it's perfectly okay to come to this class by yourself. We want you to use this program and all of the material we're going to be giving you in a way that works for you. That's a message you'll probably hear from me over and over again in here. So you can bring someone with you—and you don't have to! That is another one of the many ways that you can decide how you want to use this program.

Now I want to emphasize something about the name of this class, Solution Focused Anxiety Management. I want you all to hear clearly that it's not called "solution focused anxiety *elimination*." Of course, "anxiety elimination" is what people want! So it's important for you to be an "informed consumer." This class isn't going to claim to teach you how to make all of your anxiety disappear, but it *will* teach you how to be stubborn enough not to let it get in the way of things you want to do. You don't have to wait for anxiety to totally go away to be able to do things, both the tasks of daily living and some wonderful, amazing things.

We're real informal in here. If you need to take a break, just feel free to step out any time and come on back in.

Our one rule is confidentiality: What you hear about other people's lives stays in this room, and you can expect that same confidentiality from everyone else. But any principles or information you learn may be shouted from the rooftops! And what you discover about yourself can be shared or kept private, in whatever combination, and in whatever way feels right for you.

What questions can I answer for you now?

(Instructor may invite sharing of first names here, if desired.)

PHYSICAL REACTIONS AND COPING TECHNIQUES

Today we're going to be talking about physical reactions and some ways of dealing with them. When confronted with a stressor, people—and not just people, animals too—may have certain physiological reactions. Our bodies make chemicals that produce these reactions. These reactions may seem maladaptive, but they have a purpose: They are the body's preparation for dealing with a stressor.

In our caveman-ancestors' days, if a tiger is coming out of the jungle to eat you, it's totally adaptive to have your adrenaline flowing so you can either go after the tiger or run very fast in the opposite direction. In fact, those of our ancestors who didn't have enough adrenaline flowing maybe got eaten by the tiger, and they didn't live to pass along their genes to the next generations. It actually makes a fascinating theory about why there's such a high incidence of anxiety in the population!

So, now I'm going to invite you all to consider this question: What are some of the things that the good old human body does in response to stress? This could be your own body, or other people's. These can be things you've experienced personally, and they can also be things you've observed in other people or heard of. We're going to see how many we can come up with today.

(The instructor picks up a marker, stands at the board,[1] *and waits for someone to speak. Usually this happens almost immediately. As participants generate reactions, the instructor lists them on the board. Usually the list soon includes many of the following.)*

Your heart starts to pound.
Your breathing gets fast.
Can't concentrate.
The room starts to spin.
Feel like you have to get out of there.
You sweat.
Face and neck get red and blotchy.
Stomach starts to hurt.
Headaches.
Weakness.
I can't swallow.
My hands start to tingle.
You feel like you're going to faint.
You can't think of anything to say.
Your voice wavers.
I start to cry.

(The instructor might notice that some reactions might not technically be "symptoms of anxiety." That doesn't matter. If someone says it, it goes on the list. If no

[1] This might be a blackboard with chalk, whiteboard, or flip chart with markers, depending on the setting. In some settings, an overhead projector, PowerPoint, or other electronic media may be used. Throughout this book, using "board and markers" refers to any of these.

one speaks, or little is generated, the instructor might prompt, with questions like the following.)

What has anyone ever noticed happens to your heart when you're under stress?

What else has anyone noticed in the chest?

Where else in your body have you noticed changes?

(For reactions where some people may experience "too much" of something while others might experience "too little" of the same thing, the instructor might invite awareness of that phenomenon by asking something like this.)

So, what happens to your sleep when you're under stress?

(Someone will probably say "You can't sleep." If someone else does not spontaneously say "I sleep all the time. I don't get out of bed," the instructor might ask this.)

I'm curious if anyone has ever had the *opposite* thing happen to your sleep, that you sleep *more*? What else is like that, where some people do more of it when they're under stress, and some do less?

(This usually generates conversation about eating, energy, being around other people, talking, feeling slowed down or "speeded up." The instructor might prompt the class to consider these things. There might be a comment like this.)

It's like the saying: "The same fire that melts the butter hardens the egg."

(If this "saying" brings blank stares, the instructor might explain.)

It means that the same external thing, the heat on the stove, creates opposite reactions in different substances. You've never heard that one? Well, you're hearing it now!

(When a number of sensations and reactions have been listed, the instructor asks this.)

When a bunch of these things start happening, what starts going through your mind about what might be happening to you?

(The following are now added to the list by the instructor, if not spontaneously mentioned now [or previously].)

Sometimes people feel like they're having a heart attack, or a stroke.

Or like you're losing it, going crazy, that someone is going to take you away.

Or that you're dying.

This stuff can be scary!

What all this means is that everybody is different, and some people respond more strongly in some systems of their bodies than in others. It's like how some people sunburn more easily than other people do. Like, if all of us in this room were out in the sun for the same amount of time, some of us might get browner, and some of us would get redder, and some of us would get freckles, and some of us might not notice any difference. It doesn't mean anyone's skin is any better than anyone else's. It just means we're all different.

And sometimes there's a part of your body that's always been sensitive to stress. You might think of it as a physical predisposition. An example would be if someone is a "stomach reactor." Maybe that person remembers that, as a little boy, he always got low-level tummy aches before tests. Then, maybe in high school he couldn't eat before a big game. Maybe it wasn't a huge, big deal, but as he thinks back, he might recognize that his "stomach thing" was always there a little. So maybe now, as an adult, he's having it in a more intense way. Why might that be? Well, there are a number of possible reasons. Maybe he's meeting a stressor at a time when his resistance is already low because of fatigue or illness. Or maybe there was some recent change in his life or conflict with somebody or financial problems—or some combination of those things, because sometimes it seems as though everything is happening to you at once. But, for whatever reason, or combination of reasons, he might have his stomach reaction more intensely than he ever did before.

So, all of these reactions we just wrote on the board can be *normal* reactions to a stressor, and *they are not necessarily dangerous*. Now, I have to emphasize here: I am most definitely *not* saying that reactions like stomach pain and chest pain and dizziness can't be dangerous! Because they definitely can be. And if *anyone* here is having a physical symptom that you are concerned about, or a change in a medical condition that hasn't been checked out by a doctor, then you definitely should get that checked out. But I suspect that a lot of you *have* been checked out by a doctor or at the emergency room—that's actually one of the things that sometimes leads people to come to a class like this. They get examined and told that they are medically okay, that it was "just anxiety." Has that happened to anyone? *(Pause. People frequently nod here.)*

Yes, lots of people get referred to this class after seeing their doctor. They've been told they're okay, medically, but that's *really* hard to believe, because the reactions are still there. Right?

(Again, some people may nod.)

So I guess what I'm saying is this: If you've been told you were okay—which, of course, means at the time you were checked out, with whatever test was done—and that your reaction was probably "anxiety," your doctor may well have been correct. *Every one* of those reactions that we have on the board is sometimes a physical response to stress or a reaction that some people have when they are under stress.

And there is something else about all those physical reactions that feel so scary. They are what we call *time limited*. That means that they will stop on their own.

So now we're going to do a little experiment to demonstrate what "time limited" means. I want to invite everyone here to take one of your hands and make a fist. Just hold it for a little while, a few minutes or so.

(The instructor demonstrates and pauses to allow anyone who wishes to do so.)

And as you hold your fist, you might notice any thoughts or physical sensations or emotions that you have. You might observe them and watch them change.

(The instructor waits a bit longer and then says this.)

Who would like to say out loud what you're aware of?

(Comments here frequently refer to tightness, sensations spreading up one's arm, feeling one's fingernails against the palm, and awareness of warmth or coolness [another opportunity to comment that "the same fire that melts the butter hardens the egg"]. Sometimes people describe thinking about "what one sometimes does with a fist" or feelings of anger. The instructor normalizes this.)

(Without drawing attention to it, the instructor loosens his or her own fist. The instructor might now erase the board, turning back to the class to inquire.)

What are you aware of now? What's changed? You might allow yourself to notice: What's different from 30 seconds ago?

(Fatigue in the hand and arm and loosening the fist will probably now be reported. If no participants have explicitly asked whether they should still be holding the fist, the instructor now might say this.)

(Smiling) You all are so polite! No one has asked how long you're supposed to do this! But that's actually the *point* of this: Your hand knows how to let go. It will do it all by itself. I notice that for some of you, that's already happened. And for others, it's starting to happen now. And for those of you who haven't loosened your fist yet, you can trust that it will go loose on its own. In its own time. See, I don't have to worry that any of you are going to make little cuts on the inside of your hands with your fingernails. Oh, I suppose that if after you made a fist and let go, you made another one, and then another one, maybe you could hurt yourself. But with that first fist, eventually, the muscles in your hand just will let go. They do it on their own, *all by themselves*. And so will the muscles, and the nerves, everywhere in your body. All those parts that tighten up, that feel as though they will stay tight

forever, that fire off when you're having a huge panic attack, will let go *all by themselves.*

(The instructor pauses again. People are letting go of their fists, wiggling their hands.)

So, like we said, all of these reactions that we had on the board, that you all came up with, that are so yucky and scary: We're saying that they're normal reactions to stress. And they're usually not dangerous. And they're time limited; they stop on their own.

But when these reactions happen, sometimes even once, or maybe a few times, we human beings don't know that they're normal and not dangerous. We don't know that they are time limited and will go away on their own. Or even if we've learned it, we don't *know* it, inside. Because it's scary! We get frightened that the reactions are going to happen again or keep going forever.

It goes like this: There's a stressor and then a physical reaction.

(On board)

Stressor ———————→ Physical Reaction

And then the mind flashes "danger."

(Add arrow and "danger.")

Stressor ———————→ Physical Reaction ————→ Danger

And when the mind flashes "Danger," the body has its physical reaction again, but now at a higher intensity. Now the mind really says "Danger!" louder. Then a person starts thinking, "What if I lose control?" "What if I go crazy?" "What if I make a fool of myself?" It becomes a vicious "spiral," like this.

(Add the spiral.)

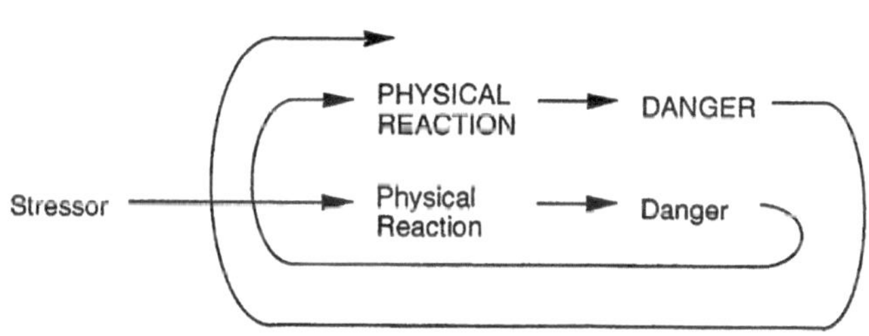

Figure 3.1 Diagram of stressor, physical reaction, and "danger."

And that "spiral" becomes the feeling of *panic.*

(Add the word "panic.")

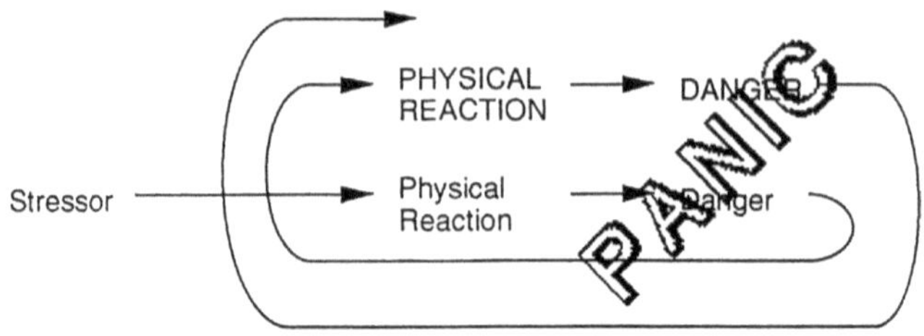

Figure 3.2 Diagram of spiral of panic.

An Australian psychiatrist, Claire Weekes,[2] called the fear of the original stressor the "first fear" and the concern about having a panic attack the "second fear."

(Add the circle around "stressor → physical reaction," and add "first fear" and "second fear" to the diagram.)

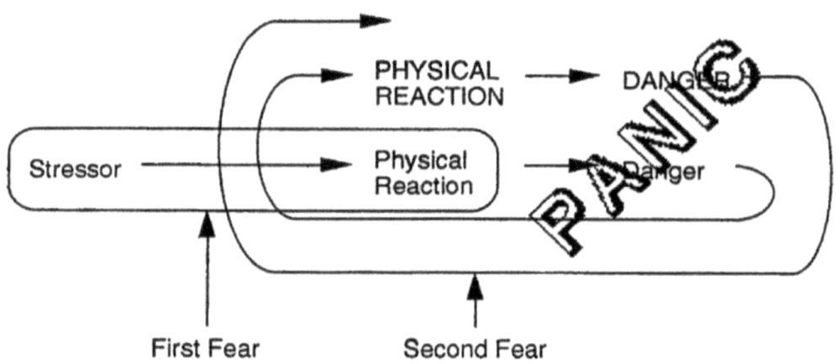

Figure 3.3 Diagram of first fear and second fear.

The physical symptoms that come with the first fear will come in a wave and will *always* die down if you just wait. Your body may flash fear from time to time, but the panic will not mount (remember the "making a fist" experiment) *if* you don't fall into the trap of "stoking the fire" of your "first fear" with more "second fear" and more adrenaline.

Now some of you, at this point, may be thinking: "*What* stressor? For me, there's no particular stressor. My sensations just come up out of nowhere, 'out of the blue.'"

(Instructor crosses out the word "stressor.")

[2] See Weekes (1978) in References.

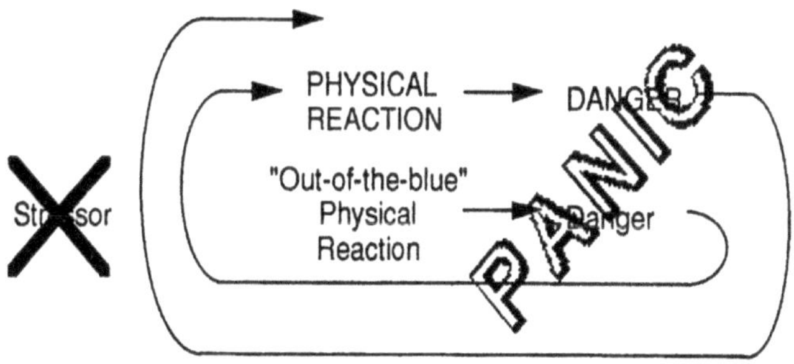

Figure 3.4 Diagram of panic without obvious stressor.

If you happen to be a "body reactor," your body may have been reacting to some situation or fear without your mind having a chance to label what it was you were reacting to. Sometimes it can be useful to scan over what has been going on or what is coming up in the future to see whether you can label the "first fear" or concern that your body may have been reacting to.

But if you can't label a precipitant, don't struggle to do so. Panic attacks that come "out of the blue" are called *spontaneous panic attacks* and are *very common*. The physical symptoms will often pass if you don't keep worrying about their happening again.

So I invite you to remember this term: *body reactor*. My definition of a body reactor is someone who just tends to get a lot of the feelings we wrote on the board before. Are you one? Lots of people are—and if you are, that's a tremendously useful thing to know about yourself.

Now, you might be thinking: Isn't *everyone* a body reactor? Doesn't everyone get these reactions? Well, to some extent, yes. But I think some of us "get" them to a greater degree than other people do. Someone talked about people who "couldn't get a panic attack if their life depended on it." And I'm thinking of someone I know who says "I don't get panic attacks. I *give* them!"

There's also a variation of body reactor that I call *mind reactor*, and that would be someone who tends to worry or obsess a lot. We talk a little more about mind reactors in the other sessions.

You can also think about being a body reactor as something that's "distributed on a bell-shaped curve."

(Instructor draws the following.)

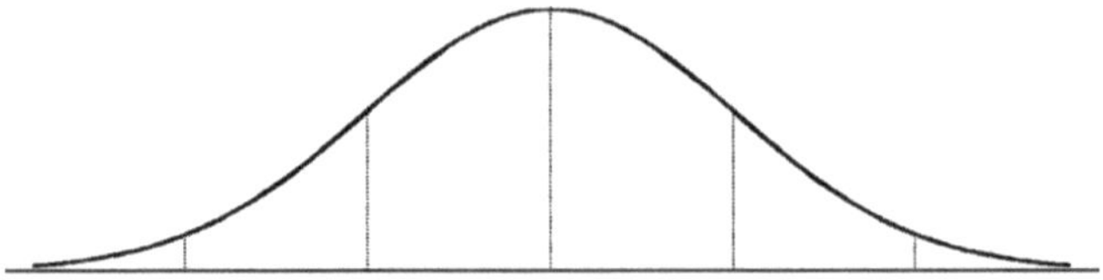

Figure 3.5 Bell curve.

It's like with height. If the average American man is, say, 5′9″ tall, then about two-thirds of all men are going to be between 5′2″ and 6′4″—this is just approximate—with a few at the "tails of the distribution" who are shorter or taller. *(Point to the ends of the curve.)*

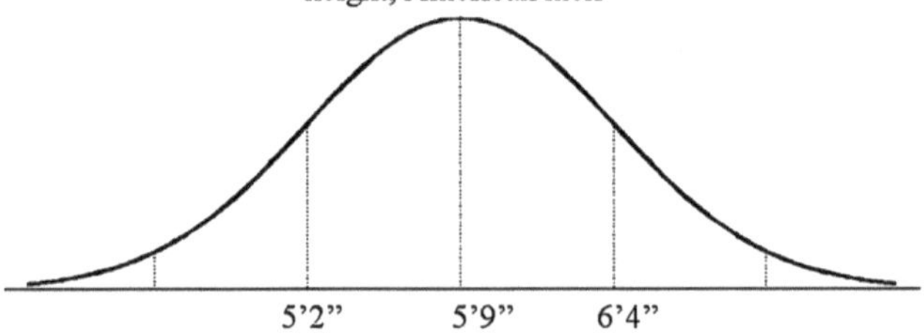

Figure 3.6 Bell curve, height.

Now I invite you to think about something like inborn athletic ability. We might assume that this too is distributed on a bell-shaped curve. Imagine that someone's ability is here.

(Erase "height" and the "feet and inches," and add "athletic ability" and dot to curve.)

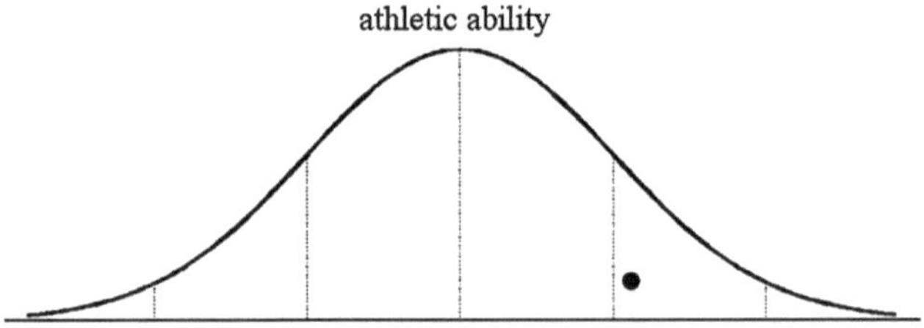

Figure 3.7 Bell curve, strong athletic ability.

If someone's "dot" is near the high end, that person has a "range" in which he or she can move.

(Add range to drawing.)

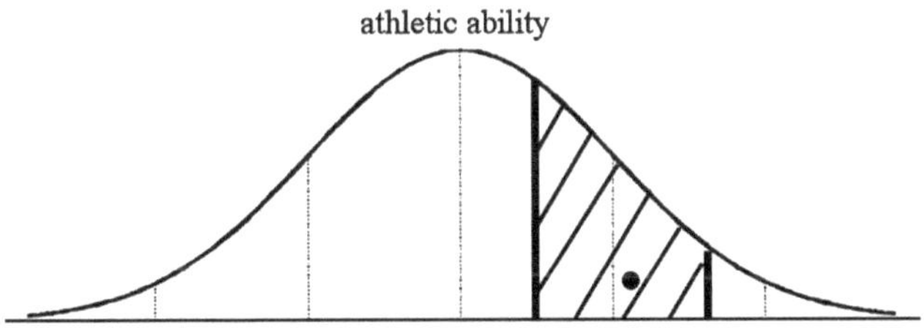

Figure 3.8 Bell curve, strong athletic ability and range.

Like, if this person gets a lot of coaching and practice, he or she may perform up here.

(Indicate on curve by adding arrow.)

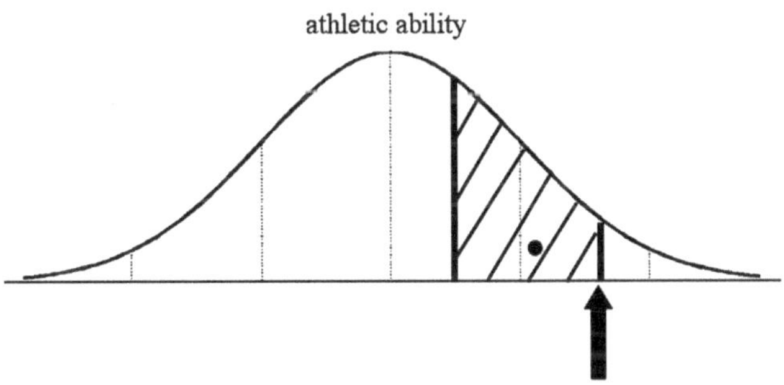

Figure 3.9 Bell curve, strong athletic ability, performance with support.

And even without special training or opportunity to practice, he or she might still be above average.

Then think about the people whose "dots" are down here.

(Erase area at top of curve and add dot below average.)

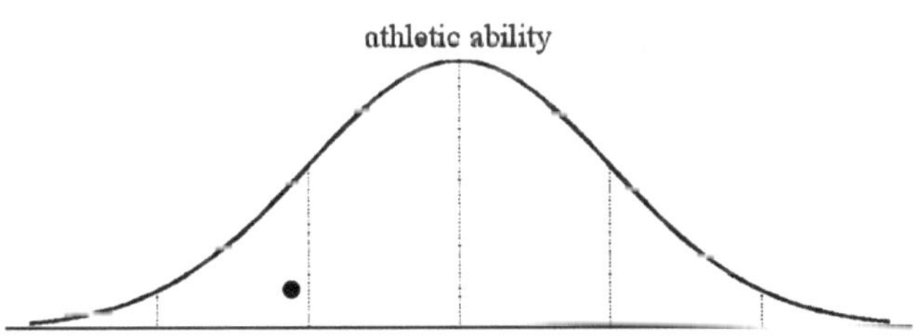

Figure 3.10 Bell curve, less strong athletic ability.

They also have a range to move in.

(Add range.)

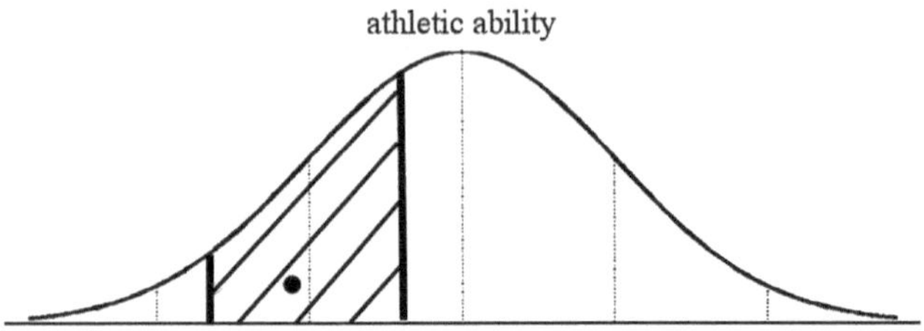

Figure 3.11 Bell curve, less strong athletic ability and range.

If they get teased and stay away from practice because they feel awkward, their skills may be pretty low.

(Add arrow to indicate low end of range.)

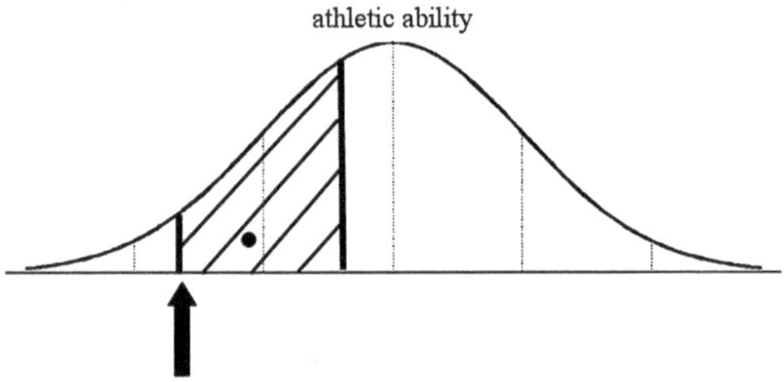

Figure 3.12 Bell curve, less strong athletic ability, performance without support.

But if they get encouragement and extra support, they may perform almost up to average.

So if we look at the curve of "autonomic reactivity," most people who come to this class have a "dot" somewhere near the high end.

(Erase "athletic ability" and add "autonomic reactivity" at top and dot to right of center.)

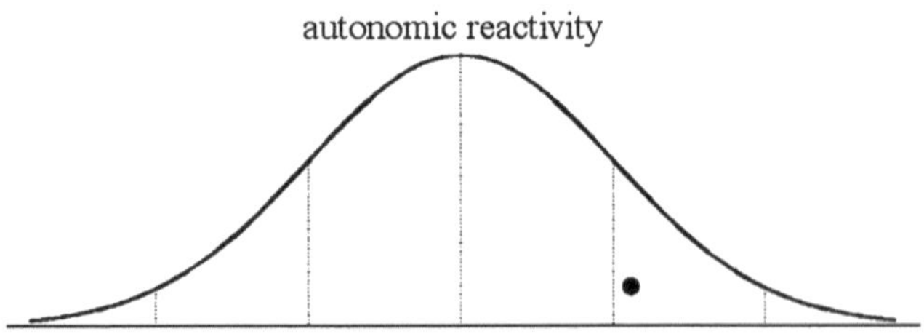

Figure 3.13 Bell curve, autonomic reactivity.

Your "dot" may never be way down at the low end, but you may be able to move your functioning toward the center by doing some of the things we talk about in here—and by doing other good things that you discover. Your life may be different in some good ways when you are functioning closer to the middle of the bell-shaped curve.

And by the way, you probably don't want your "dot" all the way at the low end. Do you know what they call people who have their "dots" way down at the low end? Psychopaths. They're the people who have so little autonomic sensitivity that they don't learn from experience.

Anyway, body reactor or mind reactor, here is an interesting thing about this concept: People sometimes tell us that it is the most significant thing they remember from Topic One.

So, if you are a "body reactor," then the next step is to learn some *coping techniques,* to deal with those body reactions. There are lots of different kinds of coping techniques, and for each one there is probably a group of people who insist that "this one is the best." Our position is that there is no single best coping technique. Different things work better for different people, and in different situations. So the best plan may be to learn a whole range of strategies and to approach them in the same way you would approach the food at a smorgasbord or salad bar: You try what interests you, and you come back for more of what you like.

There are two main categories of coping techniques to learn, and we are going to call them the *physical* techniques and the *thinking* techniques. Of course, none of them are "only" physical or mental; there is always some overlap. But in general, they can be grouped in that way. The *physical* techniques are the ones that mainly emphasize things that you do with your body: your muscles, your breathing, your general level of tension, things like that. The *thinking* techniques are the ones that emphasize what you think and say to yourself in your head.

We are going to review five physical techniques today, and we talk about the thinking coping techniques in two weeks, in Topic Three.

Physical Coping Technique #1: Instant Relaxation, or the Belly Button Technique

Instant relaxation, or the belly button technique, is one of the easiest and most effective techniques to use. It supports calm breathing and decreases the likelihood of hyperventilation, and you can use it any time, any place.

So—I invite you to get your "equipment" ready. You need your belly button, your hand, your eyes, and your lungs. Put your thumb in your belly button, rest your hand on your stomach, look at your hand, and breathe so that you can see your hand move.

(Instructor demonstrates.)

Okay, it's your turn.

(Instructor pauses, looks around room.)

Look at your own hand; don't look at me right now. Watch your hand move. *Breathe* until you see your hand move. *Breathe* until you see your hand move. That's right.

(Pause to allow people to experience this.)

Now shift your gaze up slightly so that you can still see your hand, but now you can just barely see it, in the lowest part of your field of vision. Breathe until you see your hand move. Breathe until you see your hand move. That's right.

(Pause again.)

And now lift your gaze. Look up a little more. Maybe pick a spot on the wall across from you and focus on it. Now you can't actually *see* your hand any more, but you can *feel* it. *Breathe* until you feel your hand move. *Breathe* until you feel your hand move. That's right.

(Pause again, as people do this.)

And now for the "advanced technique": I invite you to move your hand away and breathe until your stomach moves. *Breathe* until your stomach moves. *Breathe* until your stomach moves. That's right. That's all there is to it.

(Demonstrate, and pause again, so that people may practice this.)

That's right. And you might continue to breathe that way, *breathing* until you feel your stomach move, as you listen to me talk. What's so elegant about this advanced technique is that in addition to it being *instant*, it's *inconspicuous*. Why, for all you know, I might have been doing this the whole time we've been talking today, and you would never know it!

I'm curious: Is anyone experiencing a slowing of breathing or a calming feeling right now? *(Instructor looks around the room. Probably some people will be nodding, whereas others will not.)*

For some people, this slows down their breathing, and the feeling of calm spreads through the body. It doesn't happen for everyone, because different things work for different people. And if this one doesn't work for you, that's perfectly okay. You'll choose something else.

But if some calming is starting to happen for you right now, you might be wondering: *Why* does this work? Well, the answer comes from the fact that our brains need oxygen to function. When we are under stress and need oxygen the most, we often breathe shallowly. So we're taking in *less* oxygen, at the very moment when we need it the most! Breathing so that you can see your hand move assures that you will breathe deeply and take in the oxygen you need to deal with the stress at hand. And I don't know about you, but when I'm under stress, my little brain needs all the help it can get!

And this can prevent hyperventilation. Now, you may have heard that you can also prevent hyperventilation by breathing into a brown paper bag. Maybe so, but can't you just see you getting your bag out of your pocket at a job interview or a party?! What's so elegant about this technique is that you've got it instantly available—any time, any place. I may joke about "get your equipment ready," but knowing it's there any time you need it is pretty cool. Think about it: Knowing that you have a tool that's with you everywhere you go, that works immediately, and that is completely inconspicuous can add to your sense of control. And that's really powerful, since sometimes part of what's so devastating about feeling anxious is that we may feel so *out* of control.

Now, let me tell you about a time when this belly button technique may *not* work. That's when you are right in the middle of a panic attack. We're going to talk in a minute about something you *can* use in the middle of panic. But this one, this instant relaxation, is more something to do *before* a big panic attack happens, sort of as a "preventive" technique. It's sort of like the medicine people take for migraines when they first feel one coming on, or like medicine to prevent seasickness. It doesn't always stop the feelings once they're happening, but it can be really powerful when you use it ahead of time.

Actually, belly button breathing is a really good habit to get into doing regularly. Some people like to put a little sticky note on their computer monitor or refrigerator door that says "Breathe."

I know a music teacher who notices that when her students are tense, they hold their breath and don't play as well. She tells her students, "Remember to breathe!" On one level, that's almost funny. I mean, breathing is involuntary; we're breathing all the time, whether or not we're conscious of it. On another level, though, it's really profound advice. When you're under stress or overwhelmed or panicking or can't think of what else to do, sometimes a simple, straightforward direction is exactly what you need. So I paraphrase that wise music teacher: If you ever don't know what to do, remember: Breathe.

Physical Coping Technique #2: Claire Weekes' Four Concepts ("The Wave")

Remember how we said a little bit ago that there are some tools that can be especially useful when you're in the middle of a panic attack? This next method is one of them! "The Wave" is one of the most powerful techniques you can use to ride through panic attacks, so anyone who ever gets panic attacks, here's one for you.

This tool comes to us from Claire Weekes,[3] the Australian psychiatrist we talked about before. It has some words in it, but the words describe what you do with your body, so I think of this mostly as a physical technique. Here are the words:

- *Face*: Don't run away.
- *Accept*: Don't fight.
- *Float*: Don't tense up.
- *Let time pass*: Don't be impatient with time.

I want to invite you to understand what this means by envisioning the shape of a wave on the ocean. It builds, it crests, and it falls.

(Instructor draws the shape of a wave on the board.)

Figure 3.14 Shape of a wave.

The next one is just the same. If you've ever surfed or swum in the ocean, or watched people do so, then you know that you can't fight a wave. Well, you can try, but the wave will always "win." It's bigger than you are.

Now I want to invite you to visualize the shape of a wave of anxiety. Its shape is just the same. It builds, it crests, and it falls. And trying to fight *that* wave—like we do when we say, "Go *away*, stupid feeling"—works just about the same as trying to fight the wave on the ocean. And that means that it doesn't work very well.

So, it has been said that the most powerful technique you can use with the wave of anxiety is learning to *ride* the wave, instead of fighting it. You let the sensations come, to crest, knowing, trusting, that they'll diminish. You're like an expert surfer, riding the wave, going over that point of no return. Even at that moment when you're temporarily out of control, you remember that you've been here before, that you'll come down on the other side and be okay.

[3] See Weekes (1978) in References.

(The instructor now adds to the picture a stick figure of a surfer, on surfboard, on the crest of the wave. It might be noted that instructors with the least drawing ability may be most effective here. The more primitive the drawing, the better, because imperfect drawing models doing other things imperfectly—a concept that emerges in multiple places in solution focused anxiety management.)

Figure 3.15 Surfer on wave.

Now I want to show you another way of thinking about the wave.

(Instructor erases the surfer and adds a line to represent the beach and a stick figure walking down the beach.)

Figure 3.16 Person on beach with wave.

Now let's put you walking down the beach, and let's imagine that this is a really big wave. Maybe it washes over you, and you might even fall down or get the wind knocked out of you or scrape your knee. But you immediately get up and run a little bit back on the sand, away from the water.

(Add dotted lines to show where the knee is hurt and the person is moving inland.)

Figure 3.17 Person on beach, briefly overwhelmed by wave.

And the wave, being a wave and doing what waves do, goes back out to sea.

(Then add the arrows that show the wave moving back out to sea and the person continuing down the beach.)

Figure 3.18 Person on beach, briefly overwhelmed by wave, now recovering.

So this is like when that wave of anxiety washes over you, and for a minute you lose it, but the wave, being a wave, moves away, and even if you're a little shaken up, you're okay again.

Why is this such a powerful technique? The answer is this: Once you learn to ride the wave, or let it wash over you, you know that when these sensations come, you have a *plan*. And you might notice that I said *when*, and not *if*, because if you're a *body reactor*—remember "body reactor," that I was telling you about a little bit ago?—chances are that these sensations *will* come back. But rather than having to live in fear of it, like "Oh, no! What am I going to do if it happens again?" something has shifted. Something is different. What's different is that you now have this elegant skill, to remember, in your body, in your bones, at a kinesthetic, feeling level. And that can make a tremendous difference.

This is sort of an intangible concept, so I want to ask you: Am I saying this clearly enough that you have a sense of what I'm talking about?

(Instructor waits for nods or puzzled looks and invites a little discussion or elaboration if needed.)

Physical Coping Technique #3: Autogenic Training

The next technique is *not* an instant technique. It takes at least five minutes to do. And it's done best with your eyes closed. So please don't do this one while you're driving on the freeway! It's not the best choice for a job interview, either! But it can be great to do just *before* those activities. This technique is called Autogenic Training.[4] "Autogenic" means you do it yourself. The "auto" part is like the "auto" in "automobile," meaning "self-drive," and "genic" means "to do," so this is a good thing you do for yourself.

Autogenic Training is a set of sentences that you say silently in your head, and if your body feels like doing what's in the sentences, it does so. The way we'll practice it in here is that I'll say the sentences out loud, and you'll follow along silently, and again, if your body feels like doing what's in the sentence, it will. The sentences are all in the readings for this session, so please don't feel as though you have to memorize them as you're hearing them.

(Instructor softens the lighting in the room if it is possible to do so.)

Now let me show you how to sit when you do Autogenic Training.

(Instructor demonstrates while saying the following.)

You might want to uncross your legs. If you have papers or a book or anything else in your lap, you might put your things on the floor. Your hands might rest comfortably on your thighs, fingers slightly curved, palms down—or maybe it's more comfortable to have them slightly up—it doesn't matter. You might want to close your eyes. If you do that and you're wearing contacts, you might remember to blink every once in a while.

By the way, you can also do Autogenic Training at bedtime. Some people find it a comfortable and gentle way to get ready for sleep. If you do it then, it's suggested that you do it lying on your back rather than on your tummy or your side. That lets the blood flow freely and comfortably through your whole body.

Now, closing your eyes: My breathing is becoming calm and regular. My breathing is becoming calm and regular.

[4] See Luthe & Schultze (1969) in References.

(The instructor's voice slows and softens, although it is loud enough to remain audible.)

Breathing calm and regular. *Breathing* calm and regular. *Breathing* calm and regular. My breathing is becoming calm and regular.

My right arm is heavy. My right arm is *heavy.* My right arm is *heavy*—heavy and limp, like an old rag doll. If I were to lift it up, it would flop right back down. My right arm is *heavy.*

My left arm is heavy. My left arm is *heavy.* My left arm is *heavy*—heavy and limp, like an old rag doll. If I were to lift it up, it would flop right back down. My left arm is *heavy.*

My right leg is heavy. My right leg is *heavy.* My right leg is *heavy*—heavy and limp, like an old rag doll. If I were to lift it up, it would flop right back down. My right leg is *heavy.*

My left leg is heavy. My left leg is *heavy.* My left leg is *heavy*—heavy and limp, like an old rag doll. If I were to lift it up, it would flop right back down. My left leg is *heavy.*

My right arm is warm. My right arm is *warm.* My right arm is *warm*—warm and comfortable. Warmth is *flowing* down my arm, into my hand, into my fingers. My right arm is *warm.*

My left arm is warm. My left arm is *warm.* My left arm is *warm*—warm and comfortable. Warmth is *flowing* down my arm, into my hand, into my fingers. My left arm is *warm.*

My right leg is warm. My right leg is *warm.* My right leg is *warm—warm* and comfortable. Warmth is *flowing* down my leg, over my knee, into my foot, into my toes. My right leg is *warm.*

My left leg is warm. My left leg is *warm.* My left leg is *warm—warm* and comfortable. Warmth is *flowing* down my leg, over my knee, into my foot, into my toes. My left leg is *warm.*

My *arms* and *legs* are *heavy* and *warm.* My *arms* and *legs* are *heavy* and *warm.* My *arms* and *legs* are *heavy* and *warm.*

Heartbeat calm and regular. My heartbeat is *calm* and *regular.* Heartbeat *calm* and *regular.* Maybe I can feel it right now; maybe I can't; it doesn't matter. My heartbeat is *calm* and *regular.*

My abdomen is calm, relaxed, and comfortable. My abdomen is *calm, relaxed,* and *comfortable.* My abdomen is *calm, relaxed,* and *comfortable.*

My forehead is cool. My forehead is *cool* and *comfortable.* My arms and legs are *warm*, and my forehead is *cool.*

I am *calm, relaxed*, and *comfortable.* I am *calm, relaxed*, and *comfortable.*

(Instructor continues, slightly more slowly and softly.)

Breathing calm and regular.

My *arms* and *legs* are *heavy* and *warm*.

Heartbeat *calm* and *regular.*

My abdomen is *calm*, *relaxed,* and *comfortable.*

My forehead is *cool.*

I am *calm, relaxed,* and *comfortable.*

And now, continue on your own, silently, not worrying about the exact words, saying in your head sentences similar to those I have said.

(Let voice become barely audible now.)

Breathing calm and regular…

(Instructor pauses for two or three minutes, letting class practice in silence.)

(Softly) And then in a minute or so, but not quite yet, as you get ready to bring your attention back to this room, you might say to yourself in your head, "I am alert and refreshed and energized, just like after a good night's sleep." Of course, if you're using this *before* sleep, you won't want to say that. Instead, you might want to think, "I am calm and relaxed and ready for sleep."

(Brightly, a little louder) And now, as you take a deep breath and get ready to open your eyes and stretch like a cat waking up from a nap, you might say to yourself: "I am alert and refreshed and energized, just like after a good night's sleep."

(Demonstrate a big stretch. Pause as people open their eyes. Some people may be stretching. Look around the room, making eye contact and smiling as appropriate.)

Did anyone feel any increased relaxation as you were doing this?

(Some people will probably nod.)

I had the thought, as I was watching you all just before, that if you were all hooked up to biofeedback equipment, or EKGs, or things like that right now, we'd be seeing lots of people's blood pressure and heart rate and muscle tension and things like that moving in the "healthy" direction.

When you were doing this on your own, did anyone notice that your thoughts moved away from the sentences? If so, that's perfectly okay. You don't need to force yourself to feel or think any particular thing. When your mind drifts, what you absolutely *don't* want to do is to get mad at yourself, like "Bad! You should be on your left big toe right now!" You can gently direct your thoughts back to the sentences if you like, or you can just let your mind wander. The sentences are just a starting point from which you can move, if you like.

And you can add sentences about other parts of your body—such as your shoulders or the back of your neck: "My shoulders are relaxed and comfortable" or "My jaw is heavy and loose."

If you like visual images, you can add an image, too—anything you find beautiful or relaxing. One image that actually uses and deepens the sensations of "arms and legs warm, and forehead cool" is to visualize yourself outside, under a patio umbrella, overlooking the ocean or mountains or any other place that is special. You might be stretched out on a comfortable chaise lounge. You might imagine that your head is shaded by the umbrella and your arms and legs are in just the right amount of sun. Your arms and legs are warm, and your forehead is cool.

It's sometimes said that Autogenic Training is good for most people to do regularly, even if they don't have anxiety problems. And if you *do* experience anxiety, and prefer not to take "pharmacological" medicine for it, a physician I know once suggested the "non-pharmacological prescription" of doing Autogenic Training twice daily for a month, doing it as faithfully as if you were taking a pill and noticing how it makes a difference.

Physical Coping Technique #4: "Just Because"

The next tool I want to tell you about is another "instant" technique. And this is one you can use with anger as well as anxiety. So anyone who ever gets angry or irritated—and, of course, that's none of us here today *(smiling, to convey that "Of course, we all experience anger sometimes")*—this is one for you. Now, this one includes a sentence you say to yourself, but I include this tool with the physical techniques because it really emphasizes what you do with your body. Here is the sentence:

> *Just because*—and here you insert whatever is going on, for instance, "So-and-so is being a pain in the neck," "This bridge is high," "I'm home alone," or whatever—it doesn't mean I have to do this to my body. Now *relax*...

And you make that your cue to exhale, you take a deep breath and exhale again, and you immediately take your body into a state of relaxation, similar to what you've experienced through Autogenic Training, while lying on the beach, or in any other way.

Now you try it—I'll say it again—and you fill in the blank. Ready? Here we go:

> *Just because...(Instructor pauses, maybe gestures with hand to indicate "fill in the blank.")*...it doesn't mean I have to do this to my body. Now *relax*. Exhale, inhale a big breath, now exhale again, and let your whole body go limp.

(Pause, allowing participants to do this.)

That's right. Let's do it again. Again, you fill in the blank, either with the same thing as last time or something different—your choice. Ready?

Just because...(Again, instructor pauses, maybe gestures with hand to indicate "fill in the blank.")...it doesn't mean I have to do this to my body. Now *relax*. Exhale, inhale a big breath, now exhale again, and let your whole body go limp.

(Again pause, allowing participants to do this.)

That's right.

Now, as I was watching you, I noticed that some of you closed your eyes while you were doing this. That's fine—I didn't say *not* to do so—but it's my experience that lots of people say: "I can relax fine in this class or in my bedroom at home. It's when I'm out there in the world, with people, with traffic, with 'stuff,' that I lose it." So I want to point out that this is a technique that you can use in two different ways. You can do it with your eyes closed, and it's also one you can use when you need your eyes wide open and all your wits about you.

So I want to invite you to try it one more time. And this time, I invite you to pick a situation in your life where it might be helpful to be able to have your eyes wide open and your mind alert. Ready?

Just because...(Instructor pauses, maybe gestures with hand to indicate "fill in the blank.")...it doesn't mean I have to do this to my body. Now *relax*. Exhale, inhale a big breath, now exhale again, and let your whole body go limp.

(Pause, allowing participants to do this.)

That's right.

I want to say one more thing about "Just Because." If you think about it, you will see that the sentence in this technique is *absolutely accurate*. The fact that something unpleasant, stressful, or frightening is occurring doesn't mean that you *have to* tighten up your body. Your tightening up your body doesn't make you any better able to handle whatever is going on. In fact, it may have just the *opposite* effect. You're probably just raising your blood pressure and your heart rate and making yourself *less* able to handle whatever is going on.

Now, it makes perfect sense that we tighten up. It's sort of a conditioned response. It's like tightening your stomach as if you're bracing for a blow. But if we've learned to do that, we can also learn the opposite: to use these situations as "cues" to relax.

By the way, this is the same technique that sports psychologists and performance psychologists teach to athletes and performers so that they can transform that burst of adrenaline into a prepared readiness to perform. So when you use this technique, let's say that you're probably in some rather well-paid company!

Physical Coping Technique #5: Mindfulness and 54321

Mindfulness is a concept that you may have heard of, because it gets talked about a lot these days. It's a concept that comes from some Eastern philosophies, and recently it's been embraced by Western medicine and psychology. Mindfulness is riding through whatever is going on, any sensation, any thought, any feeling. You don't judge it; you don't tell it to go away; you just let it be. And you watch it change. It's like watching clouds in the sky: The whale becomes a bunny rabbit, and then the bunny's ears fall off, and it becomes a fish, and the fish turns into a little wisp of white fluff that just drifts away.

When I first learned about mindfulness, they gave everyone in the room a little box of raisins, like we put in kids' lunches. Now, I don't have any raisins for us today, so we'll just pretend I'm passing around a "virtual" bowl of raisins and inviting you to take one. You hold it in your hand. You notice its little wrinkly surface, its color: Dark purple? Brown? Black? You sniff it. You put it on your tongue. You notice any taste: Tart? Sweet? You chew, swallow. You notice any thoughts, feelings, memories: "I hate raisins"; "This is so weird to eat just one raisin"; "I remember my grandmother's raisin cake"—whatever. You just watch one thought or image or feeling morph into another.

And now I might invite you to notice some other sensation. It might be the chair against your back, the pressure of your hand on your leg, the sound of an airplane or a car outside. It's just there; it's not good or bad; it just *is*. And, as you notice it, it turns into something else.

Let's try that for a minute now. You might want to be aware of your breathing. *(Pause)*

Maybe the sensation of the chair against your back. *(Pause)*

Or the temperature in the room. *(Pause)*

Or something in your body. *(Pause)*

Or a thought. *(Pause)*

Notice it change. *(Pause)*

And you might notice your breath again. *(Pause)*

And you notice what else is there. *(Pause)*

And how it's different from just a moment ago. *(Pause)*

And you might be curious about where else you might want to experiment with this. *(Pause)*

A few years ago, the January cover story of a news magazine, *U.S. News and World Report,*[5] was about 50 good things to do for yourself in the coming year. And one of them was "learn to meditate." And I thought the article was funny and also rather profound. The writer was talking about trying to relax, meditate, use this mindfulness thing, and she started thinking something like this: "Did I take the garbage out? That gray sweater I saw on the Internet would go great with my new jeans." And she said to herself: "Stop it! Here I am trying to relax, and I'm thinking about this stupid stuff!"

And the person who was helping her with this said something like this: "You let your mind go *wherever* it wants to go. And that includes the garbage and the sweater." That's precisely what mindfulness is about: letting your "monkey mind" climb and wander wherever it wants to go.

And when you get good at it, you can do this with any thought, any feeling, any sensation—including the ones that come with panic, like your heart beating too hard. And when you can do it with those things, when breathing too hard or the image of you losing it just morphs into something else, like "My knee itches" or "Oh, someone's texting me," that changes it, and that can make a tremendous difference.

54321

Now, 54321 is a technique that uses a kind of guided mindfulness that can help you relax your body and your mind. This technique comes from Betty Alice Erickson, who is the daughter of psychiatrist and hypnotist Milton Erickson. This version has been adapted from those taught by Yvonne Dolan and Chuck Holton.[6]

Here is how it goes. In a relatively quiet (but not completely quiet) setting, with your eyes open, you pick a spot on the wall across from you. You focus your gaze on something. Moving your eyes around that spot, you say—and this can be aloud, softly, if you're in a place where it's appropriate to speak out loud, or silently if you're not—five things that you *see*. For instance, if I were doing this now, I might say, "I see the window." "I see the chair in the corner." "I see the gray backpack on the floor." *(Instructor speaks softly and slowly. He or she might choose objects actually visible in the room.)* Let's see, is that five yet? It's very common and perfectly okay to lose track of how many you've done.

Then you say, aloud or not, five things you *hear*. So I might say, "I hear the sound of the heat or air conditioning." "I hear a car outside." Again, you

[5] See Kotz (2007) in References.

[6] See Holton (2000) in References.

might not be sure when you've said five. And if it's fairly quiet, this might take a little longer. That's okay.

Then you say, aloud or not, five things you *feel* in your body, sensations or other things you're aware of. "I feel my fingers on the paper." "I feel the chair against my legs." "I feel my glasses on my ears." If there is some sensation that is uncomfortable, it's fine to include that. It's just one of the five.

And then you go back and say *four* of each thing: four things I see, four things I hear, four things I feel. And then you do *three* of each, then two, and then one. It's fine to repeat. And it's fine to get confused about where you are. And if you like, when you finish with one, you can go back to five again. You may find yourself repeating things, and that's just fine. And the process continues, as long as you like. At some point you might discover that instead of actively doing it, your awareness is just drifting. Again, that's just fine.

Sometimes people do a variation of 54321 silently before sleep. If your eyes are closed, you might not want to include five things you *see*. Instead, you might pick five things you're *thinking*. Like, I might be saying silently, "I wonder if it will rain tomorrow." "I hope my mom got home okay." "I have to charge my phone in the morning." Again, if there's something you're worried about, including it is fine. It's just one thought among many. Noticing five things that you hear may take a bit longer in a quiet room at night, and that's just fine.

Would you like to try it now? With lots of us together, let's do it silently. I invite you to notice five things you *see. (Pause to allow participants to do this.)* And now, five things that you *hear. (Another pause)* And now, five things that you *feel* in your body. *(Another pause)* And so on. Again, 54321 is a little exercise for experiencing mindfulness.

AN INTERESTING PERSPECTIVE

Now I want to add something that may surprise some of you: the fact that some professionals in the anxiety management world[7] *don't* always recommend using all the physical coping techniques we've talked about today. You might ask: Why not? The answer is this: Sometimes people feel very relaxed, very comfortable, after using some of these methods. And consciously or unconsciously, they start thinking: "I've found the cure for my anxiety. I'll just use my Autogenic Training, or whatever, and I won't be anxious any more." Without realizing it, they've just slipped into an "anxiety elimination" mindset. And then when it doesn't work, or it doesn't work

[7] See Wilson (2009) in References.

well enough, they get critical of themselves, or of the program, and they just stop trying. It's my experience that this is most likely to happen with people who are bright and highly motivated, so any of you who fall into that category might want to be aware of this perspective.

Now, I should say that this caution doesn't apply equally to all five of the methods we've talked about today. It's probably a little *more* of a concern with belly button breathing, Autogenic Training, and "Just Because," and somewhat *less* of a concern with the wave and mindfulness. The reason is that with the wave and mindfulness, you're *expecting* that some discomfort may well be there and that you will ride through it. With the others, there tends to be more of a hope that you'll keep the sensations from happening. In particular, with panic and worry and some obsessive thoughts, sometimes the reactions *do* happen, even when you use the physical coping tools. So, in the spirit of solution focused anxiety management, not anxiety elimination, that's something to keep in mind.

So, you now might be confused! Here we've been talking about and practicing these techniques, and now I'm telling you that some people don't recommend them! Am I giving you a mixed message?

In a way, maybe so. But let me tell you how I put this all together. Obviously, I wouldn't have spent all this time sharing these tools if I didn't think they had some value. The physical coping techniques have been around for a long time, and they are helpful to many, many people. The most important thing is to do what works for you. So it's absolutely appropriate to use these tools, and to notice what you discover. But if you try one, and it doesn't work, and you find yourself getting frustrated or critical of yourself, that's a signal that you might put that tool aside, at least for a while, and experiment with something different.

It's almost time for us to wind down, so now I want to give you all some time to ask questions, or share reactions, about anything we've talked about in here today. To get our discussion started, I might ask: What other techniques for physical relaxation has anyone experimented with?

(Instructor facilitates discussion, as time permits, following what participants want to discuss. No one is forced to talk. This may be an opportunity to remind people of "You can—and you don't have to.")

SUGGESTIONS FOR PRACTICE

Now I want to give you some ideas for taking these ideas with you, to experiment at home with what we've talked about in here today. Please use *any* ideas or suggestions from this class in a way that works for you!

First, I want to invite you to review the readings for this class. These cover what we talked about in here today.

(These are Appendix A *in this book and on the companion website.)*

Second, I want to invite you to sample any—or all—of the physical coping techniques, or others you've used in the past, and notice what you like. Remember, nothing works for everyone, and there are probably things that work for you that we couldn't possibly know—but that you can discover. So, notice what works for you!

The third part is optional, because it involves having a panic attack—and I don't want to tell anyone that you "have to" go out and have a panic attack! So what I'll say is that if you *do* have the "golden opportunity" to have one, you might notice how it feels different, and how you ride through it differently, as a result of what you've learned in here today, consciously and unconsciously, and as a result of being here with all these nice people who sometimes have the same kinds of experiences you do.

END OF SESSION FORM AND FEEDBACK

Now we have our short form for you to fill out.

(Instructor distributes End of Session Form [p. 22, in Chapter 2; also the final page of the learner readings for this session, in Appendix A], or equivalent designed for the practice setting. If this form has been duplicated, participants can keep one copy, while the instructor collects the other.)

And then we'll go around, and everyone can say very briefly what they most want to remember from today.

(After forms are complete and collected)

Our tradition in here is that anyone who is "graduating" goes first. Who is "graduating" today?

(Instructor facilitates "going around and saying what I want to remember." Instructor may choose to make brief comments about common themes that have emerged.)

So, for our "graduates," we wish you the best! And for the rest of us, we'll see you next week!

CHAPTER 4

Instructor Notes for Topic Two: Behavioral Techniques

WELCOME AND INTRODUCTION

(Instructor may want to bring to this session 3″×5″ note cards and copies of the End of Session Form. This form is p. 22, in Chapter 2; it is also the final page of the learner readings for this session [Appendix B]. Or the instructor may use an equivalent form, tailored to the specifics of the practice setting.)

Welcome to Solution Focused Anxiety Management! I'm delighted you're all here today! We are going to be celebrating and building courage, and this is an awesome thing you're doing for yourself, being here today. Just being here takes courage and is a step in the right direction!

For those of you who are here today for the first time, I want to go over what we do in here. We go around and share first names, although if our class is so big that we will never remember them, we may decide to skip our introductions. Then I present some information about managing anxiety. That part is mostly me talking, for two reasons. First, there are a lot of things I want to be sure to have enough time to tell you. Second, in a class on anxiety, there are sometimes people who wouldn't feel comfortable if they felt as though they "had to talk." So, as far as talking out loud in here goes, "You can—and you don't have to." By the way, "You can—and you don't have to" is a phrase that you're going to hear again and again in this class because it applies to so many things!

Anyway, after the information part, we take some time for discussion, questions, whatever people want to talk about and that we have time to talk about. Then we end with a short form for you to fill out, and by going around and everyone having a chance to say aloud, if you want to, what you want to remember or take with you from today. We do the same thing every week. There are four different information presentations. Every time you'll be encouraged to do some reading, and parts of that material repeat exactly what I'm presenting. We do that because some people have requested it in the past, so you don't have to feel as though you have to take notes. After people have been to all four classes, they're welcome to go through the series again, either right away, or at a later time, if they ever want to.

Solution Focused Anxiety Management
http://dx.doi.org/10.1016/B978-0-12-394421-4.00004-8

Significant others are welcome and encouraged to come with you to the class, too, if you would like them to do so. Many people find that the more that someone in their lives understands about anxiety management, the better! If someone in your life isn't here today, it's fine to repeat a session to bring him or her along. And, of course, it's perfectly okay to come to this class by yourself. We want you to use this program and all of the material we're going to be giving you in a way that works for you. That's a message you'll probably hear from me over and over again in here. So you can bring someone with you—and you don't have to! That is another one of the many ways that you can decide how you want to use this program.

Now I want to emphasize something about the name of this class, Solution Focused Anxiety Management. I want you all to hear clearly that it's not called "solution focused anxiety *elimination*." Of course, "anxiety elimination" is what people want! So it's important for you to be an "informed consumer." This class isn't going to claim to teach you how to make all of your anxiety disappear, but it *will* teach you how to be stubborn enough not to let it get in the way of things you want to do. You don't have to wait for anxiety to totally go away to be able to do things, both the tasks of daily living and some wonderful, amazing things.

We're real informal in here. If you need to take a break, just feel free to step out any time and come on back in.

Our one rule is confidentiality: What you hear about other people's lives stays in this room, and you can expect that same confidentiality from everyone else. But any principles or information you learn may be shouted from the rooftops! And what you discover about yourself can be shared or kept private, in whatever combination, and in whatever way feels right for you.

What questions can I answer for you now?

(Instructor may invite sharing of first names here, if desired.)

BEHAVIORAL TECHNIQUES

Today we're going to be talking about something that I bet you already know: As we get more familiar with something—like how to use a new phone, for example—the more comfortable we usually become with it. If you've ever had that experience, then you've discovered on your own the basics of the behavioral techniques that experts encourage people to use for specific anxiety problems.

EXPOSURE AND HABITUATION

There are two basic principles here: They're called *exposure* and *habituation*. *Exposure* means you get yourself to experience the situation, place, sensations, thoughts, behavior, whatever, that's scary to you, and *habituation* means you stay there long enough for it to lose its power, so it's not such a big deal anymore.

What I'm going to show you next is how to use our basic formula, exposure and habituation, for phobias, where a person is avoiding certain places, situations, experiences, or sensations. Then we're going to talk about variations on that theme that you can use for some other kinds of anxiety, such as panic attacks, obsessive compulsive disorder, social phobia, and worry, which is sometimes called generalized anxiety.

THE COMMONSENSE AND THE COUNTERINTUITIVE

(On board):

Commonsense
Counterintuitive

Sometimes I think about how anxiety management is a fascinating combination of the commonsense and the counterintuitive. Commonsense is just what it says, common sense. Everyone knows what that means. Counterintuitive is one of those big words where it isn't always as clear what it means, so I want to define it: Counterintuitive is the *opposite* of what you might expect. It's like putting salt in the cookies or sugar in the soup. It's like driving into a skid instead of away from it. It feels as though it doesn't make sense, as though it might make things worse instead of better, but it's actually a critical ingredient of the solution.

Sometimes it helps people to think about the counterintuitive in terms of what you do when you're sailing a boat. Imagine a sailboat with a beautiful big white sail. The person sailing it wants to sail over here. *(Instructor points to the right.)* But the wind is coming from that same direction. It can't catch the sail; the sail just flaps, and the boat stops moving. So the sailor has to point the boat this way *(pointing straight ahead)* for a little while, and then this way *(pointing behind)* for a little while, going back and forth between those directions in order to get the boat to the destination. To the person just learning to sail, this sometimes *feels* "wrong," like "I want to go west but I'm pointing my boat south." But trying to go directly west doesn't work. The sailor has to do the counterintuitive.

COURAGE LADDERS

So today we're going to talk about things that are both commonsense and counterintuitive. The first part, doing things a little at a time, is very commonsense.

If you have a bad experience with something or are afraid of it for some other reason, you stay away from it. That means you never get a chance to learn that you can handle it, that it can be okay. So the way to learn it can be okay is to approach it a little at a time. This is definitely a commonsense approach. It's like learning to do anything else—playing an instrument, playing a sport, lifting weights (start light, go a little heavier), teaching a child to swim. Most people don't throw the child into cold, deep water or high surf. Instead, they have the child paddle around in comfortable, safe, shallow water, so that he or she can learn from personal experience that water is safe. Then, gradually, the child is taught how to go in a little deeper.

The same thing is true for adults.

(Instructor draws the following diagram.)

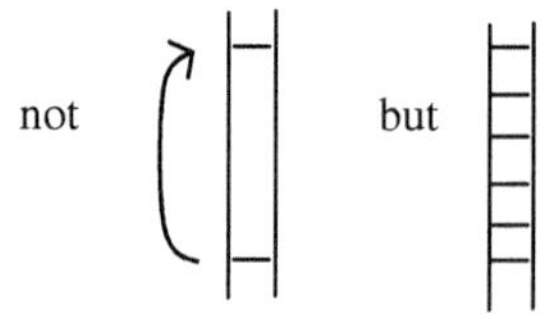

Figure 4.1 "Ladders" need many rungs.

If you're down here *(pointing to bottom rung of the first ladder)* and want to get up here *(pointing to top rung, first ladder),* you can't "jump"; that doesn't work. You need lots of little steps, and the more there are, and the closer together they are, the better it will be.

I call this a *courage ladder.* A courage ladder is a list of situations to enter, starting with the safest and gradually making them more challenging.

Today I'm going to show you how to make and use a courage ladder. We'll make one together, and then those of you who will be using one for your own situation will have a chance to make your own.

You *can* make a courage ladder by simply listing the steps on a piece of paper. When we talk about it in here, I prefer to make a series of note cards, one item on each one, because the most helpful way of doing this includes continually thinking of and adding new items. Of course, with a computer or iPad or other device, you can easily add to an ordinary list. If you happen to have one of those devices with you today, please feel free to use it, but what I'm going to show you will be the basic "low-tech" way.

The steps in a courage ladder need to be small and very specific. For example, in the case of a person who is afraid to leave the house, "going to the grocery store" isn't an ideal courage ladder item. Why? The reason is that there is a big difference between going to the corner store for one item at 10:00 a.m. and going to a big supermarket for a week's groceries at rush hour!

Now I want to show you how to make a sample courage ladder, going from "easy" to "hard."

(Instructor draws the following boxes on the board.)

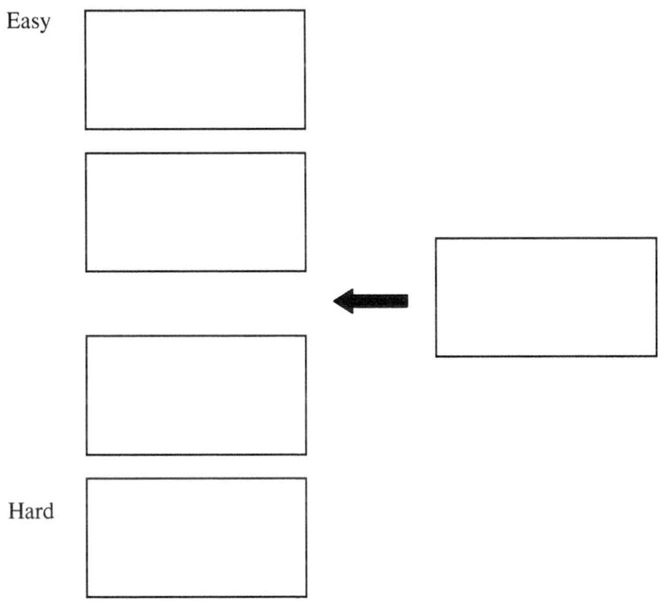

Figure 4.2 Note cards for courage ladder.

We're going to create an example of part of a courage ladder for someone who is just starting to leave the house and be with people. The first "baby step" might be to walk out on the front porch for two minutes, about 10 a.m., with her husband in the house, and no neighbors around.

(Instructor writes this, or shortened version of it, in "easy" box. As each additional step is described, the content is added to the next box.)

Then the next step might be to walk to the mailbox to get the mail, when no one is around. *(Add to next box.)*

Walking to the mailbox for mail, when you see that one neighbor is around, and saying "hello," even though it's scary, might be the next step. *(Add to next box.)*

Next, the person might walk around the block with her husband and smile and say "hello" when they see a neighbor outside. *(Add to next box.)*

Walking around the block alone and planning to say "hello" if she meets someone could be the next step. *(Add to next box.)*

The next step is a little harder: Walk to the store—and this might be a neighborhood grocery, not a huge supermarket—at 9 a.m., for a loaf of bread. *(Add to next box.)*

Now let's look at what might be part of this person's courage ladder later on.

(Instructor adds more boxes, or if there is not room on the board to do so, erases the words in the existing boxes.)

Go to PTA meeting Thursday evening. It's a lecture, so you won't have to talk except to say "hello." *(Add to next box.)*

Here is a possible next step: Stop in at Mary's party Saturday night for about half an hour. Tell her you will only be able to stay a short time. *(Add to next box.)*

You might notice how these steps include detail, specific names and places, and they include "setting things up" so that it will be easier to keep the steps small.

And a next step: Telephone your sister and invite her to meet you for coffee. Suggest a specific time and place. Expect to feel your heart pound while calling—and do it anyway. *(Add to next box.)*

You might notice that *expecting* the sensations is specifically added here. Actually, for some people it's a helpful reminder to add this piece to *every* step on the courage ladder!

Here is a next possible step: Think about two things. First, remember something special you've shared with your sister in the past. Second, imagine it's a few hours after your time with your sister, and you're reflecting back on your time with her, and feeling glad you went, and remembering what you did to make that happen. That's a lot to write in one little box, so I'm going to shorten it to this: "Remember something special. Imagine feeling glad, how you did it." *(Add that, or some other abbreviated version, to next box.)*

Keep the date with your sister! *(Add to next box.)*

That evening, think back on your time with her and what you like best about how you handled it. *(Add to next box.)*

And this might be a next step: Walk around Community College with your sister and ask for information on classes. *(Add to next box.)*

The next step might be this: Sign up for a class at Community College. *(Add to next box.)*

And the process continues. Now, this might be obvious, but it's worth saying directly: All of this is an example, and there is absolutely no implication that all people who are growing their courage in the area of getting out of the house will have the same steps or do them in the same order. For someone else, going to a party might be more difficult than signing up for a class. Everything is individually tailored to the details in your life: people and places and, maybe most important, the things that are special about them and about you. So I can't say, "Okay, here is Courage Ladder Number Three for airplanes" or "Here is Courage Ladder Number Twelve for public speaking phobia." Every courage ladder is different, and it's custom designed *for* you and *by* you. Getting some ideas from someone in your life or from me or from a therapist sometimes helps to keep the steps small and specific, but no one knows the details that matter as well as you do. So if there is a "design team," you are its most important member!

And there is another thing. For some people, really important steps on the courage ladder might include planning how you'll acknowledge to someone in your life that you haven't called him or her for a while. The courage ladder might include anticipating what that other person might say or do, and how you plan to respond, even if it's hard. It might include taking a little break and coming back to things later. And a really elegant courage ladder might include some steps on what to do when things don't go as you've planned, or when events bring something into your life before you've had a chance to take the steps that would ideally get you ready for it.

And, as we said before, courage ladders definitely include both expecting things to be hard and reflecting back on your victories!

Now we should probably talk about what you do with a courage ladder once you have it. The most elegant thing is to *do* those things you just wrote down. You can do this fast or slowly, a little bit at a time. You might wait for a while and take many steps in quick succession. As with everything else, you have to take your steps in a way that works for you. But whatever your pace, experts on skill acquisition tell us that to grow your courage, *you do have to do the things on your courage ladder, and that there is really no good substitute for this.* Sometimes that means doing them even when you don't feel fully ready. We'll be talking a little more about that in a few minutes.

I want to tell you about some research done a few years ago on people who went through classes like this.[1] People were contacted about six months after they finished the class and were asked how they were doing. Some of them were doing great, and some of them were doing about the

[1] See Quick (1983) in References.

same. What made the difference? The ones who were doing better were the ones who had actually done the things they wrote on their little note cards. Maybe this is one of the commonsense pieces here: The people who did the things on their courage ladders got more experience, and they got more and more comfortable, and that helped them to be the ones who got the best results.

TOOLS FOR PANIC ATTACKS

Can you make a courage ladder for panic attacks? Yes, you can. Now we're getting into one of the variations. With panic attacks, experts suggest that people benefit tremendously from "exposing" themselves to two things. First, it can be really helpful to spend time in the place or situation where the panic happens. Second, and sometimes even more powerful and important, is exposing yourself to the *sensations* in your body that you fear and hate the most. Experts sometimes use the term "interoceptive exposure"[2] to describe deliberately bringing on the sensations.

So, how do you do it? Well, suppose you really hate that feeling of your heart pounding. You might think: What action could create that? For some people, this one does: running up the stairs. How might you do that a little at a time? Well, you might go up one flight of stairs, and then two flights of stairs. Every time, you feel your heart pound. You hate it, but you remember: "This is my practice. This is what the class said I would feel." And you notice that gradually your heart slows down, and the sensation subsides.

Now, suppose the scariest thing for you is feeling dizzy. You might think about whether there's anything in your life that could deliberately create that. One thing that some people have discovered is sitting in a swivel chair and spinning around a few times. You might feel dizzy or nauseous, but that's exactly what you want to create. You stop, you wait, and gradually the feeling starts to go away.

Some people who get anxious describe feeling that things are unreal. This is sometimes called "depersonalization." One expert suggested that staring real hard at something, just something like the back of your hand, can bring on this feeling. Then you look away, look around you, see the familiar surroundings, and things start feeling real again. You can do the staring for gradually longer periods of time.

One really common thing that happens when we get anxious is that our breathing speeds up, or we hyperventilate. You might think about how you could deliberately breathe faster. For some people, a really easy way to do that

[2] See Craske et al. (1997) in References.

is to pant, like a dog. You feel your breathing speed up. You hate it! Then you just breathe normally, and you wait. And your breathing slows down again.

Now this next part might sound totally bizarre, but experts tell us this: When you're doing this and succeed in "bringing the sensations on," you *actively welcome* them and even try to *increase* them!

Now, you might be thinking that this is the strangest and most unpleasant thing you've ever heard. After all, you're here because you want to *get rid of* these feelings, and here I am telling you to deliberately *increase* them? Yes, that's exactly what I'm saying. And I know that it sounds *so* weird. But now I want to invite you to remember how we talked a little bit ago about the commonsense and the counterintuitive. As you probably have noticed, this interoceptive exposure part, deliberately bringing on what you hate and fear most, is counterintuitive. It's the *opposite* of what you might expect. And even though it may feel so unnatural, just like sailing the boat in a different direction seems to be, some people find it one of the most useful things they can do to take the power away from panic.

TOOLS FOR "OBSESSIONS AND COMPULSIONS"

Now I want to describe how people sometimes use all this, our exposure and habituation tools, when what they want to change is thinking too much about something, or doing too much of something, such as washing their hands or checking the locks all the time. Sometimes people call these their obsessions or compulsions. But you don't have to give these things "psychological labels" in order to change them. Here, the first thing experts might suggest that you do is to pick the thought or behavior you want to decrease. You pick just one thing. Once you've selected it, then you *delay* or *postpone* doing it. You do this really briefly, maybe just for a couple of seconds. Then you postpone it just a little longer, and then a tiny bit longer. Maybe it feels weird to postpone it, but you discover that you can do it anyway. Or maybe it doesn't feel as hard as you thought it would! You let yourself be curious and just notice what you discover. And then maybe you start postponing it for increasingly longer intervals. The technical name for this is "exposure and response prevention,"[3] because you're "exposing" yourself to whatever is hard for you to tolerate, and you're "preventing" your typical response. And that helps you to become "habituated," to learn that you can tolerate longer and longer intervals without the thought or the behavior.

[3] See Huppert & Roth (2003) in References.

So, you experiment with this. And then, whenever you don't want to postpone it any more, you go ahead and think your thought or do your behavior. Some experts add another piece here: You go ahead and do your regular behavior, or you think your usual thought, but you change something about the *way* you do it. How might you do that? For a thought, you might *sing* it or say it in Pig Latin. For a behavior, when at any point you are done postponing it—for now, at least—you might do it in slow motion, or you might decide to change some aspect of it. Some people who would like to wash their hands less frequently have discovered the trick of squeezing the soap pump with the hand that they don't usually use for that, or picking up the cake of soap with the other hand. Most of us always use the same hand to approach the soap, so this is a really easy way to do something different. Some people discover wonderful and creative ways to "mess with" the habit they want to change.

Dr. Reid Wilson, who is an expert in these things, told this story.[4] He was working with a woman who wanted to spend less time checking that she had turned off the stove. He invited her to do this: *(Instructor pantomimes, in slow motion, checking four burners),* and to say to herself, very slowly *(Instructor speaks slowly and softly here)*: "I'm checking burner number one. I'm checking burner number two. I'm checking burner number three. I'm checking burner number four. I'm checking the oven. I'm checking the broiler." Then he suggested that she do this: *(Instructor sticks out tongue, puts thumbs in ears, and* ***loudly*** *shouts)* "Blablablablabla!" *(There may be laughter from the class here.)* The woman came back to the therapist and told him that she had tried it, and that whenever she did that, she *never* forgot that she had checked the stove!

TOOLS FOR SOCIAL SITUATIONS

Another really common kind of anxiety is discomfort around other people. It might be hard to speak up in a class or a meeting or to go to social gatherings. People who struggle with this anxiety may worry that other people are looking at them or judging them or making fun of them, and it feels horrible. So they stay away from places where they think that this is going to happen. There may be a sense of being a little shy, but sometimes it feels worse than shyness. Sometimes this gets called social anxiety, or social phobia.

[4] See Wilson (2002a) in References.

When you're growing your courage for social situations, you use the same tools we've talked about before. Here, too, the important ingredient of the solution is going into whatever social situation is hard, a little at a time. You talk to people a little at a time. You start with people who seem "safer." That might be someone you already know, or it might be a stranger. There's no fixed formula, because what's easier depends on your interests and strengths. You might start by asking someone a question. Here is a hint: Try an open-ended one, where the other person is likely to respond with more than "Yes" or "No" or some other one-word answer.

Here is one little exercise that lots of people find useful when they are feeling shy about being in a place where people usually talk to each other. You imagine that you are an expert on shyness and are, in fact, the "second shyest" person in the room. Your mission is to see whether you can discover the one person in the room who is shyer than you are. When you think you have figured out who that might be, you go over to that person and say something that will make him or her feel more comfortable. Some people discover that rather than trying to "hide" their shyness in that situation, they openly acknowledge it by saying something like "I'm *so* not good at small talk." That's sort of counterintuitive, isn't it? It's so different from trying to *hide* your anxiety or pretend you're super comfortable. Very often, the other person says, "I'm not good at small talk either"!

Whatever method you use, it sometimes helps to *expect* that it might be uncomfortable—and that you're going to do it anyway. And you might be surprised: It might be easier than you anticipated. It might be fun! Or it might be hard, and you might feel really proud that you did it anyway. You may never *love* big parties or giving talks or signing your name in public, but you learn that when you have to, or the situation really calls for it, you can do it. Accepting that you don't have to love it is actually another valuable ingredient of the solution!

TOOLS FOR "WORRY"

Now I want to spend a few minutes talking about worry. Some of us have always been "worriers." We may expect that the worst is going to happen. We might feel anxious when something familiar is about to change. We might feel tension in our bodies a lot of the time. This is sometimes called "generalized anxiety." Now, when people worry a lot, what do you think other people tend to say to them?

(Instructor pauses, in case anyone answers aloud.)

They usually tell them not to worry—like, "Don't worry." This is an example of a "commonsense" suggestion that, for lots of people, doesn't work well enough! So we have some tools that invite you to do some things that are different.

Our expert, Dr. Wilson, observed that people who get anxious "worship comfort" and "worship certainty."[5] That's an interesting way to put it, isn't it? So, why might that be? Why might some of us feel so attached to comfort and certainty, or want things to stay the same as they've been in the past? Well, one reason might be that some of us are "body reactors" and "mind reactors." You may have heard me talk about that in Topic One. Or if you haven't yet been to that class yet, you'll be hearing more about it in a few weeks.

So, if your body or mind is "hard wired" to react really strongly to things, in a way it makes *no difference* what the particular *content* is of the worry, or the obsession or the sensation, for that matter. It's as though that content—the place you have to go next week, how cold it will be tomorrow, for example—just happened to "be there," and your mind "grabbed it," like little "Pac man guys" grabbing something, just because it was there.

(Instructor gestures with hand, pantomiming grabbing little things.)
Reid Wilson[6] suggested this four-part idea:

1. Act *as if* the content were irrelevant.
2. Accept the worry, obsession, sensation, whatever it might be—this is useful for panic too, when it comes—like,
   "*Of course,* I'm having all these thoughts (sensations, doing this over and over); this is what my body (or mind) does!" Or, if it's helpful for you to give a name to what you're experiencing, you could say it like this: "*Of course,* I have these sensations, fears, thoughts—I have generalized anxiety disorder (OCD, panic disorder)!"
3. *Seek out* uncertainty.
4. *Seek out* discomfort.

It's interesting: We often say that people might learn to "tolerate" uncertainty and discomfort, but it's also been suggested that "tolerate" is almost too weak or "wishy-washy" a word. You don't just want to *tolerate* the uncertainty and discomfort. You want to *match* the "terror" of the anxiety with an equally strong emotion—such as "excitement": "All right, an opportunity to practice!" and "disappointment": "Aw, it went away. I really didn't get a chance this time. Bummer!" Again, this might sound *totally weird* to you, but I bet you can guess what I'm about to say: that this is another example of

[5] See Wilson (2002b) in References.
[6] See Wilson (2002b) in References.

the counterintuitive. And it seems to be that *grasping* this concept and then actually *doing it* are what predict success with worry. Some people who have studied this tell us that it's not the severity of the anxiety, or how long or short someone has experienced the anxiety, that matters. Instead, it's "getting this" that seems to make a difference. And that's pretty good news for people who worry a lot or who have felt anxious for a long time.

Now I want to share an interesting question you can ask yourself when you worry: Is the thing I'm worried about right now more *signal* or *noise*?

(Instructor draws on board.)

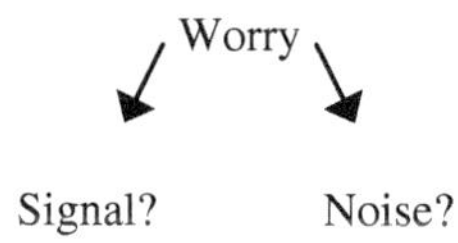

Figure 4.3 Worry: Signal or noise?

You know how when you're listening to the radio or a recording, sometimes you hear static? The music is the signal, and the static is the noise. So, with anxiety, we would say that when your concern is more of a "signal," then there really *is* something going on that's valid and legitimate to worry about. And a lot of the time, that is absolutely the case! And when there is truly something of concern that might be happening soon, then you can do some extremely useful and important things to get ready for it.

(Add to board.)

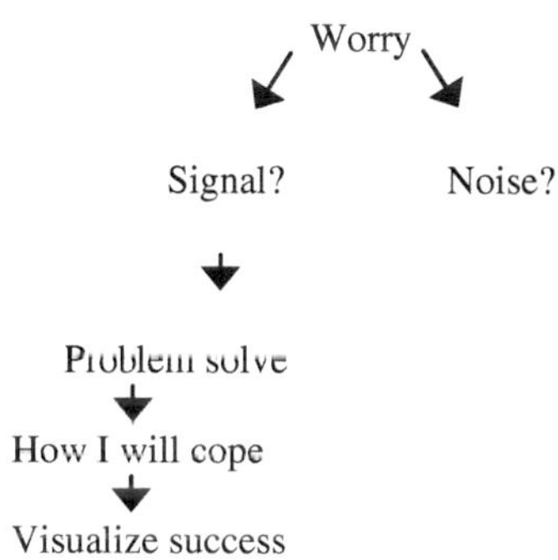

Figure 4.4 Worry: Signal leads to coping.

You can problem solve. You can plan how you'll cope if things are difficult. You can visualize the near future, when the hardest part of this is behind you. Someone once said that if you spend the afternoon worrying, what you have at the end of the afternoon is a headache. If you put a pen, pencil, phone, or computer mouse in your hand while you worry, what you have at the end of the afternoon is a plan. So I'm inviting you to transform your worry into a plan.

Now, if you decide that your anxiety is more "noise," you can use a lot of the things we talk about in some of the other sessions, such as our physical coping techniques and thinking coping techniques. And there are some ways of using our "exposure" tools that we're talking about today, too. One little way you can "expose" yourself to uncertainty and discomfort that has been suggested is this: When you're in a restaurant, and you're looking at a menu and not knowing what to order, you might push yourself to make a decision in 20 seconds, and look for the discomfort that comes with the possibility that you didn't pick the "best thing"![7]

By the way, if you can't decide if the worry is "signal" or "noise," at least one expert[8] suggests you should play it safe and treat it like a signal. You assume that it's a legitimate thing to be concerned about, and you plan for how you will cope with what might come up. Isn't it interesting that an expert on anxiety would take that "conservative" position?

There is actually some fascinating research that suggests that some people actually perform *better* on tasks if they take the time to anticipate what might go wrong and plan how they might handle it. If they *don't* take the time to do this, they actually feel worse and perform worse! Sometimes this is called "defensive pessimism," and there is a whole website on it (www.defensivepessimism.com)[9] if you would like to learn more about this perspective. Again, this is an example of a place where a counterintuitive approach works better for some people than the commonsense message of "Don't worry."

WRITE, READ, AND SHRED

And then there's "Write, read, and shred." This is a wonderful technique for worry and obsessive thoughts. Here's how you do it. You get a pad of paper—lined paper is best—and a pen or pencil, and you set a timer, like a kitchen timer, for 10 to 20 minutes. Do this early in the day, by the way. You set your timer, and you start writing what you're worried about. You can actually write anything you want, for that matter. The only "rule" in this technique is that you're supposed to keep writing until the timer goes off. If you run out of things to write, you're supposed to just keep copying what you've already written—like a kid in school writing "I will not throw spitballs at the teacher.

[7] See Wilson (2002b) in References.
[8] See Wilson (2002b) in References.
[9] See Norem (2001) in References.

I will not throw spitballs at the teacher." You don't stop writing until the timer goes off. Then you read it, silently, to yourself. And then you shred it. If you don't have a shredder, you're supposed to take a pair of scissors and cross cut it in little, tiny pieces and throw them away. This isn't a journal you keep to read later or to bring to your therapist or, heaven forbid, for your grandchildren to find some day. That's also why you never do this on your computer and just delete it, because with modern technology, there's always a chance something could be retrieved. You are physically destroying what you've written. In fact, this technique used to be called "Write, read, and burn," but then someone decided that it was better not to tell people to play with matches. There seems to be something symbolic about physically cutting up and getting rid of your worry. And it's symbolic that you do it again the next day. And the next day. This combination of writing your worry and getting rid of it becomes part of your routine. It's—sorry for the gross analogy—sort of like your emotional bowel movement. You just get it out of you.

TOOLS FOR ANXIETY ABOUT MEDICAL PROCEDURES

Now I want to talk about some things you can do for anxiety about medical procedures and appointments, which, actually, most people have, to some extent. After all, not many people actively look forward to going to the doctor or the dentist. Almost everyone finds shots and blood tests uncomfortable. And lots of medical procedures are downright unpleasant and scary. It's really normal to not like those things! But when your anxiety interferes with taking good care of your health or getting the care you need, growing your courage and coping are really good and important things you can do for yourself. In lots of ways, the exposure and habituation things we've been talking about today are applicable here just as they are with any other fear. When people learn that they can tolerate a dental procedure, for instance, it might be easier to go to the dentist the next time. Sometimes it helps to openly acknowledge to the medical provider that you might get anxious or might wince or make a noise—there's that counterintuitive thing again. Some people find it helpful to have detailed information, from the doctor or the dentist or lab tech, or from a handout, or from the Internet, about what's going to be done. Other people would rather not know the details. This is one of those situations in which the same thing doesn't work for everyone, and you need to discover what works for you. Some people like to distract themselves while a procedure is going on. You can count backward, find right angles in the room, or anything else. Whatever you do, it *definitely* helps to remember to breathe!

WHEN "PURE" EXPOSURE ISN'T APPLICABLE

I said a minute ago that in lots of ways, exposure and habituation are applicable with medical fears. But there's also a slightly different way you might use our tools here. The reason is that there are some things, and some medical procedures fall into this category, that you can't do—or wouldn't want to do—a little at a time. Pure exposure therapy means exposing yourself to something in real life. That works best, whenever it's possible and practical. But, as we just said, some situations simply *can't* be approached "a little at a time." For example, no one would tell somebody to deliberately have five unnecessary minor surgeries in preparation for major surgery!

So, when exposure in "real life" is something you just wouldn't do, the next best thing may be to *imagine* being in the situation. And this may include imagining the "worst-case scenario." This may actually be easier to do than you might think, because people who experience anxiety tend to have *wonderful* imaginations! After all, they can imagine all kinds of terrible things! So, I want to invite you to use that excellent imagination to visualize yourself *coping* with whatever is going on. That absolutely doesn't mean that you have to like it! But you are doing it. You're getting through it. You're tapping strength and courage that are already solidly inside you. You already know how to do that. You've done it far more times than you may realize. And you already know how to do boring, distasteful, and uncomfortable things. You might remember that you've taken out the garbage. You've probably paid taxes and insurance premiums. In school, you've studied for and taken tests. You may have kept an appointment with the urologist or the gynecologist. It wasn't something you loved, but you did it. You got it over with, and that was better for you, in some way, than avoiding it.

Sometimes, when we're imagining doing something that's really scary and playing that "video in our mind," we consciously or unconsciously "stop the action" at the worst possible moment, such as when we're freaking out or can't possibly imagine it getting any worse. In this technique, you *don't* stop the action there. Instead, you force yourself to keep the video going. You play it out to the end: What happens next? And next? And next? *After* you have that horrible panic attack and they take you to the emergency room? *After* you get fired from your job? You finish the video, and you include the part where, even if your knee is bruised or your pride is bruised, someone else has created far more drama than you have, and you've picked up the pieces and moved on.

BEING ANXIOUS AND DOING IT ANYWAY

Sometimes when people listen to all this, they're thinking something like this: "Well, maybe I *should* do all that stuff—the imagining, the courage ladder, the bringing it on. But I'm not ready. I'm way too anxious right now. I need to wait till I'm ready." On one level, that's absolutely something to be aware of and to respect. After all, everyone changes at his or her own pace and in his or her own way. But, at the same time, I want to add this: If you wait until you're fully comfortable or "ready" to do this, do you know how long you'll be waiting? *(Instructor pauses. If no one spontaneously answers the following, the instructor continues.)*

Way too many people discover that when you wait until you're 100% ready, you're waiting forever! So, experts often encourage us to push ourselves to do *a little bit more* than we're ready for. Someone once said it like this: Being anxious and doing it anyway aren't mutually exclusive. It's sort of like walking and chewing gum: You can do both at the same time.

Here is an even more "physical" example: Have you ever been in your car, either driving or riding, and you had to go to the bathroom? There was no place to stop, and you had to "hold it" for a while? Almost everyone has been in that situation some time, and I bet you drove, or were a passenger, safely, and appropriately, even though you "had to go." If you've done that, and most of us have, then you already know *from your own experience* that it's possible for you to have both psychological and physical discomfort—and to do something safely and appropriately at the same time.

DISCOVERING AND BUILDING ON HOW YOU LEARN

Now we're going to discover how you best learn things. All of us, if you think about it, have an amazing amount of life experience, learning so many new things. And we all have our individual ways of learning. So I want to invite each of you to think about a new skill you learned at some point—either recently or a while back, it doesn't matter—that was a significant piece of learning. Maybe it was something like learning to use a computer, or a cell phone, or a digital camera. Maybe it was learning to play a sport, or an instrument, or learning to speak a different language, or to do woodworking. Maybe it was learning to drive a car. Maybe it was learning how to take care of a baby. Maybe it was learning how to put in contact lenses. Whatever it was, allow yourself to remember what worked for you in learning that thing. What were the critical ingredients? Observing others? Practice, over and over again? Reading? Time alone, to make as many mistakes as you needed to make? What was the hardest part? The most fun? Did the learning happen gradually, a little at a time, or was there an "aha" experience, when suddenly you knew what to do? I'm going to be silent for a minute and allow you to enjoy remembering how that skill grew.

(Instructor allows class to take a minute or so to reflect silently on this.)

BUILDING COURAGE LADDERS

Now it's your turn. We're going to take a few minutes to start to build our courage ladders, right in here. So I want to invite you to create some little, tiny steps, the smaller the better. Remember that the courage ladder concept is one you can use to build all kinds of changes, from very behavioral ones to more internal or interpersonal ones. You can build a courage ladder for the sensations of panic, or to practice worrying and then doing something anyway. Of course, if there's not some something in your life to increase right now, please don't feel as though you *have* to build a courage ladder today. For some people, the courage ladder is a tool to keep in your toolbox, for whenever you need it later.

(Instructor passes around 3″×5″ note cards, encouraging participants to take five to ten cards [not just one].)

Sometimes a good way to start your courage ladder is to write one really easy item on one note card and then one really hard one on another, and then you work forward and backward. Add a card where you *imagine* you taking a step, before you actually do so. Then there's the card where you actually do it. Then add the card where you tell yourself: "I did it!" We probably won't have enough time to finish everyone's courage ladder while we're together today, but this will get you started. So as you all begin, I'm going to come around, and if it's okay, peek over your shoulder and add my thoughts.

(After allowing a few minutes for people to begin, the instructor goes around to each person and asks whether it is okay to read what has been written. If so, the instructor comments on good ideas that have been expressed, answers questions, and adds any thoughts about specific steps.)

Wow, I'm struck by the creative ideas and steps you all have come up with. What a lot of courage and strength we have in this room today!

It's almost time for us to wind down, so now I want to give you all some time to ask questions or share reactions about anything we've talked about in here today. To get our discussion started, I might ask: What are some areas where you realize, as we talk about it today, that experience and practice have already helped you to get braver?

(Instructor facilitates discussion, as time permits, following what participants want to discuss. No one is forced to talk. This may be an opportunity to remind people of "You can—and you don't have to.")

SUGGESTIONS FOR PRACTICE

Now I want to give you some ideas for taking this with you, to experiment at home with what we've talked about in here today. Please use *any* ideas or suggestions from this class in a way that works for you!

First, I want to invite you to review the readings for this class. These cover what we talked about in here today.

(These are Appendix B in this book and on the companion website.)

Second, I want to invite those of you who started courage ladders to keep building them. Notice how once you start thinking of little steps, you recognize more and more of them. Keep adding baby steps, and remember that the tinier and more specific they are, the better! Remember to include on your cards you visualizing yourself getting through the hard parts, and remember to include cards that remind you to celebrate what you've done!

And if you have a courage ladder, I want to invite you to start to take some steps on it. Not big ones—just little, tiny ones. Notice how you use what you already know about how learning best happens for you. Notice how you learn, and change, even when it's hard, and celebrate your courage!

And finally, for all of you, I want to invite you to notice some of those times when you experience some discomfort, or distraction, of some kind, and somehow "do something anyway." An example might be: You're watching television, and you have a gas pain. It's not so bad that you have to get up and go to the bathroom, but you can feel it. You keep watching your program, and the feeling subsides. Or, you're walking across your bedroom, and you stub your toe. It hurts! You hop, and yelp, and maybe mutter your favorite four-letter word. But you continue wherever you were going. Or you're washing dishes. A song on the radio stirs a memory. Tears well in your eyes. And you keep washing the dishes through the tears. Or you go to your mailbox for the mail. You see a letter you are definitely not looking forward to opening. Your heart pounds. You have the urge to throw it away. But you carry it into the house and open it. Or your breathing starts getting short. You feel as though a panic attack is coming. But you ride the wave, and your breathing calms down.

Do you get what I mean? Think of your own examples, of the amazing ability you already have, in so many areas, to have discomfort and do something anyway. Pay attention to how you do that and what that teaches you about "being anxious and doing it anyway."

END OF SESSION FORM AND FEEDBACK

Now we have our short form for you to fill out.

(Instructor distributes End of Session Form [p. 22, in Chapter 2; also the final page of the learner readings for this session, in Appendix B], or equivalent designed for the practice setting. If this form has been duplicated, participants can keep one copy, while the instructor collects the other.)

And then we'll go around, and everyone can say very briefly what he or she most wants to remember from today.

(After forms are complete and collected)

Our tradition in here is that anyone who is "graduating" goes first. Who is "graduating" today?

(Instructor facilitates "going around and saying what I want to remember." Instructor may choose to make brief comments about common themes that have emerged.)

So, for our "graduates," we wish you the best! And for the rest of us, we'll see you next week!

CHAPTER 5

Instructor Notes for Topic Three: Thinking Techniques

WELCOME AND INTRODUCTION

(Instructor may want to bring copies of the End of Session Form to this session. This form is p. 22, in Chapter 2; it is also the final page of the learner readings for this session [Appendix C]. Or the instructor may use an equivalent form, tailored to the specifics of the practice setting.)

Welcome to Solution Focused Anxiety Management! I'm delighted you're all here today! We are going to be celebrating and building courage, and this is an awesome thing you're doing for yourself, being here today. Just being here takes courage and is a step in the right direction!

For those of you who are here today for the first time, I want to go over what we do in here. We go around and share first names, although if our class is so big that we will never remember them, we may decide to skip our introductions. Then I present some information about managing anxiety. That part is mostly me talking, for two reasons. First, there are a lot of things I want to be sure to have enough time to tell you. Second, in a class on anxiety, there are sometimes people who wouldn't feel comfortable if they felt as though they "had to talk." So, as far as talking out loud in here goes, "You can—and you don't have to." By the way, "You can—and you don't have to" is a phrase that you're going to hear again and again in this class because it applies to so many things!

Anyway, after the information part, we take some time for discussion, questions, whatever people want to talk about and that we have time to talk about. Then we end with a short form for you to fill out, and by going around and everyone having a chance to say aloud, if you want to, what you want to remember or take with you from today. We do the same thing every week. There are four different information presentations. Every time you'll be encouraged to do some reading, and parts of that material repeat exactly what I'm presenting. We do that because some people have requested it in the past, so you don't have to feel as though you have to take notes. After people have been to all four classes, they're welcome to go through the series again, either right away, or at a later time, if they ever want to.

http://dx.doi.org/10.1016/B978-0-12-394421-4.00005-X

Significant others are welcome and encouraged to come with you to the class, too, if you would like them to do so. Many people find that the more that someone in their lives understands about anxiety management, the better! If someone in your life isn't here today, it's fine to repeat a session to bring him or her along. And, of course, it's perfectly okay to come to this class by yourself. We want you to use this program and all of the material we're going to be giving you in a way that works for you. That's a message you'll probably hear from me over and over again in here. So you can bring someone with you—and you don't have to! That is another one of the many ways that you can decide how you want to use this program.

Now I want to emphasize something about the name of this class, Solution Focused Anxiety Management. I want you all to hear clearly that it's not called "solution focused anxiety *elimination*." Of course, "anxiety elimination" is what people want! So it's important for you to be an "informed consumer." This class isn't going to claim to teach you how to make all of your anxiety disappear, but it *will* teach you how to be stubborn enough not to let it get in the way of things you want to do. You don't have to wait for anxiety to totally go away to be able to do things, both the tasks of daily living and some wonderful, amazing things.

We're real informal in here. If you need to take a break, just feel free to step out any time and come on back in.

Our one rule is confidentiality: What you hear about other people's lives stays in this room, and you can expect that same confidentiality from everyone else. But any principles or information you learn may be shouted from the rooftops! And what you discover about yourself can be shared or kept private, in whatever combination, and in whatever way feels right for you.

What questions can I answer for you now?

(Instructor may invite sharing of first names here, if desired.)

THINKING COPING TECHNIQUES

Sometimes when people have coped with a tough situation and you ask them how they did it, they say something like this: "I remembered that even though it feels like 'I can't stand it,' I *have* gotten through it before."

Sometimes a thought popping into your head soothes you. It reminds you of your strengths or of a different perspective, and you feel better able to cope. If that has ever happened to you, you have discovered on your own something that modern psychology has written a whole lot about! Those are the thinking coping techniques, sometimes called "cognitive" techniques. That is what we will be talking about today: another "tool in the toolbox" to experiment with and discover whether it fits for you.

So, *thinking* coping techniques are sentences or phrases you say to yourself in your head, or they might be images you visualize, that support you as you approach a frightening situation. That's really important, because when we are feeling anxious or scared, we sometimes say things that *increase* rather than decrease our anxiety. For example, if a person keeps thinking, while on the way to a meeting, "I know I'm going to blow it; I won't have a thing to say; I'm going to feel like an absolute fool," he or she will probably feel *more* anxious by the time he or she gets there.

And we sometimes say things like that to ourselves in our heads without being fully aware that we are doing so. And we may not realize at that moment that we can do something different. So learning about thinking coping techniques reminds us of something we probably already know: You can, and you probably already do, use your thoughts and images to support your courage and strength. Today we'll be talking about noticing how you do that and doing more of it.

So, here is the background for this. We sometimes assume that certain external events make us feel and do certain things.

(Instructor writes on board.)

External	→	Feelings
Event		Behavior

Figure 5.1 Common assumption about events, feelings, and behavior.

And we're going to start with an example that *doesn't* directly involve anxiety. Lots of people feel happy and energized when the sun is out, the sky is blue, and it's a nice clear day. And their "behavior," or things they do, might include smiling and chatting with people in their lives. Whether they realize it or not, they may assume that the "sunny day" is the reason for their good mood.

(On board)

External	→	Feelings
Event		Behavior
Sunny day		Happy
		Smile, chat

Figure 5.2 Common assumption about events, feelings, and behavior: Sunny day example.

But sunny weather doesn't produce good moods for everyone. For instance, one woman hates sunny days. She knows she gets irritable and snappy when the sun is out. And she knows why this is. She grew up in Switzerland, where the weather is often rainy and cloudy. On the rare days when the sun was out, people abandoned their responsibilities and "went out to play." Now she lives in southern California, where the sun is out most of the time. She still feels pressure to "be outside" and "go somewhere" when the sun is out, and she feels as though she never has time to do inside things such as working on her quilting and baking bread. She feels irritated, and her behavior, or what she does, includes sulking and snapping at people in her life.

(On board)

External	→	Feelings
Event		Behavior
Sunny day		Irritable
		Sulks, snaps

Figure 5.3 Effect of sunny day on Swiss woman.

So the process *isn't* a simple cause and effect thing, in which the external event directly leads to the feelings and the behavior. The exact same external thing, a sunny day, sometimes produces radically different reactions in different people. The reason is that external events—and internal reactions, too, something we're going to talk about in a few minutes—have certain *meanings* to us. They trigger thoughts and images almost automatically. Sometimes these get called "automatic thoughts," and those reactions can have a lightning-fast impact on how we feel and what we do.

(Add to board.)

A	→	B	→	C
Event		Automatic Thoughts Meaning		Feelings Behavior

Figure 5.4 A-B-C model.

So, for our Swiss friend, for example, a cloudy day might trigger this: "All right! A great day to stay inside! I think I'll work on my quilt today." And she's happy, smiling, chatting with people in her life.

(Add the following to board.)

A	→	B	→	C
Cloudy day		All right! A great day to stay inside! I think I'll work on my quilt today.		Happy Smiles, chats

Figure 5.5 Cloudy day example for A-B-C chart.

And when she wakes up in the morning and it's sunny, her automatic thought might be this: "Oh, crap. Sun's out again. Have to go somewhere. Never get to do what I really want to do." And she's irritable, sulking or snapping at people.

(Add the following to board.)

A	→	B	→	C
Sunny day		Oh, crap. Sun's out again. Have to go somewhere. Never get to do what I really want to do.		Irritable Sulks, snaps

Figure 5.6 Sunny day example for A-B-C chart.

So, the challenge is this: If she wants clouds and gets sun, is there anything she might say to herself in her head at Point B so that at Point C she might feel and do something different? Yes, there is. And I want to share with you a powerful and amazingly useful two-part formula that helps you to make that crucial change at Point B. Step One is to "accept." And there are two things you accept: first, the reality of the situation, and second, how you feel about it. Step Two is to say "But—." And after the "But—," you add something like this: "I'm going to be *stubborn* enough not to let that external thing stop me from what I really want to do." And that can make a *big difference* in how you feel and what you do.

(On board)

Accept: Two things:

a. the *reality* of the situation, and

b. your *feelings* about it;

But … stubborn … not ruin day

So, for our Swiss friend, "I wanted clouds, but got sun" is the "reality" of the situation. And "I don't like it!" is the feeling. Or, maybe the "feeling" is a mixed one, like this: "Part of me likes it and is actually tempted to go for a walk, and part of me doesn't like it because I *always* go for walks and never get to do quilting and inside stuff."

Now, let's add Step Two of our little formula: "But—I'm going to be stubborn enough not to let the weather stop me from what I really want to do. It's way easier to stay home when it's gray outside, but I really want to quilt today. I think I'll sit in this sunny window and work on my quilting."

(Instructor writes the following chart on board.)

A	→	B	→	C
Sunny day		1a. I wanted clouds and got sun.		Mixture of irritation, amusement, pride, satisfaction.
		1b. I don't like it. Actually, mixed feelings		
		But—stubborn, do quilting anyway		Quilting!

Figure 5.7 Sunny day example with two-part formula.

Look at what has happened at Point C. After using our little formula and looking at it differently, she *is doing* her quilting. That's what she wanted to do! The *feeling* might still include a little irritation, but now there might also be some amusement at her dilemma, and there might also be some pride and satisfaction in how she worked it out. She came up with her own creative solution! She didn't have to move back to Switzerland to do what she wanted to do, and she didn't have to be depressed and resentful. That's *really different* from where she started out.

Now, you might notice that I've used the word "stubborn" a few times. I'm wondering if anyone in here today (in addition to me!) has ever had the word "stubborn" applied to you? *(Instructor pauses, looks around room for nods indicating "Yes," nodding in response.)*

You know, it's interesting: Sometimes when people call us "stubborn," they're not saying it as a positive characteristic. But in solution focused anxiety management, stubbornness is a significant strength. The reason is that it can be an *advantage*, when it comes to managing anxiety, to have a touch of "stubbornness"—or persistence or determination, maybe, if you'd rather call it that. You can use that strength to be stubborn enough *not* to let anxiety get in the way of what you truly want to do.

Now I want to share an example involving anxiety. This time we'll make our external thing at Point A an elevator, since sometimes people who feel anxious have trouble with elevators. So I'm going to invite you to consider three possible scenarios. *(Instructor writes the following on board.)*

A	→	B	→	C
Elevator				
Elevator				
Elevator				

Figure 5.8 Elevator example I.

The first one will be someone who is afraid to ride on an elevator. This person's feeling at Point C is probably fear, and the behavior is to avoid. *(Instructor fills in C on first row on the chart.)*

A	→	B	→	C
Elevator				Fear Avoid
Elevator				
Elevator				

Figure 5.9 Elevator example II.

Now, think about someone who doesn't mind elevators. Those of you who are fine on elevators might think about this: What's your *feeling* when you go up to an elevator? *(Pause briefly.)* I would guess that for most of you it's probably pretty matter-of-fact or neutral. You're not super happy or particularly upset. Right? *(Pause briefly, waiting for possible nods.)* And your behavior? For most of us, we push the button, and when the door opens, we get on. *(Instructor fills in C on second row on the chart.)*

A →	B →	C
Elevator		Fear Avoid
Elevator		Neutral Get on
Elevator		

Figure 5.10 Elevator example III.

Now let's talk about the really important third possible scenario: a friend who is learning to *manage* a fear of elevators. This person probably still has some fear, maybe a little less, but here, the behavior is that he or she gets on. *(Instructor fills in C on third row on the chart.)*

A →	B →	C
Elevator		Fear Avoid
Elevator		Neutral Get on
Elevator		Fear (a little less) Get on anyway

Figure 5.11 Elevator example IV.

This combination of *fear and approach* at Point C is one of our favorite definitions of *courage*. Those of us who feel sort of neutral about elevators aren't doing anything particularly "courageous" or remarkable when we ride on them. But our friend who has some fear *and does the feared thing anyway* is demonstrating *courage*. And I know that when I facilitate this class, I meet some pretty remarkable and courageous people.

(Instructor pauses to highlight this and looks around room, smiling.)

Now let's go back to our chart and fill in what each person might be thinking at Point B. In our first scenario, the person in the elevator might be thinking something like this: "This thing is going to get stuck. I'll be trapped in there for hours. I'm sure it will happen! And there's nothing I can do about it!" *(Fill in B of first row.)*

A →	B →	C
Elevator	I'll be trapped! I'm sure it will happen! There's nothing I can do about it!	Fear Avoid

Figure 5.12 Elevator example V.

There might be an intense focus on three things: how very dangerous it is, the high probability of something bad happening, and how helpless they feel to do anything to make it better.

(On board)

↑ danger
↑ probability of bad things happening
↑ helplessness

Now, people who don't mind elevators—what do you think they are thinking about? *(Pause briefly.)* It might just be some random thought. Or it could have to do with the person they're about to visit, what you might call their "destination." So they might be thinking, "Am I on time?" "Should I text my friend to let him know I'm on my way up?" "I hope they've got the air conditioning on in there!" "Did I bring all the ingredients for the potluck?" They might be happy or excited or concerned about something, but it's not the elevator they're focusing on. The elevator is just a means of getting there. *(Add "destination" in B of second row.)*

Elevator	Destination	Neutral Get on

Figure 5.13 Elevator example VI.

Let's talk about what the thoughts might be at Point B for our courageous friend who is afraid but gets on anyway. Maybe our friend is using our little formula. First, the "reality" of the situation is this: Elevators *do* sometimes get stuck. One *could* get trapped. Maybe part of the reality is that this actually *has* happened to our friend in the past. And the "feeling" is "I'm scared!" Maybe it's also "I'm embarrassed about being scared" and also "I really want to change this."

Next, our friend might use our step of saying, "But—I'm going to be stubborn enough to not let my fear control my life." And our friend might add something else. If fear *grows* by "turning up the volume" on the details of danger, on the probability of bad things happening, and on feeling helpless, *(Point to this on board, or write it again.)*

↑ danger
↑ probability of bad things happening
↑ helplessness

Then maybe fear *diminishes* by "turning *down* the volume" on those things. *(Add "down arrows.")*

↑ danger ↓
↑ probability of bad things happening ↓
↑ helplessness ↓

And courage *grows* when we do this:
(On board)

↑ safety
↑ probability of good things happening
↑ strength, ability to cope

So our friend might remember things that help keep us safe and the likelihood of good things happening (or bad things ending). He or she might remember the many strengths that empower us and enable us to cope when things are tough. Our friend might remember, "I know that elevators really don't get stuck very often. And if this one does, I actually know some things I could do. I could call my friend on my cell phone. Sometimes phones work in elevators, so it's worth a try. Or I could push that little 'attendant call' button. I can remember to breathe. I can do that even if it's scary."

(Fill in B in third row of chart. The completed chart now looks like this.)

A →	B →	C
Elevator	I'll be trapped! I'm sure it will happen! There's nothing I can do about it!	Fear Avoid
Elevator	Destination	Neutral Get on
Elevator	1a. It could get stuck. b. I'm scared! 2. But—it probably won't. And if it does, I will use cell, call button, breathe, remember that I can do this!	Fear (a little less Get on anyway)

Figure 5.14 Elevator example VII.

Now let's do an example in which the thing at Point A is a *sensation*. This is incredibly valuable for anyone who gets *panic attacks*. In this example, at Point A, the person might be having chest pain. And the immediate thought at Point B is, of course, "Heart attack!" At Point C, of course, is intense fear, and whatever we do when we feel very afraid.

(Instructor erases other example and begins the following chart on board.)

A →	B →	C
Chest pain	Heart attack!	Intense fear

Figure 5.15 Chest pain example I.

Now watch what happens when we use our formula. "The *reality* of the situation is that my chest is hurting. It *could be* a heart attack. It could also be one of those stupid panic attacks. When I was at the emergency room the last time this happened, they did an EKG and told me my heart is fine, and that this is panic. The *feeling* is that I'm scared. And I *hate* it when this happens. And I'm *confused*. I don't know if I should call an ambulance or wait it out. Crap!" (Excuse my language!) Isn't this combination of feelings what happens lots of times?

Okay, here is Step Two. "But—I need to remember that this probably is one of those 'expletive deleted' panic attacks I hate so much. Okay, breathe. I can still think. I can remember that they told me I'm a 'body reactor.' I can wait for it to pass. I can call my friend. I can use my brain. If I want some advice on what to do, I can call that emergency phone service that my healthcare offers and tell them what's going on. I've been through this before. I do know what to do."

A →	B →	C
Chest pain	Heart attack!	Intense fear
Chest pain	1a. My chest hurts. It *could* be a heart attack. It could also be panic. The reality is that right now I don't know which it is. b. I'm scared! And more! 2. But—I need to remember: I'm a body reactor. It probably will pass. I'm not helpless. Breathe! Use your brain. Call healthcare provider if you need to.	Fear (a little less) Sense of control

Figure 5.16 Chest pain example II.

And now, our friend may still feel scared, but it's very, very different from totally freaking out. There's empowerment, and soothing, and a plan.

(Instructor completes chart above.)

This is so incredibly important because we may not always be able to change certain things that happen out in the world. We also may not be able to control our first, immediate reaction, or certain sensations in our bodies. But we *can* learn to see things in a different way. You probably already do so, maybe more often than you may realize. And that can make a tremendous difference in how you feel and in what you do.

Now I want to show you another way of writing this. You can make a grid like this.

(Erase what is on board and begin the following chart.)

Thoughts Now (might increase anxiety)	Alternate Thoughts (might decrease anxiety)

Figure 5.17 Thoughts now and alternatives grid I.

Now we're going to look at a copy of a few pages from our readings for today. *(This is Worksheet C.1, the Solution Focused Anxiety Management Automatic Thoughts and Alternate Perspectives Worksheet in Appendix C, on p. 263 of this book. Instructor verifies that everyone has a copy of this form that he or she can write on.)*

I want to invite you to turn to page 263, where we have the two columns, just like on the board. In the left column, we have a bunch of things that people sometimes say to themselves in their heads that end up making them more anxious than they want to be. Then on the right, for each one of those thoughts, there are a couple of alternatives, things that you might say instead, that could empower you or give you a different "take" on them. Now, I'm going to read these aloud, and I invite you to follow along silently. Here's how I'll do it. I'll read "Thought Number One" on the left, and then go to the right column and read some alternatives for that one. Then I'll go back to the left and read "Thought Number Two," and then go right and read some alternatives for that one. And so on.

So, as you follow along, when we get to any thoughts on the left that "sound like you," you might want to put a mark next to them, in the left margin. And when one of the alternatives on the right seems as though it might be useful to experiment with instead, you might put a mark next to that one, in the right margin, like this.

	Thoughts Now (might increase anxiety)	Alternate Thoughts (might decrease anxiety)	
	1. xxxxxxxxxxxxx	1a. xxxxxxxxxxxxxxxxx	
	xxxxxxxxxxxxxxx	b. xxxxxxxxxxxxxxxxx	
		c. xxxxxxxxxxxxxxxxxx	
x	2. xxxxxxxxxxxxxxx	2a. xxxxxxxxxxxxxxxxxxx	
		b. xxxxxxxxxxxxxxxxxx	x

Figure 5.18 Thoughts now and alternatives grid II.

(Instructor checks with the class to be sure that everyone understands and has access to the worksheet.)

Okay, here is the first one: Oh, "expletive deleted"! Weird physical symptoms again. I bet I'm going to lose it.

And here are some alternatives: I need to remember: I'm a body reactor. These feelings will build and crest and then come down on their own, just like they always do. The fact that they're here right now doesn't mean I'm going to lose it. These feelings don't always turn into a full panic attack any more. Now that I know what they are, they aren't as scary as they used to be. And if you're taking medicine: Now that I have this medicine in me, the sensations don't scare me as much. The medicine helps them just drift away.

By the way, these alternatives are only suggestions. The best alternatives are usually the ones you come up with or realize that you are already using! For all of these that we're doing together, when you think of another one that fits for you even better—it might be a variation of one of ours or a brand new one—I invite you to add it to your list. And please feel free to share it with the rest of us if you like! So, what else might be useful to remember for this one? *(Instructor pauses, to give participants a chance to add a thought, in writing and/or aloud.)*

Here is the next one. I'm getting anxious. I'm not going to be able to function (speak, drive, take this exam, stay in this room).

And here are some alternatives. Yes, I will. I've done it before. It's like "walking and chewing gum at the same time." The discomfort I feel at first will subside. Hang in there. You can do it. And what else, for this one? *(Pause)*

And the next one: I can't go. I'll fall apart.

And the alternatives: That's how I feel right this minute. I can allow that to be there, and get ready to go, even with my feelings, and watch the feelings change. What do I need to do to nurture myself right now? What will be more helpful: a little "push" to go, even in the presence of my anxiety, or a little "permission," to take my time—or both? And what else, for this one? *(Pause)*

Okay, here is the next one. I take pride in my high standards, and I'm not measuring up. And some alternatives: Yes, it's hard for me when I don't do as well as I'd like. I need to be really gentle and nurturing to myself right now. I can ask myself: What is the single most important thing I can do right now to feel proud of how I handled this? If I've made an error, I can acknowledge it, with self-respect and dignity, and get things back on track. I can remember: "What do they call the person who graduated at the bottom of the class in medical school? Doctor." And what else, for this one? *(Pause)*

Okay, here is the next one. If I can't do it perfectly, I'd rather not do it at all.

And some alternatives: It's uncomfortable for me when I'm imperfect, but I can remember that I don't have to be perfect in order to do a good job. Pushing myself to be perfect sometimes becomes counterproductive because so much energy goes into worrying that it can detract from my performance. When something goes imperfectly, I can get back on track. Being able to recover seamlessly may be an even more important skill than doing it perfectly in the first place. And requiring perfection contradicts everything we know about skill acquisition and climbing courage ladders. And there is this quote from Elbert Hubbard[1]: "The greatest mistake you can make in life is to be continually fearing you will make one."

Talking about this one reminds me of an exercise some experts suggest for people who consider themselves "perfectionists." The exercise is to deliberately do two things "imperfectly" every day. One should be so small and subtle that no one but you notices it. The other one doesn't have to be so big that it totally messes up your work, appearance, relationships, finances, or anything, but it's supposed to be big enough that someone else might notice it. The idea is that, just like when you walk on the sand on the beach in the summer and get "good calluses" on your feet, you sort of desensitize yourself to being imperfect. There's also the story that gets told about beautiful

[1] See Hubbard (2012b) in References.

Oriental rugs: It's said that each one has a small mistake deliberately woven into it. Isn't that an intriguing thought? And what else, for this one? *(Pause)*

Here is the next one. I can't help it that I have a short fuse when I get anxious. After all, I have a chemical imbalance!

And some alternatives: Yes, I get irritable. But that doesn't give me license to lash out at other people. And lashing out usually doesn't get other people to change much anyway. They just start telling me that I have an "anger problem," and the focus shifts away from whatever I wanted to express. Instead, I look like the bad guy! And it's *not* completely true that "I can't help it": If someone said, "Hey, you get a hundred thousand dollars if you can keep from lashing out," I bet I could do it—even if I do have a chemical imbalance. And what else, for this one? *(Pause)*

Okay, here is the next one. I've always been a sensitive person. I can't handle rejection or criticism or people being mad at me.

And here are some alternatives for this one. Yes, criticism and conflict are hard, but I *can* cope with them. I've done it before, and I can do it again. And I need to remember that people may not approve because of *their* issues. It isn't always because something's wrong with me. Relationships are resilient, and even though it might be hard to remember right now, sometimes disagreement and working it through make relationships stronger. Sometimes I'm sensitive, but I have more strength inside than other people realize—and maybe more than I realize, too. And what else, for this one? *(Pause)*

Okay, another one. There's something very wrong with me.

And some alternatives: It sure feels like that when these reactions happen! I need to remember that experts tell us that anxiety can manifest itself in lots of different ways. I can get checked out medically if I have concerns that there's something medical going on that I don't know about. I can remember that if I've been diagnosed with an "anxiety disorder," the thing that is "wrong with me" has a formal name, and that I'm here: I'm doing something about it; I'm getting treatment for it. And what else, for this one? *(Pause)*

Here is the next one. Calm down. Don't worry about it.

And some alternatives: That's *way* easier to say than to do! Given my style, and how I'm "hard wired," I probably *will* worry sometimes, and maybe more than other people do. If my worry helps me to prepare, or to handle it when things are hard, then I'm using it in a productive way. I think about *many* different things—some of them are things I worry about, but lots of them have nothing to do with my worries. And some of my thoughts are pretty creative! And what else, for this one? *(Pause)*

And the next one: I can't handle it if things don't go the way I want them to. Someone once said we all have a little two-year old inside, and that little person has a temper tantrum when he or she doesn't get his or her own way! I sure know that little person inside me, and I bet you know him or her inside you, too.

And here are some alternatives. I can treat myself the way I would lovingly nurture a two-year-old: I would hold that frustrated little person tight and say, "I understand. It's okay." I can remind myself, "You don't have to like it, and it's okay to fuss a little if you need to. And after you fuss, you *will* get through this." What can you do to help yourself make things even a little bit better, both now and a little way down the road? And what else, for this one? *(Pause)*

Here is another one. I need things to be just a certain way, and I lose it when things are different.

And some alternatives: Yes, structure and order and routine support me a lot, and it *is* harder for me when things are different. But I understand that about myself, and that insight helps me to cope. It helps me so I *don't* "lose it." I'm practicing strengthening my "flexibility muscles." And what else, for this one? *(Pause)*

Here is the next one. I can't handle uncertainty or change or when things go wrong.

And some alternatives: I don't like those things, but I actually have more capacity to tolerate them than I may give myself credit for. After my initial reaction subsides, I will use the resources, internal and external, that support me. I can remember my sense of humor. To paraphrase Elbert Hubbard,[2] "Life is one damned thing after another." And in the words of John Lennon,[3] "Life is what happens to you while you're busy making other plans." And what else, for this one? *(Pause)*

And another one: I'm socially inept.

Here are some alternatives for this one: If social interactions are difficult for me, I can grow my skills with practice. I can smile. I can ask questions. I can ask other people about themselves. I can listen. And I can remember that being quieter is okay. And what else, for this one? *(Pause)*

Another one: After what happened to me before, I can't do it (go there, try that) again.

Some alternatives for this one: Of course I'm apprehensive. But I care too much about doing this *not* to go back. It *will* be hard at first. It's

[2] See Hubbard (2012a) in References.
[3] See Lennon (1980) in References.

important enough to me to do this that I'm going to tolerate the discomfort. And what else, for this one? *(Pause)*

Here is the next one. I'm too anxious to practice.

And some alternatives for this one: Although it absolutely feels that way, practicing is actually one of the very best ways of growing my skills and comfort and confidence. The more I do it, even with my discomfort, the better I will get, and the less anxious I will be. There is the counterintuitive again! And what else, for this one? *(Pause)*

And another one: The worst possible thing is going to happen. I just know it will.

Here are some alternatives for this one: It *feels* that way, but I need to remember that *feeling* that something bad will happen doesn't mean that the bad thing *will* happen. The reality is that I absolutely don't know at this moment what the future is going to bring. Whether for better or worse, I cannot predict the future! It's true that the worst *could* happen, even if the probability of it is low. But the *possibility* of something bad happening doesn't mean that there is a high *probability* that it will. The best could happen, too, and there could be an outcome that is in between. So I need to remember that I've tolerated uncertainty before, and I can do it again. I have more ability to tolerate "not knowing" than I sometimes give myself credit for. And what else, for this one? *(Pause)*

And another one: If there is something bad that might happen, I can't stop obsessing and thinking about it.

And some alternatives for this one: It may *feel* as though worrying prevents bad things from happening, but it actually doesn't. What *does* help is planning and problem solving and anticipating how I might avoid trouble—and planning how I'll cope with it and support myself if something bad does happen. When worry visits me, I need to use it as a reminder to start that problem solving as soon as possible. Or, if this isn't the best time to do problem solving, I can allow the thoughts to "just be" and then allow them to drift elsewhere. Or I can distract and soothe myself. Or I can write my worries or worst fears, or share them with a trusted person if that helps me. I can decide what I need right now and do what works for me. And what else, for this one? *(Pause)*

Here is another one. I can't stand being alone. I have to have someone with me.

And here are some alternatives for this one: I may not *like* being left alone. It's lonely, and sometimes I worry, but I *can* stand it. Sometimes being alone is actually fun. I can do exactly what I want and don't have to worry about anyone else! And what else, for this one? *(Pause)*

Here's the next one. My anxiety is a result of very real past trauma, so it's going to be with me forever. Some alternatives for this one: Reality now is different from reality then: Something may have been necessary for survival once, but *not* now. I learned that old response; in the same way, I can learn a new response now. The past is not an excuse. A trauma may leave a scar forever, but an arm or leg with a scar can still work and play—and so can I.

I want to elaborate on that last thought a little bit because I think there absolutely are some experiences that leave emotional scars, sometimes permanent ones. And that's why I think the analogy of physical scars is so powerful. We all have scars on our bodies. When we see them, sometimes we remember what happened. And sometimes we are more careful in certain ways. But just as physical wounds heal and don't have to be the most interesting thing about us, memories of emotional injuries don't have to be deal breakers either, and they don't have to stop us from doing the things we care about and the things we want to do. And what else, for this one? *(Pause)*

Here is another one: Avoiding is better than facing it. If I don't put myself out there, at least nothing bad is going to happen.

And some alternatives for this one: Well, on one level, it may be true that nothing bad will happen, but on another level, if something truly needs to get done eventually, avoidance only postpones the inevitable. It's still hanging over me. I will feel better when I get it over with. And if this is something I really *do* want to do, or maybe part of me wants to do, I'm going to feel frustrated and disappointed in myself. And there is another part to this, too: For some situations, choosing not to do something is absolutely a legitimate option. I can choose *not* to do something for now and change my mind later. I can—and I don't have to. And what else, for this one? *(Pause)*

Here is the next one. My anxiety is going to show. People are going to be able to tell how anxious I am. I'll be humiliated.

And now some alternatives for this one: Telling others about my situation, in self-respect and dignity, when *I* choose to do so, is a way of taking control and creating a safe environment for myself. Self-disclosure usually enhances relationships, while concealing detracts from them. And self-disclosure frequently results in others acknowledging their own fears, which may be more like mine than I realized.

I want to tell you about someone who came to a class like this one. This woman was very frightened by her panicky feelings and very fearful of anyone at work discovering that she had them. Before coming to the class, she had never met anyone else who got panic attacks. That was what she thought, at least. So, after she came to the class and heard other people describing feelings exactly like her own, she screwed up her courage and told a co-worker that sometimes she felt anxious. Her friend said, "You know, we were so concerned. We saw you turn green and suddenly leave the room, and we wondered what was happening to you. We didn't want to say anything, but we wondered if you were doing some kind of street drugs or selling drugs, and you had a beeper that was going off or something. I'm so glad you told me! It's just panic attacks. I used to get those, too."

The woman was horrified that people had been thinking that! Never in her life had she used or sold street drugs! What people had "filled in" or assumed was far worse than the reality of the situation. The woman told this story in her class the next week. And after that, when she felt a little anxious at work, she immediately told people that she was having one of her "garden variety panic attacks," and she asked them to please bear with her. Isn't that an interesting story? And what else, for this one? *(Pause)*

Another one: I *have* to be in control. I can't stand it when I'm *not* in control.

And some alternatives: There are people and situations and sensations in my body that sometimes I just can't control, however much I wish I could. To accept these moments when I temporarily feel out of control is really the ultimate control. If you think about it, this is a pretty powerful existential statement. And what else, for this one? *(Pause)*

Now, take a moment to look over the sentences we just read together. Notice which sentences resonate for you, since, of course, different things stand out for different people. Which are your favorites? *(Invite discussion.)*

Now, I want to mention what I *don't* suggest that you do with all this: I don't want anyone to go out of here feeling as though you have to memorize multiple pages of automatic thoughts and alternatives! Instead, I invite you to simply notice what resonates for you. And, as we said before, you might discover that the thoughts or images that make the most difference are the ones that you have come up with!

I want to share an example from the author of these materials that illustrates that it isn't always what's in the books that makes the most difference. She tells this little story: When she was first learning to drive, she started to develop a bad habit of stepping on the brake rather than the gas when she was in an entrance lane. Someone who was helping her learn to drive said,

"Scurry along, now." And for some reason, that phrase stuck in her head. Even when that person wasn't in the car, she started saying to herself "Scurry along, now," and she stepped on the gas. She says that she will never know why that particular phrase stuck in her mind. The person who was helping her learn to drive was generally supportive and said lots of helpful things. That phrase was only one of many. But she says that this was the phrase that helped her—more than any book or list of automatic thoughts or class could have done.

So, I invite you to notice the phrases or sentences that someone says to you, or that you say to yourself, that help you the very most.

There's one more thing I want to point out about that phrase, "Scurry along, now," that worked for our author. It has the flavor of something one might say to a child. And clearly the author wasn't a child then, if she was driving. But I don't think that tone is a coincidence. If we think about it, most of us *do* know what to say to a child, or a dear friend, or maybe anyone else in the world. Actually, many of us have a kind of "double standard": We can be so nurturing to a child—and so mean to ourselves! So, if you ever can't think of what you might say to yourself at Point B, or on the right side of our little grid, think about what you might say to a child. People sometimes talk about discovering one's "inner child," and you can nurture the "child" within you.

So, if memorizing is *not* the way to use all this, what *do* we suggest you do with all these thoughts and alternatives? One way to use this information, if it interests you, is to experiment with "catching yourself in the act" of having the thoughts or images that get you more anxious than you would like to be. When you notice one, you might experiment with saying an alternative in its place. It may well feel awkward, and it probably won't eliminate discomfort entirely.

But gently reminding yourself of the alternative is worth experimenting with. That's true even if you do so awkwardly, self-consciously, and even if you don't fully believe it. Even if you just do it as a half-hearted exercise, the process might decrease the intensity of your distress. And as this happens, you might notice other thoughts and feelings. You might notice a sense that you can tolerate it, or some calm. Or there might be something else, something that we haven't thought of yet. You might experiment with this on your own and be curious about what you discover.

Now we're going to take a few minutes to practice this process. We'll do an example together, and then I'm going to invite each of you to create your own example.

Notice that I've divided my right column into two parts, one for accepting the reality and the feelings, and one for the "But—," just like in our little two-part formula.

(Draw the following grid.)

Thoughts now	Alternatives	
	Accept a. Reality b. Feeling	But...

Figure 5.19 Thoughts now and alternatives grid with "Accept" column.

Here is our example. This is a man who is worried about an important sales presentation tomorrow. As he thinks about it, he is sweating and feeling his heart beat faster and faster. His thoughts snowball, growing more and more catastrophic. Here are some of his racing thoughts: "I won't be able to answer their questions." "I'll have a panic attack during the presentation." "They'll laugh at me." "We won't get the bid." "I'll be fired." "My wife will leave me." "I'll be homeless."

(Instructor adds these to the left column of the chart.)

Okay, let's do the first one: "I won't be able to answer their questions." What's the reality for that one? "True. They may ask things I don't know about." And how might I feel if that happens? "I'm probably going to get uptight. I hope I don't get defensive, but I might." Okay, what's the "But—?" for this one? "Well, I may be calmer than I think. I'm going to go over my PowerPoint tonight and anticipate what they might ask. And if there's something I can't answer, I'll let them know that it's a good question and that I'll get back to them with the answer."

(Instructor fills in the remaining two columns of the chart for this one.)

Okay, let's do the next one: "I might panic." The reality for that one? "Yes, I might. That's happened before when I get anxious, and it could happen again." And my feeling about it? "It's really embarrassing. I hate it when that happens." And the "But —?" "I need to remember what I learned in the class: Sweating doesn't always turn into massive panic. Sheesh, politicians on TV sweat all the time. It isn't always as noticeable as it feels. Last time my buddy said he couldn't even tell. And if I do get anxious, it will pass. I'll excuse myself and take a break if I need to."

(Instructor fills in the remaining two columns of the chart for this one.)

Okay, the next one: "They'll laugh at me." The reality for that one? "True, they might." And the feeling? "That would be humiliating." But—? "They probably won't. These guys know we're under pressure. And they're good guys. Sheesh, I sure wouldn't laugh at someone who was anxious. Let's give them the benefit of the doubt. And if someone does laugh, I'll ignore it. Or maybe I'll laugh, too."

(Instructor fills in the remaining two columns of the chart for this one.)

Okay, let's do the next one: "We won't get the contract." The reality here? "True, that's possible." And the feeling? "I'll be bummed. And obsess about what I did wrong." But—? "I know we don't get all the ones we bid on. But I'm going to do my best. If we don't get it, that sucks, and, knowing me, I'll probably mope and go into my cave for a while, and lick my wounds. And then it's off to the next project."

(Instructor fills in the remaining two columns of the chart for this one.)

Here's the next thought: "Management is going to be pissed. They're going to fire me for screwing up." The reality for that one? "It could happen. Guys get fired over less than that." And the feeling? "That would be pretty devastating."

Are you starting to see a pattern here, by the way, in all these variations of "It could happen" and "It's pretty scary"?

And the "But—?" "Well, they're not going to be thrilled, but I'm probably not going to get canned over this one thing. I can remember that no one likes the Monday morning quarterbacking that happens after an embarrassing defeat, but we do it, and we suck it up, and go on."

I want to add another piece here. Sometimes a job or a school turns out to be different from what we expected. Sometimes it isn't the best fit for us. If some situation in our lives constantly asks us to do something that's hard for us—such as someone who has a fear of heights having to climb telephone poles every day—then maybe moving on, even if it's hard in the short run, is absolutely for the best. We humans have amazing resilience: We look for a new job. We pick up the pieces and do what needs to be done.

(Instructor fills in the remaining two columns of the chart for this one.)

Okay, the next one: "Once I don't have a job and can't pay the bills, my wife (husband, girlfriend, boyfriend, etc.) is going to leave me." The reality here? Again, "True, it's possible." And the feeling? "Talk about devastating. One loss on top of another!" And the "But—?" "Well, she probably won't. That's probably me going overboard with every doomsday scenario from some corny classic country and western song. The *way* more likely thing is that we'll take good care of each other. We'll talk about what we have to do, and about how we're going to get through this."

But just like with the last one, it's absolutely true that relationships do end sometimes, and it's not always because we want them to. So: "If my relationship ends, for whatever reason, I may mourn, rage, feel as though I've hit bottom. Although it may feel inconceivable at the time it happens, I will probably love again. With or without my partner, I will go on."

(Instructor fills in the remaining two columns of the chart for this one.)

"No job, no money, no relationship... I'll lose my house... I won't be able to afford another place to live... No one else (job or relationship) will want me... I'll be homeless..." This may sound like an exaggeration. But when the catastrophic thoughts and fears keep snowballing like this—as sometimes they do, when we get really, really anxious—the process is the same. The reality is that even if it's unlikely, that thing we fear the very most *could* happen. And the feeling is dread, a horrible, horrible fear. And the "But—" is the same, too. "That 'worst' isn't likely to happen, but if it does, I will expect to feel intense pain, and I will go on to use my resources, my strength, my creativity, and I will write the next chapter in the story of my life."

Does anyone know what is sometimes suggested that you should do if you ever find yourself homeless? *(Instructor gives class a few minutes to respond. People frequently volunteer excellent ideas, including contacting relatives and friends, finding roommates or other temporary living situations, and exploring public housing and other community resources.)* The answer is: You find a box. One of those big ones, like refrigerators come in. You move it to a sheltered place, where other people have similar boxes. And you create a safe place for yourself.

By the way, I share that with you today *not* because I expect that any of you are about to become homeless! Instead, I share it as a kind of metaphor. Whatever you worry about most, whatever your deepest, darkest catastrophic fears may be, what I am saying is this: If "the worst" happens, take a small, concrete step. Do something to take care of yourself. That is the first step in your solution.

(Instructor fills in the remaining two columns of the chart for this one. The completed chart now looks like this.)

Thoughts now	Alternatives	
	Accept a. Reality b. Feeling	But…
I won't be able to answer their questions.	True. Uptight, maybe defensive.	I might be OK. Will review PowerPoint, say "That's a good question."
I'll have a panic attack during the presentation	I might. Embarrassing.	Sweating doesn't always mean full panic. Politicians sweat! Not always noticeable. It will pass.
They'll laugh at me.	Yes, they might. Humiliating.	They probably won't. I wouldn't! I can ignore, laugh too.
We won't get the bid.	Possible. Bummed, obsess.	I'll do my best. OK to lick wounds; then—next project.
I'll be fired.	Could happen. Devastating.	Probably not. But if so, suck it up, look for new job, go on.
My wife will leave me.	Possible. Devastating.	Probably not (me going overboard…) we'll talk, plan. If worst happens, mourn, go on.
I'll be homeless.	Could happen. Dreadful	Not likely. But if so, after pain, write next chapter. Start with big box!

Figure 5.20 Thoughts now and alternatives grid with "Accept" column: Example.

(If there is time to do so, the class might suggest and complete another example together. The instructor ensures that the "Accept" column includes both the "reality that the bad stuff might happen" and a feeling of upset or fear about it. If the "Thoughts now" column includes "I'll die," the "But" column can include "Probably not today. But if I do, do I have a will or a trust? Have I told the people in my life how much I care about them?")

Now it's your turn. You can use a copy of our worksheet. *(This is Worksheet C.2, the Solution Focused Anxiety Management Thoughts and Alternatives Worksheet, on p. 273 of Appendix C of this book).*

(Instructor checks to be sure everyone has this or an equivalent worksheet. As participants write their own examples, instructor circulates and shares individual encouragement and ideas with those who are willing to have the instructor view what they are writing. When everyone is done, the instructor says the following.)

I am struck by the profound and creative thoughts people have come up with. *(Look around the room, making eye contact.)*

So, now that you have done this, what feels different about this perspective from what other people have suggested to you about this before? *(Almost invariably, someone points to the center column: the validation that the bad stuff absolutely* ***could*** *happen. If no one spontaneously mentions this, ask if anyone has noticed this.)*

That's *very* different from the messages most of us have usually gotten about this before. For lots of us, if someone *only* tells us—or we say to ourselves—"Chill out" or "Don't make such a big deal about it," it doesn't silence that worry inside: "But what if it *does* happen?" Because the bad stuff absolutely *could* happen. Taking a moment first to recognize and accept that fact helps us to see that we're not weird or crazy for wondering about it. Once we do that, in a way we're better able to consider the alternative: a scenario in which even if the worst happens, we find a way to mourn, cope, and go on.

It's sometimes said that in behavior therapy, the first "wave" said: Change your behavior. Then there was a second "wave" that said: Change your thoughts. That was the "cognitive" part. And now there's a "third wave" that says this: It's not just about changing your thoughts. It's also about changing your *relationship* to your thoughts. This is the acceptance part, or the mindfulness part. So we talk about changing our behavior *and* our thoughts *and* our relationship to our thoughts. And we might add to all of that: You have to discover the unique things that work for *you*. In here, we think of all of these things as ingredients of the solution!

It's almost time for us to wind down, so now I want to give you all some time to ask questions, or share reactions, about anything we've talked about in here today. To get our discussion started, I might ask: What are some areas where you realize, as we talk about it today, that thinking about things in a different way has already helped you to get braver?

(Instructor facilitates discussion, as time permits, following what participants want to discuss. No one is forced to talk. This may be an opportunity to remind people of "You can—and you don't have to.")

SUGGESTIONS FOR PRACTICE

Now I want to give you some ideas for taking this with you, to experiment at home with what we've talked about in here today. Please use *any* ideas or suggestions from this class in a way that works for you!

First, I want to invite you to review the readings for this class. These cover what we talked about in here today.

(These are Appendix C in this book and on the companion website.)

Second, I want to invite you to notice your thoughts. Notice the ones that support your courage and coping and appropriate caution and choice. Remember where you learned them, and if there was a caring person in your life, either in the past or in the present, who said supportive things to you, you might imagine that that person is with you now. That person might be cheering you on and reminding you of how you got through before. And if you discover thoughts that make you more fearful than you would like to be, you might consider what you would like to say to yourself instead. Or you might consider what you would say to a little child who was scared, and say that to yourself. And as you do that, you might notice how that makes a difference.

END OF SESSION FORM AND FEEDBACK

Now we have our short form for you to fill out.

(Instructor distributes End of Session Form [p. 22, in Chapter 2; also the final page of the learner readings for this session, in Appendix C], or equivalent designed for the practice setting. If this form has been duplicated, participants can keep one copy, while the instructor collects the other.)

And then we'll go around, and everyone can say very briefly what he or she most wants to remember from today.

(After forms are complete and collected)

Our tradition in here is that anyone who is "graduating" goes first. Who is "graduating" today?

(Instructor facilitates "going around and saying what I want to remember." Instructor may choose to make brief comments about common themes that have emerged.)

So, for our "graduates," we wish you the best! And for the rest of us, we'll see you next week!

CHAPTER 6

Instructor Notes for Topic Four: Life Issues and Anxiety

WELCOME AND INTRODUCTION

(Instructor may want to bring copies of the End of Session Form to this session. This form is p. 22, in Chapter 2; it is also the final page of the learner readings for this session [Appendix D]. Or the instructor may use an equivalent form, tailored to the specifics of the practice setting.)

Welcome to Solution Focused Anxiety Management! I'm delighted you're all here today! We are going to be celebrating and building courage, and this is an awesome thing you're doing for yourself, being here today. Just being here takes courage and is a step in the right direction!

For those of you who are here today for the first time, I want to go over what we do in here. We go around and share first names, although if our class is so big that we will never remember them, we may decide to skip our introductions. Then I present some information about managing anxiety. That part is mostly me talking, for two reasons. First, there are a lot of things I want to be sure to have enough time to tell you. Second, in a class on anxiety, there are sometimes people who wouldn't feel comfortable if they felt as though they "had to talk." So, as far as talking out loud in here goes, "You can—and you don't have to." By the way, "You can—and you don't have to" is a phrase that you're going to hear again and again in this class because it applies to so many things!

Anyway, after the information part, we take some time for discussion, questions, whatever people want to talk about and that we have time to talk about. Then we end with a short form for you to fill out, and by going around and everyone having a chance to say aloud, if you want to, what you want to remember or take with you from today. We do the same thing every week. There are four different information presentations. Every time you'll be encouraged to do some reading, and parts of that material repeat exactly what I'm presenting. We do that because some people have requested it in the past, so you don't have to feel as though you have to take notes. After people have been to all four classes, they're welcome to go through the series again, either right away, or at a later time, if they ever want to.

Solution Focused Anxiety Management
http://dx.doi.org/10.1016/B978-0-12-394421-4.00006-1

Significant others are welcome and encouraged to come with you to the class, too, if you would like them to do so. Many people find that the more that someone in their lives understands about anxiety management, the better! If someone in your life isn't here today, it's fine to repeat a session to bring him or her along. And, of course, it's perfectly okay to come to this class by yourself. We want you to use this program and all of the material we're going to be giving you in a way that works for you. That's a message you'll probably hear from me over and over again in here. So you can bring someone with you—and you don't have to! That is another one of the many ways that you can decide how you want to use this program.

Now I want to emphasize something about the name of this class, Solution Focused Anxiety Management. I want you all to hear clearly that it's not called "solution focused anxiety *elimination*." Of course, "anxiety elimination" is what people want! So it's important for you to be an "informed consumer." This class isn't going to claim to teach you how to make all of your anxiety disappear, but it *will* teach you how to be stubborn enough not to let it get in the way of things you want to do. You don't have to wait for anxiety to totally go away to be able to do things, both the tasks of daily living and some wonderful, amazing things.

We're real informal in here. If you need to take a break, just feel free to step out any time and come on back in.

Our one rule is confidentiality: What you hear about other people's lives stays in this room, and you can expect that same confidentiality from everyone else. But any principles or information you learn may be shouted from the rooftops! And what you discover about yourself can be shared or kept private, in whatever combination, and in whatever way feels right for you.

What questions can I answer for you now?

(Instructor may invite sharing of first names here, if desired.)

LIFE ISSUES AND ANXIETY

Today's session is a smorgasbord of ideas that experts have discovered are sometimes useful to people who are growing courage, coping, appropriate caution, and choice in their lives. Some of the ideas may be familiar, and some may be new. And for some of the topics, at first you might be a little curious about how the idea is connected to solution focused anxiety management. Or if today is the first time you're here, you may find yourself wondering: Where are the tools for relaxing my body, changing my thoughts, or doing things a little at a time that I thought we would be learning about? The answer is: They are in the other sessions! So I invite you to approach everything we talk about today in the same way that you eat a piece of watermelon: Spit out the seeds and chew and swallow any of the parts that fit for you!

THE PROS AND CONS OF MANAGING YOUR ANXIETY

The first piece we're going to talk about is the pros and cons of managing your anxiety. We do so because a really important step in growing courage is making the active decision to do it! Of course, you *already* know a lot about courage, even *before* you deliberately decide to increase it. But even when courage is already present, making the decision to increase it can be a powerful and important step, and it's worth talking about.

Now, it often helps people to make and support a decision to change if, around the time they're contemplating the change, they anticipate the pros and cons of making that change. This is the same kind of thing that lots of us do, either deliberately or without fully realizing it, in everyday decisions. For instance, suppose you're deciding whether or not to get a dog. You go over the pros and cons, maybe in your head, maybe in conversation with other people. You might even make a little chart, like this.

(On board)

Pros	Cons

Figure 6.1 Pros and cons: Basic grid.

So, I want to invite you all to help us brainstorm here. What are some reasons a person might want to get a dog?

(Take some time to allow participants to respond. Ideas usually include things like these: companionship; protection [a watch dog might bark at intruders]; fulfilling a longstanding wish; re-creating an experience that was special in the past, perhaps in childhood; providing a special experience for children or seniors [bonding, taking responsibility]; creating an opportunity to meet people [including other dog owners]; exercise while dog-walking. As ideas are generated, the instructor adds them to the chart.)

Now let's brainstorm the other side, the cons, or concerns that one might want to think about when considering whether or not to get a dog. What can you think of here?

(Again, the instructor invites participant response. Now, ideas usually include things like these: financial considerations [including initial purchase, food, shots, vet visits, boarding during vacation]; how to find time for the dog in an already busy schedule; possible mess [dog hair, paper training]; the possibility that a child or partner who has promised to care for the dog might not do so; mixed feelings about the dog [including guilt, regret, anticipating the loss that will be experienced when the dog dies someday]. Again, as ideas are generated, the instructor adds them to the chart. The chart might now look something like this.)

Pros	Cons
Companionship	Cost of dog
Protection	$ - food
I really want one!	$ - vet, shots
Special in childhood	Plan for vacation, cost
For my child (grandma, etc.)	Time, responsibility, for walks
Ice breaker to meet people	Kids might not feed him even though they say they will
Walking the dog will give me exercise!	I might be sorry I got him and feel guilty
	Would have to face pain when I lose him some day

Figure 6.2 Pros and cons: Dog example.

Notice that you want to be as specific as possible here. And then, when you have your little chart, you think of the two sides as if each were on one side of a balance scale. You probably notice that it's not just the "number" of items on a side that makes a difference. Some items just simply are more important! And if the "weight" of the pros is greater than the "weight" of the cons, you get the dog. You know that there will be costs, financial or otherwise, but if that's the decision that feels right for you, somehow you're going to find some ways to deal with them.

The same process applies to managing anxiety. For example, consider the very common worry about driving on freeways: What are some reasons a person might want to build courage in this area? Again, I invite you to be as specific as possible.

(The instructor erases the dog example and begins a new chart, again taking some time to allow participants to respond. Ideas usually include things like these: freedom to travel to places not accessible by surface streets [these might include work, recreational destinations, visiting family, friends, shopping, medical appointments]; sense of independence, or freedom from dependence on others' schedules and availability; getting places faster and saving time; sharing driving on trips; enhanced self-esteem or feeling "the same as everyone else" [in a society where most people drive on freeways]. If some of these are not spontaneously offered, the instructor might mention them, wondering aloud if anyone has ever had this reaction. As with the dog example, as ideas are generated, the instructor adds them to the chart.)

Now we're going to do the same thing we did with our dog example: Let's brainstorm the other side, the "cons," or possible concerns or problems that might come up when you're driving on the freeway. This is sort of like the old saying "You'd better not wish for something; you just might get it," with the implication that once you've "got it," you have to deal with it. Now, this might seem like a strange thing to be deliberately talking about, especially in a solution focused anxiety management class! But being solution-focused absolutely doesn't mean that we can't talk about concerns or problems. So, in that spirit, what might happen or what might you have to handle or deal with if you start driving on the freeway?

(Again, the instructor invites participant responses. Ideas here often include concerns like these: having a panic attack; getting in an accident; financial costs [for vehicle, gas, tolls, parking]; getting lost or getting in the wrong lane; sitting in bumper-to-bumper traffic or gridlock; there may be places one doesn't really ***want*** *to go, and one "loses the reason [not driving]" for not going there. As concerns are mentioned, the instructor adds them to the chart.*

Again, if some of the preceding concerns are not specifically mentioned, the instructor might suggest them, wondering aloud if anyone has ever had this reaction. The con of "losing the reason not to go" sometimes becomes clearer with an example like the following.)

This is an example of "losing your reason not to go." Suppose that you are regularly invited to family get togethers in a city that is about two hours away by freeway. Everyone understands that you usually don't go because you don't drive on freeways and need to find a ride. You actually don't like the gatherings much anyway. So once your relatives discover that you're driving more now, you can't as easily say "I can't drive there." Maybe you'll go, and maybe you won't—an example of our "You can—and you don't have to" perspective—but regardless of which you choose, your driving has led to a dilemma you (mostly) didn't have before. As someone once said about a situation like this, "It was so easy when I just didn't do freeways!"

So, our chart for "building your courage so you can drive on freeways" might end up looking something like this.

Pros **(of building courage for freeways)**	**Cons** **(of building courage for freeways)**
Get to work—keep my job	Might panic
Get to school	Could get in an accident
Water park!	Money for gas
Be able to drive my mom to the hospital if there's an emergency (or anyone, if they need it)	And tolls
Independence	And parking…
Share driving on trips	I might get in the wrong lane and get lost
Feel normal	Deal with traffic, gridlock
Proud that I'm not letting this stop me!	Lose my reason not to go to those family things

Figure 6.3 Pros and cons: Freeway example.

Now, if you're here today primarily as a friend or relative of someone who is growing his or her courage, you can use this pros and cons process, too. You can, of course, do this for an area where you want to grow braver personally, but you can also do it this way: "the pros and cons for *you* of *him or her* being braver," in whatever area he or she is here about.

(Instructor adds another chart, as follows. If space allows, leave the first chart on the board, since more will be added to it a little later.)

Pros for me **(of my significant other building courage for freeways)**	**Cons for me** **(of my significant other building courage for freeways)**

Figure 6.4 Pros and cons: Grid for significant other, freeway example.

So let's take just a few more minutes to brainstorm what our little chart might look like if I'm here as the relative or friend of the person who is getting braver with driving. *(Pause for ideas and add them to the chart.)*

Some of the things would be exactly the same as they were on our last chart. Of course, I would love for her to feel good about herself. And it would be awesome if she could get us to the hospital if there was an emergency. And then, some other ones might have an additional "twist" to them. I'm inviting you to think in terms of what I call "good selfish" here, things that might be good for you, apart from or in addition to any good things they bring to her. What can you think of?

(Instructor invites more responses here, adding them to the chart. If not mentioned by the participants, the instructor might wonder aloud about some like these. "If she gets a job, then there's less pressure on me, and I might not have to take so much overtime." "She might be able to pick the kids up at soccer so I don't have to do it all the time." "I won't have to go along every time she needs to go shopping." Add any of these ideas in the Pros column. The grid might now look like this.)

Pros for me (of my significant other building courage for freeways)	**Cons for me (of my significant other building courage for freeways)**
If she gets a job, less pressure on me	
Share kid pick-up	
More time for me—don't have to go shopping	

Figure 6.5 Pros and cons: Freeway example for significant other, pros added.

And what might the cons be? Again, some would be exactly the same as on the first chart. "Of course, I would feel bad, and a little worried, if she has to experience panic, because I know that it's so uncomfortable and that she hates it so much." "And, of course, as is true for any of us, there could be an accident." In addition to all those, what else can you think of, again from that "good selfish" perspective, that could be cons or concerns as she grows braver?

(The instructor again invites responses here, adding each one to the chart, in the Cons column, as it is described. If not mentioned by the participants, the instructor might wonder aloud about some like these. "She might start spending more—on gas, shopping, eating out with her friends." "I might miss our time together in the car." "I might miss my role of being the driver and 'strong one'—this will be new for us." "What if she starts getting so independent that she starts spending a lot of time away from home?" "This one feels terrible to say, but what if I decide I liked it better when she had her phobia?!")

What else do any of these make you think of?

(The grid might now look like this.)

Pros for me **(of my significant other building courage for freeways)**	**Cons for me** **(of my significant other building courage for freeways)**
If she gets a job, less pressure on me	She might spend more $
Share kid pick up	I might miss my role as the"needed driver" and our time in the car together
More time for me—don't have to go shopping	She might get too independent!

Figure 6.6 Pros and cons: Freeway example for significant other, cons added.

So, now I want to invite all of you to make a grid like the one we've been using, for some area in your life where you want to grow your courage. Again, if you are here as the support person, you can do yours either for pros and cons of more courage in some area of your own, or you might consider the perspective we just talked about.

(The grid worksheet is Worksheet D.1, on p. 281 in Appendix D of this book, and participants can certainly create one on a blank piece of paper or on a tablet computer.)

Sometimes people ask: What if there aren't any cons? What if there is absolutely nothing "bad" that you can think of? I mean, someone who wants to feel less panicky might say: "What could possibly be 'bad' about not having panic attacks any more?"

Well, if there are no cons, there are no cons! Please don't feel as though you have to create them! But I will suggest one that people sometimes do experience for the "panic attack situation": What if I get overconfident, and then a panic attack comes on when I'm not expecting it? Would that feel really horrible?

But anyway, as you do this exercise, I encourage you not to be afraid to anticipate the cons. Identifying them in advance will make you better able to deal with them. To evaluate the pros, you might reflect on some of these things: What might I gain in my personal life? In social situations? At work? In how I feel about myself? In how I view other people? In little details of my world that will make so much of a difference?

And as you do this, I'm going to walk around the room, and I'll be asking you if it's okay for me to look at what you've written and share my thoughts.

(Instructor waits a few minutes for people to get started and then circulates. For participants who say that it is okay to look at what they have written, in a short one-on-one conversation, the instructor comments on their good ideas. If a participant wishes, instructor also takes a minute to brainstorm together. "Is it okay if I add my two cents?" is an example of the language the instructor uses here. After the interaction with individual participants is complete, the instructor addresses the full class again.)

Wow, what a lot of profound ideas you all have come up with! I want to encourage you to take a minute to read over your own list. You might imagine that your little chart is a balance scale, with the pros on one side and the cons on the other. As you imagine it that way, notice which side tilts down because it is heavier. We can expect that different people are going to have real different patterns: Some people may have almost no cons at all, and some people may have some fairly substantial ones. If that's the case for you, that's so valuable to be aware of, because it gives you a head start on discovering some creative ways of dealing with them. That's something we're going to address in just a few minutes.

Meanwhile, remind yourself of your pros! They're the reason you're doing this, that you had the courage and made the arrangements to come here today, to a roomful of strangers, where maybe some of you didn't know what was going to happen! Reminding yourself of your pros is a real important way to sustain your commitment to change.

Now I want to show you one more thing we can do with our little chart. Watch how I add a third column: "How I might deal with each con."

(Instructor adds a third column to the chart, as follows.)

Pros	Cons	How I might deal with each con

Figure 6.7 Pros, cons, and ways of coping: Basic grid.

For this particular exercise, we really don't pay a lot of attention to the pros. They're still there, of course, and they're wonderfully important in so many ways, but here, we're focusing on the cons and ways of coping with them. I'll show you what I mean with an example.

In the situation we did before, about driving, our first con was "I might panic." For that one, we could say any of these things: "And I might not!" "Now that I'm practicing this driving more, I'm way braver." "If my heart starts pounding, I'll treat it like a wave and ride through it." "It's like walking and chewing gum at the same time: I can feel the sensations and still drive safely." "I can get off at the next exit or pull over when it's safe." "I can—and I don't have to." What else?

(Instructor invites participant ideas here, adding them to the chart as they are generated. The process is the same for the other cons, except that now, the instructor invites participant ideas before suggesting anything. Some ideas for the remaining cons include the following. For "I could get in an accident," a coping tool might be "I will be really careful. I will remember other drivers want to get there safely, too. And if I do get in an accident, I'll, of course, be upset, but even with that, I'll somehow do what I need to do to get through it." For the added cost, one idea is "I will figure out how much I need for expenses and plan accordingly. If I have to, I will cut back elsewhere or not drive every time I want to." For getting in the wrong lane, one might take this perspective: "I'll try to plan ahead. But if I do get in the wrong lane, I'll try to move over safely. If I can't, I'll get off at the next place where I can do so safely, and then I'll get back on in the other direction.

I have my phone and GPS for backup." For being stuck in traffic, coping tools might include anticipation of the possibility, acceptance, and some music on the sound system. For "losing my reason not to go," one coping idea is to talk about it. "I can talk to them directly and let them know that I won't always be there. Even if it feels hard to resolve this, I know that our relationship will survive this, and it might even get stronger because I was honest." The completed chart might look something like this.)

Pros (of building courage for freeways)	**Cons (of building courage for freeways)**	**How I might deal with each con**
Get to work—keep my job	Might panic	Might not! Ride the wave. I can feel sensations and still drive safely.
Get to school	Could get in an accident	True. Anyone could. But those other drivers want to get there safely, too. If something happens, I will do what I need to do to get through it.
Water park!	Money for gas,	I'll have to plan where I'll go and how much I'll need for gas. If I need to cut back elsewhere, I can figure out how, or drive less.
Be able to drive my mom to the hospital if there's an emergency (or anyone, if they need it)	And tolls,	Same as above
Independence	And parking…	Same as above
Share driving on trips	I might get in the wrong lane and get lost	I will plan, and I will get off when I can. I have my phone and my GPS.
Feel normal	Deal with traffic, gridlock	Anticipate it, acceptance, and some music on the sound system.
Proud that I'm not letting this stop me!	Lose my reason not to go to those family things	I can talk to them directly and let them know that I won't always be there. I can do this, and our relationship will survive and maybe even grow stronger.

Figure 6.8 Pros, cons, and ways of coping: Freeway example.

While we're on the subject of pros and cons, I want to share with you a variation that can be especially helpful with decisions. This one is called "the cons and the cons" because it doesn't address the pros at all. We're not going to take as much time with this one, so I'll just give you a short example.

(Instructor now draws the following grid. This is done in a way that deliberately leaves space between the columns. Additional columns will be added after each "con column" in a few minutes.)

Cons of X	**Cons of Y**

Figure 6.9 Cons and cons: Basic grid.

Let's suppose a man is considering quitting a job that he finds stressful and wants to use this tool to support making a decision. On our grid we'll let quitting be X, and staying will be Y.

(Instructor adds to grid, and as each con is mentioned here, it gets added too.)

For "the cons of quitting," he might list these things: loss of income and benefits; feeling bad about himself, regretting the decision later. And his "cons of staying" might include having to deal with a difficult boss or co-worker, feeling unfulfilled, and always being tense and on edge.

(The chart now looks like this.)

Cons of quitting job	**Cons of staying at job**
No salary or benefits!	Have to deal with boss
Feel bad about myself	Feel unfulfilled
Might regret it later	Always tense

Figure 6.10 Cons and cons: Job example.

Now, you might notice that I left some space between the two columns. The reason is that now we're going to add another column: "How I would deal with each con." So now our chart looks like this. *(Add to chart)*

Cons of quitting job	How I might deal with each con	Cons of staying at job	How I might deal with each con
No salary or benefits!		Have to deal with boss	
Feel bad about myself		Feel unfulfilled	
Might regret it later		Always tense	

Figure 6.11 Cons, cons, and coping: Job example.

(Instructor adds each of the following to the chart as it is mentioned.)

So, for coping with the quitting, he might do these things. Financially, he might look for another job or use his savings. For feeling bad about himself, he might reach out to important people in his life, or he might do something fun that he never had time for when he was working. If he discovers later that he regrets his choice, he might allow some mourning for the road not taken, he might be gentle with himself, and he might find another good road to go down.

And if he stays, he might cope by thinking about what he could do to make his work more comfortable and what has helped with his boss before. He might imagine that a miracle suddenly happened, and it was that work had suddenly become more interesting, even with the current realities there. And he could calm his body and mind with some of the tools from this class.

(The chart now looks something like this.)

Cons of quitting job	How I might deal with each con	Cons of staying at job	How I might deal with each con
No salary or benefits!	Look for a job, use savings	Have to deal with boss	Reflect on what has helped before
Feel bad about myself	Reach out to people, do something there wasn't time for when I was working	Feel unfulfilled	Imagine that work has suddenly become more fun
Might regret it later	Allow mourning, be gentle with myself, find other good road to go down	Always tense	Use tools from this class

Figure 6.12 Cons, cons, and coping: Job example, grid completed.

So it's sort of like either choice has a downside—that's the cons side—but each one also has some ways of coping, taking care of yourself, getting through. Whichever fork in the road you take, there are ways you can take care of you.

I CAN'T VS. I DON'T WANT TO

Now we're going to switch gears a little bit and talk about another perspective. Suppose you woke up tomorrow and, for some reason, you didn't have your fears or anxiety any more. Once you figured that out, you, of course, would be delighted. There would probably be some things that you couldn't wait to start doing, or places you'd like to go. And there would probably be other things that you still wouldn't be eagerly anticipating. I mean, not many of us actively looking forward to doing our income tax or getting blood drawn.

So there might well be situations, or maybe certain interactions, that you avoid now "because of your anxiety" that you still would like to avoid. That's the most normal thing in the world! But you may not have had much practice recently thinking about what and whom you would *prefer* to avoid. After all, if you're in a panic, who has the luxury of contemplating "Hmm, I'm not sure I want to do this"? When you're in high anxiety mode, whether you *want* to or not is irrelevant. Instead, it's more like this: "Get me out of here! I *can't*!"

Some people find it helpful to start thinking about how they would, or *could*, get out of situations if they chose to do so. You may choose *not* to avoid things in your life 99% of the time—you may be delighted to finally enter those situations—but it's important to remember that you have the *right* not to want to do certain things—sometimes or at all—even if you're not afraid of them. It's like our perspective of "You can—and you don't have to" that we talk about so much in here.

So we're talking about transforming "I can't…" to "I don't want to." Or "I'd rather not." Or sometimes, the more accurate feeling is mixed, sort of like this: "Part of me wants to, and part of me doesn't want to, and the part that doesn't want to feels stronger right now."

(On board)

I can't…	I don't want to…
	I'd rather not…
	Part of me wants to, and part of me doesn't want to, and the part of me that doesn't want to feels stronger right now.

Figure 6.13 Can't or don't want to.

Notice the *right now* in that last one. Notice how it leaves open the possibility that the other side, the one that "wants to," may feel stronger later on.

I'm curious: Which way do you feel stronger, emotionally: saying "I can't" or "I'd rather not"?

(Allow any participants to respond, if they wish. Often many participants will point out that the "I don't want to" option feels better, more like a personal choice. But this is not always the case for everyone. For some people, the "certainty" of "I can't" feels more comfortable. As is the case for so many things, one size does not fit all!)

So here is an idea for an experiment: When the immediate thought about something is "I can't do that! I would lose it if I did that," you might want to practice substituting something like this: "Part of me wants to, and part of me doesn't want to, and the part of me that doesn't want to feels stronger right now"—in preparation for a time when you truly will feel less afraid.

Sometimes I think our society should teach a class called "Ambivalence 101" at every level of the educational system. Ambivalence is one of those big words we've all heard and may not always remember exactly what it means, so I want to give you a definition: Ambivalence means mixed feelings. And the overarching theme of my "Ambivalence 101" would be: Mixed feelings are normal!

(On board)

Ambivalence = Mixed feelings
Ambivalence 101 = Mixed feelings are normal!!

(Instructor continues.) In preschool, we would teach our kids: It's perfectly normal to *love* to go to school because they have cool toys and to *hate* to go to school because they make me lie on my rug at nap time. Or in fourth grade: I love soccer because the meets are in neat places, and I hate it when Coach yells at me. Or in high school: I want to go to the dance, but I have a zit and am afraid no one will want to dance with me.

No one teaches us that mixed feelings are normal, but they are. They are *so* very normal, and they are everywhere. So that leads me to suggest a little experiment you can do with mixed feelings. It's to notice them in all kinds of little everyday places—most of which, by the way, may be totally separate from anxiety—and to be curious about how many you can discover. They might be things like "I want to eat that, but I don't want to get fat" or "I want that new gadget, but I don't want to spend the money." Exercising your "noticing mixed feelings muscles" is wonderful practice for identifying and coping with the mixed feelings that so often come up in anxiety.

ASSERTION

Now we're going to segue in a slightly different direction for a bit and talk about the concept of assertiveness and how it interfaces with solution focused anxiety management. I bet assertiveness is a concept some of you are already familiar with. Am I right? *(Look around the room to see if there are nods.)* The process we've just been talking about, saying "I'd rather not..." or "I don't want to..." (and I *do* want to..., maybe even more important!), often is supported by assertiveness.

Assertiveness means expressing, or *asserting*, what you want, what you are feeling, or what you plan to do. Without violating the rights of anyone else, you value your own. You say what you want directly and kindly. Assertion is different from *passivity*, where you allow others to choose for you. It's also different from *aggression*, where you protect your rights but might put other people down in the process. And then there's the *passive aggressive* position, where on the surface you go along with other people but find a way to get back at them in some way later.

So here is an example of passive, assertive, aggressive, and passive aggressive handling of the same situation. Let's imagine that the situation is that a friend is asking for a ride to the airport at a time that's really inconvenient for you.

A *passive* response might be to agree to do it. You might be aware of sensations in your body, maybe your chest tightening or breathing speeding up, and there might be a flash of emotional arousal, but mostly you're aware of "not wanting to make waves" because you don't want this person to be upset with you.

An *assertive* response might grow from awareness of all those mixed feelings and sensations. You might be conscious of being torn, but on the "balance scale" of "Do I risk having someone upset with me?" versus "Do I need to pay more attention to my own needs right now?" the need to take good care of yourself is heavier. So you might say something like this: "I'm afraid that isn't going to work for me. I know it's a hassle to get to the airport, but this time I'm not going to be able to help out." You may say it in a way that conveys empathy and kindness—and that at the same time is clear. Your attitude and tone communicate that your decision about the airport trip is absolutely not a rejection of your friend. You recognize that there may be some "pushback," and that if it comes, you can tolerate it and maintain what you need to do to take good care of you. You may feel some pride that you did this, even though it wasn't totally comfortable.

An *aggressive* response might sound something like this: *(Instructor says the following in a loud, belligerent tone.)* "Are you crazy? You know I can't do it then! You just expect me to drop everything because you suddenly need something. You have a hell of a lot of nerve!"

And then there's one more: a *passive aggressive* stance. When you're passive aggressive, you do what's being requested, but you also somehow "get back at" the other person. So, in this example, you might say "Yes" and then show up a little late for the airport ride or roll your eyes or say something sarcastic or hurtful. We may or may not be consciously aware that we're doing these things.

Let's go back to our assertive and aggressive responses for a minute. Did you hear the difference between them? *(Pause, looking around room for nods.)* They're really very different, aren't they? Sometimes people feel as though the only alternative to being passive is to be aggressive or abrasive. Some of us grew up in families where it was like that, with everything either all "nice-nice" or absolutely horrible. Or maybe we saw role models being passive aggressive. If we haven't seen people in our lives do a lot of assertive responding, and if we haven't yet discovered that assertiveness eventually strengthens relationships, it naturally is going to take a little more practice to grow our assertiveness now.

You may have heard of assertiveness before. And you may be thinking that, as a concept, it certainly makes sense. But you may be wondering: What does assertiveness have to do with anxiety management?

The answer to that question is this: As people grow braver, and as they're more able to do things they didn't do in the past, they may realize that there is something they *can* do but don't *want* to do. Here's an example. This is a woman who has been afraid of elevators for a very long time. She is getting braver, and she's riding them now. Her co-workers go to lunch every Friday at an upscale restaurant on the 15th floor of a nearby office building. She has never gone along, and everyone has always understood that the reason was that she "didn't do elevators." But now, it's only a matter of time until someone sees her on an elevator somewhere and says, "Hey! You're doing elevators now. Now you can do our Friday lunches!"

She recognizes that she has a dilemma. She doesn't really *want* to eat out on a weekly basis. She thinks, "Yuck. That place is expensive. It's a lot of calories that I don't need right before the weekend, and these people are not exactly my best friends. But I have to work with them, and I don't want to seem weird or not social. Yuck. You know, it was way easier when I just didn't do elevators!"

So, she has some choices. She could be passive and just start going, even though she doesn't want to. She could be assertive and say, "I'm not really up for going every week. But I'd love to be able to join you when there's a birthday or special occasion." She recognizes that there is a "risk" here that they won't want her occasionally if she isn't a member of "the every week gang," but she knows she can tolerate that possibility and say what feels right for her. She could also be aggressive and retort, "Just because you all take two-hour lunches on company time doesn't mean I'm going to start doing that!" Or she could be passive aggressive by going along and regularly "forgetting" to bring money or a credit card, so that someone else has to pay for her.

That situation is a bit of a caricature, but I think it illustrates the point that sometimes, as we grow braver, we do face choices and decisions that maybe didn't come up for us before.

There is something else important to add about assertion. In addition to the times that it supports us in saying "No," there are the many times it reminds us to say "Yes": "Yes" to the things we want to do, to our dreams and goals (which may be different from the other person's, but not necessarily incompatible with them). Maybe we can say "Yes" to everyone's needs, if we think creatively, or outside the box. We can say "Yes" to doing things that are important to us even when anxiety has been there. Sometimes saying "Yes" might include saying "Yes" to caution, welcoming it into our lives, as one ingredient of the solution—not the entire solution, but one valuable component of it.

There is a whole lot more about assertion that we don't have time to go over together today, in a class that's primarily about anxiety management, not about "assertiveness training." The learner readings for this session include a little additional information about assertion. And if assertiveness is an area of special interest for you, there is a whole lot more out there in the world and on the Internet for you to discover.

Before we finish our little section on assertiveness, I do want to mention one final thing. Although assertion is always available for expression of *your* feelings, it doesn't always succeed in changing the other person's feelings or getting the results you want. Sometimes, no matter how assertive you are, no matter *what* you say or do, a situation or person may not respond the way you want. When that happens, you can still take really good care of yourself by recognizing that you have options. You might decide to use acceptance. You might be curious about creative ways you can make things work for you. And you can eventually decide to change a job or living situation or relationship that isn't good for you. You can take whatever amount of time you need to decide. Again, "You can—and you don't have to." Knowing how to be assertive isn't the only tool you use in your life in making decisions, but it's another "tool in the toolbox," for expressing your feelings and taking care of you.

So if assertiveness is a useful concept for your life, you can notice yourself in a whole range of different situations. Where are you already being assertive? You might be curious about instances of good assertion and ability to tolerate "pushback" that are already there, even if you haven't been paying attention to them. Noticing your good assertion will help you to continue it. And you certainly don't have to be assertive all the time! Sometimes, it feels right to make a different choice.

And, if at some point you notice that you haven't made the assertive choice, and you think you might like to do so in the future, you might let yourself think about what the assertive choice would look and sound like. Like any other skill, assertiveness grows with baby steps and repeated practice, even in the presence of discomfort.

DEVELOPMENTAL TASKS

Now we're going to shift gears again and talk a little about how life issues interface with anxiety. Sometimes people are so focused on their anxiety concerns that they lose sight of what issues they'd be facing at this point in their lives if they just had a "normal" amount of anxiety. You might notice that I didn't say *no* anxiety, because, as we talk about in so many ways in this class, *some* anxiety is absolutely normal!

I want to invite you to think for a minute about how children go through developmental stages: weaning, toilet training, separating from their parents. Well, as adults, we go through developmental stages, too. We do that regardless of whether we feel a lot of anxiety or don't feel very much anxiety. And it can be helpful to reflect on what those stages are, and which one or ones you and the people in your life are "in," and what the tasks and issues of those stages are. It also may be useful to think about how you're facing these things, and to find ways of dealing with the issues, *even if* you do still have a fair amount of anxiety at this point. You may be able to find ways of dealing with many of the issues at hand, even if you still have some fear. And once you're less anxious, or put a different spin on things, you may be able to deal with these tasks even more creatively than you are now.

We're going to talk for a few minutes about a framework that comes from Erik Erikson,[1] a Harvard psychiatrist who came up with a way of looking at what people often think about and face at different times of life. And the way we'll do it is that I'll put on the board the time of life, using the name Erikson gave it, and you all can help me come up with the issues for that season.

(On board, begin the following chart.)

[1] See Erikson (1959) in References.

Phase of Adulthood	Core Issues	Tasks and topics people address during this time of life
Adolescence (emerging adulthood)		
Young adulthood		
Middle adulthood		
Older adulthood		

Figure 6.14 Erikson's phases of adulthood.

We're going to start with adolescence. Now, some people might question whether that "counts" as adulthood, but we're going to start there anyway. Sometimes this stage is also called "emerging adulthood." So I want to invite you to reflect on the different things we think about as we move toward adulthood. For some of you, that may be where you are right now, and for others of you, you might think back to a few years ago, or about your children or grandchildren. What are some of the things that are important to us at this time of life?

(As ideas are mentioned, the instructor adds them to the third column of the chart. Ideas often include the following: relationships, looks, money, values, cars

and driving, academic performance, rebellion from parents, getting into college, deciding what is important. The instructor can add thoughts as well. If the following ideas have not already been mentioned, the instructor adds something like this.)

We think and worry about: Does the person that I like also like me? What do I want to be when I grow up? Will I get into the school I want to go to? Sometimes I think about how at this time of life, we desperately want independence, but it's a "funny" kind of independence, like: We want the car and unlimited phone and texting and data minutes, but we don't mind if Mom and Dad pay the car insurance and the cell phone bill! If your friends all have green hair, and your parents don't approve of green hair, you have to decide what color you want your hair to be.

Erikson said that the central, overarching issue for adolescence was "identity" versus "identity diffusion." The word "diffusion" basically means "all over the place." *(Instructor writes that in the second column.)* Of course, none of us emerges from adolescence with a perfectly formed identity—this is exactly who I am and where I'm going—but if you think of this as a continuum, Erikson would say that it's better to be closer to the identity end.

Now let's talk about Erikson's next stage, young adulthood. And I should mention here that there isn't a clear age boundary between the stages. For instance, Erikson might say that a 20-year-old young man who has a job and a wife and a baby may be facing more of the issues of young adulthood than a 28-year-old man who is single, living at home with his parents, and going to school. So it's what you're doing as well as how old you are that determines what stage you would be in. So, in that spirit, what are some of the things that young adults think about?

(Again, the instructor adds ideas to the third column of the chart as they are mentioned. Comments here often include the following: work, relationships, marriage or commitment, children. Again, the instructor participates in the conversation and may add this perspective.)

It's interesting: A lot of the issues that young adults face are the same ones that we talked about in the preceding stage. But there's sometimes a difference in the *meaning* of the same activity. For instance, suppose I'm 17, and I'm working in a restaurant. That may be "just a job," something that I do because it happened to be available. Now let's suppose I'm 26 and working in that same restaurant. It still might be "just a job," but it also might be more than that. Maybe I'm moving toward a career as a chef or in restaurant management. Or maybe I'm paying for graduate school, or it's my "day job" that supports me so I can do my art or music or something that's my true passion.

Although these days not everyone lives in a nuclear family with 2.5 kids and a house with a white picket fence, this is still a time of life when people may be establishing long-term relationships and having children. Or maybe they're not, and they're considering whether they want to. In careers, relationships, and passions, in some way or another, it's a time of life for "putting down roots," or getting "on the road" to some vision of the future.

There's also a kind of financial responsibility that emerges in young adulthood for a lot of people. To use our example of the car insurance and the cell phone, we're more likely to be paying for those ourselves at this time of life.

Erickson used the words "intimacy" versus "isolation" to describe the central issues of this time of life. Sometimes I prefer the idea of *commitment*—which may be to a person, but may also be to a career, philosophy, or something else—versus *lack of commitment.*

It's also worth mentioning that Erikson's original work was done with men. More recently, a psychologist from Harvard, Carol Gilligan,[2] did some research on women that suggested that for some women, intimacy actually comes *before* identity. So these stages are fluid and, like so many things we talk about in here, have to be considered in terms of what fits for you. *(Instructor adds intimacy [commitment] vs. isolation [lack of commitment] to the second column of the chart.)*

Now let's look at middle adulthood. What are some of the things that are important and that we think about at this time of life?

(Again, the instructor adds ideas to the third column of the chart as they are mentioned. Comments here often include the following: aging, reevaluating choices, midlife transitions in career and relationships. People describe multiple demands on their time, energy, and money, including children and aging parents. Again, the instructor participates in the conversation and may add the following perspective.)

If young adulthood is where you "start down the road of life," then middle adulthood is where you're partway down the road and think about whether you're where you thought you would be by this time. If, at age 20, we haven't met the perfect partner or made our first million dollars, with the "grandiosity of youth," we sometimes feel as though we have forever to get there. A few

[2] See Gilligan (1982) in References.

decades later, when something is still missing in our partners, careers, finances, or general happiness, we may go: "Aakk! Time is running out!" And that can lead to reevaluating our earlier decisions.

Work sometimes takes on a different meaning by middle adulthood. The career we were passionate about at first may feel less exciting, but we need the income and benefits. Sometimes people reinvent their careers, or they find meaning in activities or values apart from work.

Another thing that happens by middle adulthood is that the "old body" is aging. More things may be breaking down. If, when you're 20 years old, someone from your high school graduating class drops dead of a heart attack, you may have a momentary shudder but then quickly think, "That was a fluke. I'm young and healthy, so it probably won't happen to me." But when we're 45 years old and someone from our high school graduating class drops dead of a heart attack, we go, "That's my generation! That could happen to me!"

So it's interesting. If we consider what people who get panic attacks often worry about, we think about heart attacks, dying. But this is a time of life when even if we've never had a panic attack, we might be starting to think about health and mortality in a very different way.

Erikson used the words "generativity" versus "stagnation" for his central issue for this time of life. It's an interesting perspective, isn't it? The idea is that instead of being like an old, stale, stagnant pool of water, you find ways to stay "generative" or passionate about something, and that when you do that, it makes a tremendous difference. *(Instructor adds the words to the middle column.)*

And now we have older adulthood. What are some of the things that are important to us at this time of life?

(Again, the instructor adds participants' ideas to the third column. Topics here often include transition to retirement, health concerns, managing loss [widowhood, physical decline], retaining independence, relationship with the younger generation, mortality, spirituality. As with the other stages, the instructor participates in the conversation.)

Erikson used the words "wisdom" versus "despair" as the continuum for this time of life. *(Add to center column.)* The reason is that this can be a time of life when all your earlier bad habits can get intensified by loneliness, loss, new aches and pains, and the challenges of aging. But it can also be a time to have "the bumps on our personalities" smoothed out a bit by wisdom and a larger perspective of life and the life cycle.

(The completed chart may now look like this.)

Phase of Adulthood	Core Issues	Tasks and topics people address during this time of life
Adolescence (emerging adulthood)	Identity vs. Identity diffusion	We establish what kind of person we are going to be as adults, separate from family of origin while still connected to it. We may shift values in the process of establishing career, relationships, lifestyle. We find a way to balance dependence and independence.
Young adulthood	Intimacy (commitment) vs. Isolation (lack of commitment)	We consider and often make commitments to relationships, work/career/education, values. We "put down roots" or get "on the road" to a goal. We may have increasing financial responsibility.
Middle adulthood	Generativity vs. Stagnation	We reconsider earlier choices and may reaffirm them or make changes in work, relationships, and other activities. There may be multiple financial demands on us. We may be more aware of health concerns, aging, and mortality, and that awareness helps us to make choices that enhance life now.
Older adulthood	Wisdom vs. Despair	We may face retirement transitions and choices about use of leisure time. There may be losses of health, strength. Our housing needs may change. We have connections with, and get support from, the younger generation. Widowhood and bereavement bring appropriate mourning. We may be more patient. We may have a larger sense of "the bigger picture."

Figure 6.15 Erikson's phases of adulthood, issues, and tasks.

Now, you may be wondering. All of this may be very profound, but what does it have to do with solution focused anxiety management? Well, the answer is this: If you think of life as a journey down "the road of life," sometimes we hit "bumps in the road." And if you're a body reactor, guess what your body and mind are going to do when it hits those bumps: It's going to do its thing, whatever that may be. And you can recognize that and ride through it and use your tools to get back on track, and that can make a tremendous difference.

So, I want to invite you to reflect on these three questions:

1. What issues am I facing in my life these days?
2. How would I be dealing with those things if I just had a normal level of anxiety (not "no" anxiety)?
3. What does that tell me about how I might deal with those things even *with* my level of anxiety?

(Instructor writes the three questions on board.)

When we start talking about "a normal level of anxiety," people sometimes ask: What "counts" as a normal level of anxiety? I like to answer that by reflecting on how I'm repeatedly struck by how, in the same class, we might have someone who is afraid of driving but flies in airplanes without difficulty. Then there's someone else who is afraid of shots but drives just fine. If you think about the short list of things that some people are afraid of—shots, public speaking, sweating, eating, sex, swimming, losing one's job, foreclosure, having enough money to retire in times of unprecedented financial meltdown, staying at home alone, getting a haircut, crossing the street, earthquakes, hurricanes, wildfires—you'll probably recognize some places where you already have a completely appropriate degree of caution.

So, let's take a minute for everyone to reflect silently on this right now: What is an area where you feel as though your degree of anxiety or caution is *appropriate*? Not excessive, but fully appropriate. Maybe it's one of the ones I just mentioned. Or maybe it's something different. *(Give class a minute to reflect.)* Would anyone like to share aloud what you came up with?

(Instructor facilitates discussion. As always is the case in the class, no one "has to talk." This may be an opportunity to remind people of "You can—and you don't have to.")

Now I invite you to consider how you take appropriate precautions in that area and what that tells you about your capacity for healthy, appropriate anxiety. *(Instructor allows another moment or so for reflection.)*

SUGGESTIONS FOR PRACTICE

Now I want to give you some ideas for taking this with you, to experiment at home with what we've talked about in here today. Please use *any* ideas or suggestions from this class in a way that works for you!

First, I want to invite you to review the readings for this class. These cover what we talked about in here today.

(These are Appendix D in this book and on the companion website.)

One suggestion is to continue to reflect on our three questions. Again, they are: What issues am I facing these days? How would I be dealing with them with a normal level of anxiety (not "no" anxiety)? What does that tell me about how I might deal with those things even *with* my level of anxiety?

And you might consider how you already know how to take appropriate precautions, probably in so many ways, and what that tells you about your capacity for healthy, appropriate caution.

Here are a few other things to experiment with:

You might continue to think and/or write about the pros and cons of making changes—and that really interesting idea of "how I would deal with each con," or our variation about "the cons and the cons."

You might want to experiment with changing "I can't…" to "I don't want to…," or "Part of me wants to, and part of me doesn't want to, and the part that doesn't is stronger right now."

You might decide to strengthen your "mixed feelings noticing muscles"—this sort of goes along with the preceding one. As with any other skill, your awareness of mixed feelings and your comfort with them will grow with practice.

And if assertiveness is something you want to grow, you might want to notice times it's already happening. You might notice the times you use it to say "Yes" as well as "No," because those choices might be especially important. You might decide to play with assertiveness or to experiment with it, maybe at first in tiny ways, and you can be curious about what you discover.

END OF SESSION FORM AND FEEDBACK

Now we have our short form for you to fill out.

(Instructor distributes End of Session Form [p. 22, in Chapter 2; also the final page of the learner readings for this session, in Appendix D], or equivalent designed for the practice setting. If this form has been duplicated, participants can keep one copy, while the instructor collects the other.)

And then we'll go around, and everyone can say very briefly what he or she most wants to remember from today.

(After forms are complete and collected)

Our tradition in here is that anyone who is "graduating" goes first. Who is "graduating" today?

(Instructor facilitates "going around and saying what I want to remember." Instructor may choose to make brief comments about common themes that have emerged.)

So, for our "graduates," we wish you the best! And for the rest of us, we'll see you next week!

CHAPTER 7

Solution Focused Anxiety Management and Individual Therapy

SOLUTION-FOCUSED METHODS AND ATTITUDES

In many ways, solution-focused individual therapy for anxiety is like solution-focused therapy for anything else. The therapist typically begins by asking about the client's best hopes from coming here. If the answer is something like "I want to get rid of my anxiety," the therapist wants to know what will be present *instead*. Using some of the solution-focused methods described in Chapter 1 (including miracle questions, relationship questions, difference questions, and scaling questions), the therapist asks what "being rid of my anxiety" might look like. The therapist builds on the client's language and invites elaboration of detail. The therapist listens for any clues that suggest that "exceptions to the anxiety" are already happening. He or she also notices and highlights instances when the client somehow coped with a tough situation or "got back on track." The therapist might ask, "How did you do that?" Feedback at the end of the session is likely to invite amplifying "pieces of the solution" that have emerged during the conversation. Often, these things may not seem to be obviously or directly related to the problem.

As described in Chapter 1, solution-focused attitudes are conveyed throughout the process. There is an attitude that even when feelings such as fear, panic, and worry are present, there are also many good and special things happening in the client's life. People do not have to wait for anxiety to disappear (or for a complete "miracle" to happen) to be able to experience joy and interpersonal connection. The therapist communicates an expectation that the client already has multiple strengths and resources. The most elegant solutions may be expected to emerge from those "client variables," and often these variables cannot be predicted ahead of time.

Are there any "distinguishing features" about solution-focused therapy for anxiety in particular? This book offers a two-part response: The therapist uses basic solution-focused methods and attitudes *and* is informed by

Solution Focused Anxiety Management
http://dx.doi.org/10.1016/B978-0-12-394421-4.00007-3

knowledge about the many ways people grow courage, coping, appropriate caution, and choice. Here is an example. There is a training exercise called "Moan, moan, moan" (Fiske & Moon, 2011). In this exercise, done in dyads, one person "complains" for three minutes, and the other listens for strengths. Then the listener gives feedback: three strengths that he or she heard during the complaining. Here is a variation on this exercise for anxiety. The "client" is instructed to spend three minutes describing a fear or worry. The "therapist's" task is to listen for the courage, coping, appropriate caution, and choice embedded in the anxiety—and to share with the "client" what has been discovered. In individual sessions of solution-focused therapy for anxiety, the therapist acts "as if" he or she is doing that exercise.

Therapists who listen for courage notice descriptions of things that might be steps on a courage ladder. Sometimes these are tiny "baby steps," things so small that the client may not have identified them as things that "count" as steps toward change. On other occasions, the steps are huge. Therapists also know that a behavior that may not seem particularly remarkable to one person can represent a significant act of courage for another. Sometimes these courageous acts happen in the "here and now," during a session. When that is the case, the therapist has a wonderful opportunity to highlight the act of courage.

Here are a few examples of brave things that people do at psychotherapy clinics everywhere: sitting in chairs that other people have been in, taking the elevator to the second floor, remaining in a room with the door closed, telling something personal to a total stranger. When one of these courageous acts is observed, the therapist might say something like this: "So it was huge for you to drive down here today."

Solution-focused therapists assume that people have the resources, internal and external, to cope with even the most difficult of situations. They listen carefully for signs of creative coping, and when they do so, they hear amazing things. They hear women who call themselves "needle phobic" describe how they had blood drawn during pregnancy because they cared about their not-yet-born children. In response to the question "How did you do that?" they hear people describe the diverse things that have helped them to stay in line at the grocery store. ("Checking my phone," "counting stripes on the shirt of the girl in front of me," and "tickling my little boy's toes" are examples of a few of these.) When people talk about abuse, trauma, and pain they have suffered, solution-focused therapists hear stories of resilience and the ability to complete the tasks of everyday living, even in the presence of significant arousal and distraction. In response to the creative, individualized things done to "get through"—things that the therapist could not possibly have thought of—the solution-focused therapist may highlight the coping behavior. The therapist will also remember the resources this person has used before, because they are likely to be important ingredients of future coping solutions as well.

Another important thing that solution-focused therapists listen for—and hear—is active, deliberate choice. Even when people say that they are "prisoners" of their anxiety, they are still making decisions. The therapist often hears an example of a choice made (for example, "I texted him [or didn't text him]"). In response, the therapist might ask "How did you decide to do that?" It usually becomes clear that even in the presence of anxiety, people make decisions, large and small, all the time. The normalcy of mixed feelings and the perspective of "You can—and you don't have to" can emerge in individual sessions as well as in the class. For example, one client decided, "I *can* go out to meet people or do online dating. And I don't have to. Actually, even if I weren't going through all this, I don't think I'd want to be looking for a relationship right now."

A related concept is "appropriate caution." This concept is related to the idea of choice, especially when the choice is to "not do something." Although the client may be saying that he or she was "too scared" to take an action, the therapist may hear sensible, legitimate reasons behind the decision. Sometimes taking one's time and being cautious make tremendous sense, especially in light of what this person has experienced. The therapist might choose to share that perspective. Here are some additional examples of things "anxious" clients recognized during individual sessions. "I *can* take the GREs (or LSAT, or MCAT…) and fill out those applications and write the essays, even in the presence of my anxiety, and I don't have to. The cost of graduate school and the work and effort and the debt it will bring are absolutely legitimate to consider." "I *can* go back to my old church after my divorce (even though it was my wife's church originally)—and I don't have to. It doesn't have to be 'social phobia' that makes me want to visit a new congregation and meet some new people. And I can also take a break from going to church at all right now."

Right now. The therapist might highlight those tremendously important words because part of choice is the freedom to change one's mind. Choosing not to do certain things right now doesn't mean that one will *never* do them. How solution focused anxiety management uses the construct of "appropriate caution" is described in more detail in the next chapter.

ADDING PSYCHOEDUCATIONAL INFORMATION TO INDIVIDUAL SOLUTION-FOCUSED THERAPY

Some solution-focused therapists may wonder whether it is consistent with solution-focused practice and attitudes to introduce information or specific suggestions. As discussed in Chapters 1 and 9, many solution-focused therapists answer "Yes." The therapist always introduces any information or method as a *possibility*, a perspective that is "out there in the world," something that the client might be interested in. This is always done in a collaborative spirit, keeping the client the expert about whether this particular idea, experiment, or chunk of information would be useful right now.

Here is a one idea for adding information suggested by Insoo Kim Berg, as described by Fiske (personal communication, November 9, 2011):

> *At a training session in Milwaukee, I was telling Insoo that sometimes it was still hard for me not to give advice to clients. She sighed, and said, "Well, if you really can't help yourself, say what you have to say, but put 'I wonder' in front of it."*

Terry Trepper talked about it like this for sex therapy: "Making sure the solution-focused interventions and spirit are predominant, you might say, 'Some people have found doing more structured exercises to slow down their lovemaking to be helpful. Is that something you'd be interested in learning more about?'"(Trepper, in Trepper, Treyger, & Yalowitzh, 2007). In the same way, the therapist doing solution focused anxiety management in an individual session might say something like this: "There's a little exercise for worry called 'Write, read, and shred' that some people find helpful. Would you like to hear about it?"

Another alternative is to refer to the literature: "I was thinking about what the literature says about tools for the kind of panic you're describing. Want to hear the brief summary?" Or the therapist might ask, "Would you be interested in my five-minute 'lesson' on mixed feelings (stages of loss, stages of change, etc.)?" Sometimes the therapist might want to draw one of the figures from the program. He or she might say, "What we're talking about right now makes me want to draw you a little picture. May I?"

Sometimes introducing some information feels different from what was happening earlier in the session. It is certainly appropriate for the therapist to acknowledge the shift. He or she might say, "This is going to sound a little different from what we've been doing before. Is that okay?"

Another approach is to introduce a concept as something that a colleague might suggest: "If this window were a one-way mirror, and we had ten experts on anxiety disorders observing us, they might have a bunch of different suggestions—want to hear some of them?" Or, "You know, last week I was at a conference and learned about…"The therapist might offer a reference for a self-help book or a website.

After an idea has been introduced, the therapist weaves the thread back into the fabric of the solution-focused process. There might be curiosity about pieces of this information that the client already knows. Some of the tools introduced might be things that the client has already discovered. Using future-oriented inquiry, the therapist might ask, "When you do more of that, how will it make a difference?" "What will your husband notice about you?" "What will be different about your perspective?"

The therapist who is using the strategic solution focused variation of solution-focused therapy (Quick, 2008) might introduce the concept of "attempted solutions": "Understanding what you've already tried helps us build on what works, and it keeps me from suggesting something that you already know doesn't work." The conversation might segue into discussion of how well-meaning messages such as "Don't worry" frequently don't work well enough (something the client may have already discovered). The "commonsense and counterintuitive" perspective might be introduced here.

BRIEF THERAPY CASE EXAMPLE: SHEILA

The following case example illustrates solution focused anxiety management conducted in individual sessions.[1] Sheila is a 45-year-old African American woman. She is married, and she lives with her husband and her young adult daughter. Sheila has worked in the past as a clerk, but she is not working now because of medical and psychological challenges. Sheila is requesting treatment for her panic attacks. "They're horrible," Sheila said. "I try to suppress them. They make me feel like I'm having a heart attack. They make me feel like I'm going to die. That's what happened the other day. My husband was scared, too. He took me to the Emergency Room. But they told me that my heart was fine. The way I felt, I couldn't believe it could possibly be fine, but that's what they said. And they did check everything. They gave me some medicine and told me to come here."

The therapist asked Sheila, "So, since you called to make this appointment, what's better or different?"

[1] To safeguard confidentiality, names and identifying detail have been changed in all case material in this book.

This is a common solution-focused question at the beginning of a first session. It communicates a presupposition that positive changes occur between the request for service and a first appointment.

Sheila said, "I guess I feel better that I'm seeing someone for this. For the panic attacks. I mean, if that's what this is, then it's a good thing that I'm here."

Sheila's response indicates that positive change has already begun. If the therapist had begun with a more problem-focused inquiry, such as asking immediately about the panic, it might not have been immediately apparent that there have been changes for the better. Even if more details about the panic are discussed later in the session, the conversation has already identified change that can be amplified.

A few minutes later, the therapist said, "Can I ask you a strange question?"

"Sure," Sheila replied.

"Okay. What's the worst message that I could be giving you today? And I don't mean necessarily me, but that some therapist could say, that would make you go, 'I don't know about that therapist. Here I was looking forward to seeing someone about the panic attacks, but now I feel worse than before'"?

This indeed may seem to be a strange thing for a solution-focused therapist to be asking—it is specifically eliciting something negative! However, some solution-focused therapists, and strategic solution focused therapists in particular, often ask this question. The response can provide important information about the client's worst fears—and sometimes about what to avoid suggesting or implying.

Sheila's response was immediate: "That I have to feel this way for the rest of my life."

The therapist's next question asked about the *opposite* of this. The therapist smiled. "Now I want to ask you what the opposite of that would be. What would be the best or most helpful thing I could say or suggest today, that would make you feel like you got exactly what you want and need?"

Sheila smiled too. "Well, it would be nice if there could be instant relief. Or if you could tell me it will never happen again." She paused. The therapist waited. Sheila continued, "But I know that you can't say that."

"I wish I could," the therapist agreed. "What are your best hopes from coming here?"

Sheila began to cry. "It's so complicated," she said. "I'm scared, and I don't have anyone to talk to about all this. Sometimes I don't know what to do."

Sometimes clients do not answer questions about their best hopes from treatment directly or easily. The therapist now knows that one thing Sheila wants is the opportunity to talk. She probably also wants to decrease her fear and confusion. Over the course of the session, the therapist will want to discover more about what the solution will look like.

What makes Sheila's situation more complicated is that she had a heart attack three years ago. This makes her concerns very different from those of a person without a cardiac problem history, because another heart attack *is* a very real risk. Sheila has also struggled with depression, financial challenges, and relationship problems. Her husband wants her to return to work, and Sheila does not feel able to do so. She has left her husband on several occasions and then returned to him. Sheila has no one to talk to about this.

As the session continued, Sheila requested some tools to cope with the panic. The therapist offered the solution focused anxiety management class. Sheila had mixed feelings about attending. She said that she would think about the class, and she would check to see whether her husband could drive her. What she really wanted was "some ideas today." The therapist agreed to provide some possibilities. Continuing in the way described earlier in this chapter, the therapist offered some ideas, emphasizing that Sheila would be choosing which, if any, might be helpful. The ideas discussed included interoceptive exposure, courage ladders, riding the wave of panic, and the concept of the commonsense and the counterintuitive.

Sheila loved the ocean and was intrigued by the idea of "riding the wave." The therapist ended the session with the idea that when panic comes, Sheila might practice riding through it, riding the wave. She also might use her insightful knowledge of the fact that the situation *is* complicated—because of her panic, depression, relationship issues, and true cardiac condition—to help her understand that it makes a lot of sense that panic might emerge at times. When asked what she most wanted to remember from the session, Sheila replied, "Riding the wave."

Sheila began her next session by announcing, "The panic attacks are horrific." She wondered if she needed to be admitted to the hospital. "I can't drive. I can't stay alone. It makes my heart race. It feels like I'm going to die, like something bad is going to happen." Sheila was having panic attacks several times a day. "Riding the wave" helped—but the sensations returned. She said that she couldn't get to that anxiety class because she couldn't drive, and it also felt "too scary" to come alone. Her husband's work schedule did not allow him to accompany her to the class.

But things with her husband felt better. Sheila said, "He's been nicer recently." The therapist asked Sheila how she had helped that to happen. Sheila wasn't sure. The therapist encouraged Sheila to notice how she helped her husband to stay "nicer."

What was Sheila's thought about why her panic was so bad now? Sheila wasn't sure. Then she said, "Maybe it's because my daughter's school schedule is changing, and I'm going to be home alone, between the time my daughter leaves for school and when my husband comes home. Today she goes to school at one o'clock, for the first time." Sheila's husband would be home around six. That was what was so scary about today.

The therapist asked Sheila to imagine that it is this evening, and her husband is coming home, and she is feeling very proud because she made it through her afternoon alone. What will she be remembering? What did she do right after her daughter left? Sheila answered that she watched a DVD and had some granola and yogurt. She watched a soap opera on TV. Then she thought about what she wanted her husband to bring home for dinner (chicken, she thought) and called to let him know. She took a shower. When her husband got home, what did he notice about her? "Me in a better mood," Sheila said. She would be thinking, "I made it!" The whole evening would go better.

The therapist asked Sheila how she had prepared her daughter for things like the first day of school (not just now, in college, but also when her daughter was very little). Sheila remembered that they had played peek-a-boo, and Mommy had disappeared after the 15th peek-a-boo. She had let her daughter know that Mommy absolutely knew that her brave big girl could do it. What else did she give her daughter strength to do? Soccer, Sheila remembered. "Oh, she was so nervous about that. But I was there for her."

The therapist asked Sheila how long her panic attacks usually lasted. About five minutes, Sheila thought. "How do you get through that time?" the therapist asked. "A person can do anything for five minutes," Sheila replied. The therapist brought up the idea of "management versus elimination."

"I was just wondering," the therapist said, "if you can do a panic attack faster than five minutes."

"What do you mean?" Sheila looked puzzled. "Like running a race and seeing if I can break my record?"

"Hmm, how could you find that out?" the therapist wondered.

"Well," Sheila said, "I could watch the hands of the clock."

"Interesting," said the therapist. They ended the session with the plan for Sheila to use the schedule she had set for herself for after one o'clock today: Watch the DVD, have a snack, watch more TV, call her husband about dinner, and take a shower. If panic visits, Sheila would watch the hands of her kitchen clock and see how fast she could get through it. (Might she beat her "record" of five minutes?) "Or, I could call my girlfriend," Sheila added.

This was an idea that she had not previously mentioned. When the conversation invites multiple solutions, clients frequently come up with additional ideas on their own.

There was no further mention of the hospital as a possible place to spend the afternoon.

The therapist began the third session by asking, "So, what's better or different, since last time?" Sheila felt better. On a zero to ten scale, she had felt at a "two" last time. She was at a "four" today. After the last visit, she had stayed home alone that afternoon—and other afternoons since then as well. Sheila had called her friend and asked if she could come over if she needed company. She had not needed a visit that day. But she had visited that friend a few times since then. "How did you get there?" the therapist asked.

"I drove," Sheila answered. "It's really not very far."

Sheila was still not driving alone very much, but she had driven to the grocery store, mostly with her daughter—but also a couple of times alone. She said, "I just tell myself, if I'm going to have heart attack, it could happen anywhere." Her husband was being difficult at times, but Sheila was "just letting it go." She chuckled, "He can't make every little thing into an argument if I refuse to fight about it."

What was the issue or focus for today? "I want to get to the point where I can drive by myself so I can go to those panic attack classes you were telling me about," Sheila said. "I drove down here today, but not alone. My daughter was in the car. And she'll be with me on the way home later."

The therapist commented on Sheila's skills as a mom and the awesome way she had supported the daughter over the years. The daughter had grown from that scared little girl to a beautiful, competent, and caring young woman. Together the therapist and Sheila discussed how skills grow, a little at a time. In addition to her skilled parenting, what else was Sheila good at? "Well, I can cook," Sheila said.

"Like what?"

"I can make papas rellenas. Those aren't easy."

The therapist wondered aloud how Sheila might start someone cooking. "Instant pudding," Sheila said. "The 'just add milk and stir' kind."

The therapist and Sheila discussed how Sheila might build her courage ladder for driving. First, there would be lots of trips with her daughter in the car, like on the way home today, and short trips to visit her friend. Then her daughter or husband could follow in another car. Or they could be "on standby," and Sheila could call or text on her cell phone when she got to her destination. Sheila liked the idea of reminding herself that heart attacks are no more likely to happen while driving than any other time. She could pick up her daughter downtown or pick up her niece. She could remember that panic *does* subside. (Her current "record" was two minutes.) Once Sheila had had a panic attack on the way to her dad's place, and she knew she would be driving there again. Occasionally, Sheila might drive to her sister's workplace. She could drive to the pharmacy. All of these would be steps on Sheila's courage ladder.

"I have a weird idea," said the therapist. "Can I share it with you?"

"Sure," Sheila said.

"You could try a step with your passenger in the back seat," the therapist said, with just a hint of a smile.

Sheila laughed. "That is so funny. I was just thinking the exact same thing. I could tell my daughter, 'You're in the back seat on the way home today, girl.'"

The therapist and Sheila talked more about the commonsense and the counterintuitive, or "the opposite of what you would expect. It's like putting sugar in the soup, or salt in the cookies." They discussed that Sheila might *expect* a little panic while driving with her daughter on way home. "Actually," Sheila said, "I did have some panic on the way here. And I had that thought. I just said, 'Girl, you're no more likely to have a heart attack now than just sitting at home.'"

This is an example of how solutions that clients suggest for the future may already have happened.

Sheila talked about more steps for her courage ladder, including ones such as having her passenger in the back seat. The therapist brought up the idea of "You can—and you don't have to." Sheila didn't have to do all these things, at least not right away. The therapist described how even people who don't get panic attacks sometimes hate driving from San Diego to Los Angeles. They may say, "I'll go, but I won't drive. I'll only go if I can take Amtrak."

"My brother did that once," Sheila remembered. "And he's one of those people who couldn't have a panic attack if his life depended on it!" Sheila and the therapist talked about how Sheila might take Amtrak to Los Angeles, too, if she ever wanted to. "Or I just might drive," Sheila said. "I used to do that all the time."

As the session ended, the therapist said, "Between your understanding of how you'd teach someone to cook, and your idea for putting your daughter in the back seat, and all those other neat ideas, I think you really get this. You really do. So I want to invite you to be curious about some other creative steps you can come up with on your courage ladder. Just like you're a creative cook, I have the feeling you're a creative courage ladder designer."

Sheila smiled. "Getting creative with my courage ladder. I never thought of it that way. That's a pretty cool way to look at it."

SINGLE SESSION CASE EXAMPLE: JOHN

The following vignette is written in the first person by a therapist who saw John once for a single session. It illustrates (at least) two important things: first, John's tremendous courage, and second, the solution-focused attitudes conveyed by both the therapist and the system that allowed the appointment to happen.

"John had been scheduled to see another therapist for a first-time appointment an hour and a half earlier and had just arrived. I had a last-minute cancellation, so John was booked with me. John described chronic pain and increasing depression and anxiety. He is 24, he has a college degree, and he would like to get an MBA someday, but he is unemployed now. He lives with his wife of about a year, who works (providing income and his health insurance). His wife also does the shopping and other errands. A psychologist who John saw at a chronic pain management program a few months ago diagnosed John with 'social phobia or agoraphobia.'

"John said, 'I don't go out much. I pretty much stay home these days.'

"So I asked him, 'Hey John, if coming here helps you just the way you hope it will, what will be different?'

"John answered that he might go out somewhere. Where would he go? He said, 'For a walk maybe. There's a walking path near my house.'

"I asked John, 'How will that make a difference?'

"He said, 'It's something I know I should do. And something I do want to do. But I don't. I go days without going outside.'

"As I listened to him, I suddenly thought: 'This guy who just told me he never goes outside just got himself out of the house and here to the clinic.' And I thought: 'That's why he missed his appointment!' Getting out of the house is the hardest thing in the world for John—and he just did it! Talk about an act of courage! I decided to tell him that. 'I'm realizing that you got yourself here today. That was huge for you.'

"John looked at me. He said softly, 'Yeah, it really was.'

"'How did you do that?' I asked him.

"'I'm not sure. I almost didn't come. And by the time I got here, I knew I had missed my appointment. I almost didn't come in.'

"'But you did. How did you do that?' Maybe I was pushing the point with John here. But somehow, at the time, it felt like just the right thing to do."

This is exactly where solution-focused therapists "push the point"! Some might say that unless the client indicates otherwise, one cannot "overdo" the highlighting of courage and strength.

"John said, 'I don't know how I came in. I just did. I guess I just figured that since I was here, I might as well come in. I do want to get my life back.'"

Recognizing and highlighting John's courage and ability to get here even in the presence of his fear and reluctance helped John to recognize those strengths as well. Expecting reluctance and discomfort and doing something in the presence of them will be something for John to "notice and do more of."

"Thinking about John also makes me appreciate the support staff and system that didn't turn him away because he had missed the originally scheduled appointment. Our staff looked for and found a way for him to be seen. I hate to think about what it would have felt like for John if he had been turned away."

In John's situation, flexibility in the system was an ingredient of the solution.

INTERMITTENT THERAPY WITH THE CLASS: PAM

The following case example describes a woman who first came for individual therapy, then attended the class, and then returned for more individual sessions over the next two years. Pam, a 32-year-old White woman, called to request help with "panic attacks." During her telephone intake, she explained that she had always been somewhat anxious and sensitive, but it was worse now. Pam worked in the personnel department of a large company and took pride in her work. But recently, she had felt unusually anxious when her supervisor called to ask her about a change she had made in staffing. "My tongue felt too big, and my heart was beating hard," she said. Then she had the same feeling when she was in line at the grocery store. "It was hot, and I thought, 'What if I pass out?' I was buying all this stuff for the kitchen in my new condo. I had been all excited about it before, but now I just left the shopping cart and ran out of the store. I never did anything like that before. I just hate feeling so out of control."

By the time Pam saw the therapist, she was even more anxious. She was avoiding any situation that might bring on the sensations, including being in the condo by herself. Getting the condo had been Pam's dream for years, but now she was afraid to be there alone, away from her mom and stepdad (with whom she had lived before) and away from her boyfriend, Bob (who lived in the old neighborhood).

Most of all, Pam was concerned that she couldn't possibly drive to work from the condo. She had never been very comfortable driving, and she had understood when she bought the property that her new commute would require freeway driving. Until now, she had assumed she would "just do it." But the first time she tried the commute, shortly after the anxiety in the grocery store, Pam had panicked. She had pulled over and called Bob. Now he was driving her to work every day.

"But he can't keep doing that," Pam said. She was frantic. "I have to be able to drive. I have to work. Especially now that I have this condo to pay for." The fear of driving was also "spreading." "I can hardly drive anywhere anymore," Pam said tearfully.

"You said 'hardly,'" therapist said, in a puzzled tone. "Does that mean that you *do* drive sometimes?"

"Almost never," Pam sighed.

The therapist asked, "How did you get here today?"

"Well, I did drive here," Pam answered.

"You did? How did you do that?" asked the therapist.

"Well, it's not very far," Pam replied.

The presence of "exceptions" has now been established. When there is one time when the problem is absent, there is often another, and another.

What would let Pam know that this wasn't so much of a problem? "Understanding what's happening to me and whether I'm going crazy. Getting back to how I was before," she said.

The therapist asked Pam about times when that was already starting to happen, even a little. "Well," Pam said with a little smile, "you just reminded me that I did drive here today."

Because it seemed that the solution focused anxiety management class might provide Pam with some of the information she was seeking, the therapist described the program to Pam and asked whether she would like to attend. "It sounds like exactly what I need," Pam said. "I want to get back in control. I don't want to let this stop me from making this condo work." She particularly liked the fact that she could bring her mom or Bob with her to the class. She smiled, "That way I don't have to drive down here alone."

The therapist also asked Pam if she would be interested in doing a little experiment "right now" to see if she could create some control over her sensations. Pam agreed to try it. The therapist continued, "This might sound sort of weird, but some experts would say that the best way to prove to yourself that you have some control over the sensations is to see if you can make them feel more intense, or even bring them on. I'm curious: If you wanted to deliberately try to bring on one of those weird sensations, right now, in here, do you think you could do it?"

"I don't know," Pam said. "I might be afraid to try."

"Which one would you pick, as a baby step?" the therapist asked.

Pam paused, moving her tongue around in her mouth. "I think I would see if I could make my tongue bigger, like it was when I got anxious that first time."

The therapist invited Pam to try it. Pam moved her tongue around a bit. She scrunched up her face. Then she began to giggle. "I can't do it," she said.

This is an example of inviting interoceptive exposure during a therapy session.

As the session ended, the therapist told Pam that she was struck by her determination and courage—and by the fact that even with all the weird things she had been experiencing, Pam had driven here today! The therapist also highlighted Pam's courage: her willingness to go to the class, her experimenting with deliberately trying to create the kind of feeling that had been so scary before. The therapist also invited Pam to notice more times when the weird feelings in her body weren't a problem, or when they were there but somehow drifted away on their own. The therapist asked Pam what she wanted to remember from their conversation.

"Bringing it on," Pam said. "It's such a weird idea, but I want to think about it. And I think you understand how much this condo means to me. I was so scared you were going to tell me that I was crazy, like 'What could you possibly have been thinking, that you could live alone?' But you think I can do it. That feels huge to me. Thank you."

Pam and her mom attended all four sessions of the class, and one week her boyfriend came, too. By the time Pam saw the therapist again, she was staying overnight at her condo about half the time, but not yet alone. The therapist asked what would be most helpful today. Pam wanted some coaching on building her courage ladder.

"Shall we use note cards or do it as a document on the computer?" the therapist asked. Pam wanted to use note cards. Together they brainstormed "baby steps." The therapist put a big stack of note cards on the desk and gave Pam a pencil. Pam looked at Google Maps and thought of three different routes she could take to work. One of these included only a short stretch of freeway. The entrance lane was long, and she had to move over only one lane. It occurred to Pam that she could practice this route on a Sunday morning. Pam remembered two places where there were fast-food places with bathrooms, places where she could stop if she needed a break.

Pam's courage ladder also included some steps for creatively managing sensations if they happened while she was driving. She could think of driving safely while her heart was pounding as being the same as driving safely while the windshield wipers were on. She could look forward to the days when she had her period, so she could remember that she could drive even when she had cramps.

Throughout the process, the therapist invited Pam to create variations on the creative solutions she was describing. Occasionally, the therapist suggested a variation. Pam commented, "It's interesting. Your steps are way littler than mine." Pam's steps started becoming smaller and more specific as well.

For two more sessions, Pam built courage ladders and reported on her practice. The therapist heard multiple instances of courage—in driving and other areas as well. Pam described spending four hours alone at the condo on a rainy night before Bob got off work. "You mean that counts?" Pam asked. "I mean, I didn't really stay all alone all night."

"What do you think?" The therapist smiled.

Pam smiled too. "Okay, it counts."

The therapist continued to highlight Pam's courage as examples of it emerged. Pam had decided to learn to drive Bob's car, which had a manual transmission. She practiced on hills and in traffic. During a conversation about the "commonsense and counterintuitive" perspective Pam had learned about in the class, the therapist asked Pam if she would like to do jumping jacks together during the session, to see if both of them could bring on breathlessness. They did so. They discussed "taking all the time you need."

By the next session, Pam felt ready to stop her appointments for now. She wanted to remember "all the good ideas, and how small the baby steps are. And that it's so weird, welcoming the panic, but it's huge for me."

Pam returned about six months later. She was driving now, and work was going well. During the week, she usually stayed in the condo alone. Most weekends, Bob stayed over, not because she couldn't be alone, but because their relationship was deepening. But now there was a new concern. Pam's mom's house was in foreclosure, and her mom and stepdad wanted to move in with Pam for a while. "I feel so mean saying 'No' to Mom. But I really don't have space for them." Pam and the therapist talked about how Pam probably *would* feel anxious telling her mom that moving in didn't feel like a viable option. "But I do think I can do it," Pam said. "It's sort of like expecting to feel anxious on the I-805 to I-8 overpass. Like you once said, it's like walking and chewing gum at the same time."

About a year later, Pam returned. She had broken up with Bob—a hard decision, but a good one for her, she said. She was truly living alone now. She was dating, but there was "no one serious." Her stepdad had found work, and he and her mom had managed to refinance their home. Pam's job was offering some new and exciting options, but they might require some travel. "I don't think we ever talked about this before," Pam said, "because it wasn't an issue. But I'm so anxious about flying. And about staying in a hotel alone in a strange city. I mean, I *never* stay in a hotel, anywhere! And what if I'm expected to rent a car and drive on freeways I don't know? What if I have a panic attack? It brings up all my old issues—being alone, worrying, not having my support next to me."

Pam and the therapist talked about how to use the same process that had worked for Pam before. What would let Pam know that she was growing her courage for these new challenges? Again Pam came up with creative ideas. Pam decided she might experiment with staying at a hotel in a nice place near home—"Coronado or La Jolla, maybe. I've actually been wanting an excuse to do that for a while. Like a mini 'staycation,' I think they call it."

For trips out of town, Pam realized this: "I don't really have to go alone. My mom would love an excuse for a trip and would probably come with me if I invited her. I know she doesn't have the money to do that every time, but she would do it sometimes."

The therapist and Pam talked about another concept from solution focused anxiety management: "You can—and you don't have to" might become an additional "ingredient of the solution." Where might Pam most want to remember that perspective? "Definitely about renting a car in a strange city," Pam said. "I think it's absolutely appropriate, on business travel, to take an airport shuttle and cabs." She paused. "Or, who knows? Maybe I *will* decide to rent a car!"

On the plane, Pam decided that she would read her Kindle. "I never have time to read," she said. She would bring a book of Sudoku games for takeoff and landing time.

The therapist had a question. "Let's imagine that you and I are having a conversation after one of those trips, and I ask you, like I always do, 'What's better or different?' And you're telling me that you took a plane trip, and you had some weird sensations on the plane, and you're feeling really proud of how you got through them. What might you be telling me?"

This is an extremely useful and versatile question in solution focused anxiety management. It normalizes the possibility that anxiety will return, and it conveys an expectation that the client will use existing strengths and resources to cope successfully. It communicates that the therapist views this process as a victory and invites the client to do so as well.

Pam thought for a minute. "I think I will tell you that I took a Xanax. I don't take them very often, but I might use one then. And that I remembered that I *can* tolerate discomfort. I did it when I stopped seeing Bob. That wasn't easy. If I could do that, I can do other things, too."

Pam felt comfortable using this appointment as a one-time booster session. "You reminded me of all those tools. Like 'I can—and I don't have to.' And I'm realizing that that applies to taking the new position at all. And I *do* want to. And I think I realize something else: that worrying is just what I do when I face something new. It's sort of part of me. And that's okay."

Pam's realization, two years after completion of the class, reflects one of the most elegant outcomes of solution focused anxiety management: the combination of acceptance of anxiety, on one hand, and on the other, the courage and strength to do wonderful things.

CAT PHOBIA: GEORGE

George, a 66-year-old White man, who had been born and raised in England but who had lived in the USA for 50 years, had seen his therapist 2 years earlier because of mild depression and indecision about when to retire. He returned now requesting a consultation for a new concern, his cat phobia.

George said, "I don't think we talked about this the last time I was here, but now that things have settled down in my life, I want to deal with this cat thing. I don't know exactly when it started, but I've never been comfortable with cats. It feels like they're going to scratch or bite. Siamese are the worst. They just look mean. I have some vague memory of seeing a really ugly one when I was a kid, about four or five or so. It was on a street in London, I think, but I'm not really sure what happened."

George had decided to retire, and he felt good about his decision. Now he wanted to do more traveling. He said, "I know that there will be cats around. It's an inconvenience. I can't expect people to keep them away from me. So I want to deal with it."

The therapist asked what would be different when George had "dealt with it." He replied immediately, "Well, the first and most obvious thing is that I'll be able to go to my daughter's house, and she won't have to keep the cats in the garage. I'd sure like to not have palpitations when a cat is around."

"What will you be aware of instead?" the therapist inquired.

The reader might notice that George had provided a great deal of information, and there were several possible ways in which the therapist could respond. This example illustrates the therapist's deliberate choice to follow up on "dealing with it" rather than focusing on the origin of the problem.

"Oh, a damn cat," George laughed. "Just tolerate it."

The therapist wondered aloud where George already had that kind of reaction. With rats, snakes, and cockroaches, that reaction was already present.

"What lets you know that you're already starting to deal with cats differently?" the therapist continued.

George's neighbor had cats, and George had noticed that "it's already gotten better." For some reason, tan or orangish cats were easier for George. Black and white cats were harder. George also commented that he loves dogs. He said, "It's funny, I didn't grow up with dogs either, but the kids wanted dogs." How had comfort with dogs grown for him? He had discovered that they were affectionate, almost like a member of the family.

The therapist asked George where else he had grown some comfort over the years or gotten over a phobia. George remembered that he used to be afraid of public speaking. He said, "I went to Toastmasters, years ago. After the little practice talks they make you do, I tried one at work, and I thought, 'Hey, I can handle this.' Wrong! It was a total disaster." But George had been determined. "I had some opportunities professionally, and they were going to require some speaking. At first I thought, 'No way.' Then I said to myself, 'Look, man, you're 40 years old. This is a promotion. This is your kids' college education. You can do this.' I'm not the world's best speaker, and I don't love it, but I can do a decent presentation and hold my own."

George's response gives important information about his resources and strengths. These include self-talk that he had come up with on his own, viewing age or season of life as a reason to change, using external resources (Toastmasters), and willingness to do something even without excelling at it or "loving it."

The therapist asked George how he would create for himself a process similar to that which had worked for public speaking. George said, "I think if I could touch one cat, one time, I will be okay."

The therapist invited detail about where this would happen. The cat would be one of his daughter's. Which one? The little orange one. What was the cat's name? Pumpkin. Was Pumpkin a boy or a girl? George wasn't sure, and the therapist encouraged George to find out. Which part of Pumpkin would George touch? The back of the head, and he would stroke "in the direction the fur grows." Where would this occur? In his daughter's house, in the family room, near the door. His daughter would be holding Pumpkin.

Steve de Shazer said, "Hope lies in the details" (Dolan, 2009).

What would let George know he was ready to make this happen? George said that he would have a conversation with his daughter ahead of time about planning the process. He had already mentioned to her that he was "working on this."

The therapist wondered aloud, "If they had the equivalent of Toastmasters, like 'Catmasters' or something, what else would they be suggesting that you do to get ready for this? Sort of the equivalent of little practice talks?"

George thought that Catmasters might recommend some "intermediate steps." What might these be? "Well, it wouldn't be some lecture on 'It's only a cat. Don't be afraid of it,'" George said.

This is an example of a spontaneous recognition that commonsense suggestions frequently do not work well enough. Sometimes this kind of recognition provides a naturally occurring opportunity during a session to introduce the concept of the commonsense and the counterintuitive.

George thought that "intermediate steps" might include the following: finding some pictures of cats, touching those pictures, and his daughter holding Pumpkin while he walked by and said "Hi, Pumpkin." The therapist asked George whether he would like to write these steps down, and he did so.

The therapist asked whether George would like to try a first step during the session, and the answer was yes. The therapist said that if he wanted to do this, they could Google "cat images" on the therapist's computer and see what they discovered. The therapist invited George to select one picture that might be an easiest first step. George picked an orange kitten. The therapist suggested that if George wished to do so, he could approach the computer, as if he were going to touch the screen without actually doing so. George did this, grimacing a bit. Then he said, "I almost wanted to touch it and get it over with. Isn't that weird?"

As the session ended, George said, "You know, when I thought about coming for a consultation on this, I never thought we would do so much today" He had a plan, and he was already well on the way to his destination. He did not feel a need to set up a follow-up appointment. He said, "I may email you a picture of me touching Pumpkin."

THE CLIENT AS EXPERT

Like many of the clients described in this chapter, George came up with details that the therapist could not possibly have known. As discussed previously, the solution-focused attitude of viewing the client as the principal member of the "solution design team" is critical. The therapist listens for and builds on the client's language and strengths and past successes. He or she is clearly a collaborating member of that design team, offering suggestions and ideas, but the overarching attitude is that clients are the experts on what fits for them.

The following example illustrates how the components of courage may be different from those suggested in the literature. This case was described by Quick (2012):

> *Tou, a 37-year-old Laotian man, was referred by his psychiatrist for "anxiety management techniques." Tou had been on psychiatric disability for many years. He lived with his mother, and he spoke English, Chinese, and Laotian. Tou described feelings of panic, which occurred when the TV "taunted" him for being Laotian. Tou saw images and heard voices, and it felt to him "like being raped." His best hopes were for the panic to go away. What would let Tou know that the panic was diminishing? Not hearing the voices, he said, especially the ones that were in English. When were the voices less of a problem? When texting or surfing the Internet, Tou said. It also helped when he talked back to the voices, in Laotian.*
>
> *The therapist asked Tou if he would like to create a list together of things that might calm him down. They would take turns generating possibilities. Tou liked the idea of doing this. Here is the list they made together: cooking, taking his medicine, mowing the lawn, getting "back to real," thinking about the pomegranate tree in the back yard, talking back to the voices (in English or Laotian), Chinese and English music, tea, coffee, turning the TV off, telling the voices that he doesn't have to do what they say, thinking that it's okay to not be sure if he is gay or straight or "bi," walking, going to the gym, cutting his old jeans into cutoffs, remembering that sexual fantasies are normal, spending time with his dog, checking his investments on the computer, and talking to his mom. (pp. 147–148)*

This case illustrates that even when the client describes symptoms that other clinicians might not diagnose as "anxiety," if "anxiety" is the *client's* term, the therapist may choose to use it as well. In this case, after the session, the therapist thought about how different the session had turned out to be from what Tou's psychiatrist had probably expected when referring Tou for the consultation.

It might be noted that children as well as adults are often the true experts on what works for them. In the book *Therapy with "Impossible" Cases*, Duncan, Hubble, and Miller described a little girl who had been diagnosed with "separation anxiety." Although she had seen multiple therapists, she could not sleep alone in her own room. Finally, she discovered a solution that grew from her own ten-year-old world. She described it to a therapist in the following words:

> *I feel a lot better now that I came up with the solution to sleep in my own room, and I did it, and I'm proud of myself. And I couldn't be proud of myself if you told me, "How about if you barricade yourself in with pillows, maybe that'll work?" I wouldn't feel like I've done it. So basically, what I'm saying is you don't get as much joy out of doing something when somebody told you to do it. (Duncan et al., 1997, as cited in Duncan, 2010, p. 91)*

As Quick pointed out, it was "not just the suggestion but the fact that it came from the client that made a difference" (Quick, 2012, p. 83).

TAPPING RESOURCES FOR GROWING COURAGE

Sometimes significant others in one's life are wonderful resources for growing courage. One mom told her little boy, "You are like the cowardly lion in the Wizard of Oz. You feel so scared, and at the same time, you are the most courageous boy I know."

In the author's experience, multiple clients have received—and been significantly helped by—remarkably similar messages from the people in their lives who know them best and love them most. The therapist might invite reflection about this with an invitation similar to the following, which has been adapted from Fiske (2005): Think about someone who has helped you to recognize the courage you have within. This person may be in your life now, or it may be someone you knew in the past. This person may not have been around a lot, but in some small or large way, he or she helped you to recognize and grow your courage and capacity to tolerate discomfort.

The therapist might ask the client questions like the following:

- What did this person recognize about you?
- If that person were with you now, what would he or she be saying or doing?
- What can help you to access that support when you need it the very most?

What clients realize becomes like the phenomenon described by the title of a book about Milton Erickson, hypnotist and master therapist, *My Voice Will Go with You* (Rosen, 1991). The words, supportive messages, and reminders of strength that people have heard in both the past and the present can remain alive, supporting "the four Cs"—courage, coping, appropriate caution, and choice—in so many ways.

CHAPTER 8

Appropriate Caution as an Ingredient of the Solution

The strength that solution focused anxiety management calls "appropriate caution" is often underappreciated, both by people who request help with anxiety and by the therapists who treat them. Clients often simply assume that their caution is something negative, part of the problem, something to be ashamed of, something to eliminate. Throughout this book, solution focused anxiety management has been described as a program that enhances courage, coping, appropriate caution, and choice. Just about everyone who struggles with anxiety immediately recognizes how courage and coping are desirable outcomes, and most people view increased choice as a good thing as well. The value of appropriate caution may be less clear. This chapter attempts to explain it and to provide some examples of appropriate caution as an important ingredient of the solution.

DEFENSIVE PESSIMISM

The term "defensive pessimism" is introduced briefly in Topic Two of the solution focused anxiety management class. As indicated in Chapter 4, there is some fascinating research suggesting that some people actually perform *better* on tasks if they take the time to anticipate what might go wrong and to plan how they might handle it. Like some other components of solution focused anxiety management, this perspective is counterintuitive, so it is worth describing the research that supports this concept in a little more detail.

It is often assumed that students perform better academically when they worry less. Some research with bright female college students attempted to study this assumption by introducing an intervention that attempted to decrease worry and to increase belief in a positive outcome. For some of the students, the expected results were found: Decreased worry was followed by better performance. But for others, the *opposite* was the case! Some of the students seemed to perform *worse* when encouraged to inhibit their naturally occurring style, which included worry. They performed *better* when preparing for exams in the way that worked for them: a style that included significant anticipation of what might go wrong. Dr. Julie Norem, a psychologist who

Solution Focused Anxiety Management
http://dx.doi.org/10.1016/B978-0-12-394421-4.00008-5

conducted some of this research and has written about it (Norem, 2001), called this construct *defensive pessimism*. As noted in Chapter 4, a website provides more information on the topic (www.defensivepessimism.com).

Additional follow-up on the college students showed that for students who did better with "less worry," the following seemed to occur: Thinking about the positive, desired outcome (such as a high grade on an exam) led to engaging in the behaviors that were most likely to produce that outcome (studying). If a student just assumed that the positive outcome would happen on its own, without effort, and did not study, the positive outcome was far less likely to occur.

For the students who did better with "worrying in the way they always did," the process seemed to be more like this: Anticipating what could go wrong (such as a low grade on an exam) led to engaging in the behaviors that were most likely to prevent the undesired outcome (that is, studying greatly decreases the likelihood of failing a test). If the worry was so extreme that it interfered with effective preparation or study, the positive outcome was far less likely.

For both groups of students, the same behaviors—study and effective preparation—were associated with doing well on their exams. What was different was what mediated or led to the effective behavior. In the spirit of the "one size does not fit all" perspective of solution focused anxiety management, this is extremely important. Discovering and building on what works for a particular individual are critical ingredients of the solution.

Since defensive pessimism is common among people who request help with anxiety, it is worth elaborating more on the concept. In her description of the style, Norem noted that some people simply seem to have "anxious dispositions." Whether because of genetic influences, life experience (past or current), or some combination (and a combination is most likely), this is a relatively stable characteristic across time. In the language of solution focused anxiety management, these people are "mind reactors" (or body reactors, or both).

Norem wrote that people who share these characteristics often expect the worst to happen. Like the students who worried about failing their tests, they may spend a lot of time anticipating what might go wrong. They also may spend a lot of time planning how they might handle things. The time and energy that are spent considering what might go wrong and how they could fix problems help these people to prepare. The process reduces their anxiety.

Norem also pointed out that, contrary to what one might expect, defensive pessimists don't seem to be particularly depressed. They are often successful in multiple areas of their lives, and they often have meaningful relationships and satisfying careers. They may be puzzled to learn that anyone would expect them to be depressed. Defensive pessimism isn't a problem for them. In fact, for these people, it is a solution.

Anticipating disaster, thinking, and planning all help defensive pessimists to manage their anxiety. The mental "work" of going through all those worst-case scenarios—and how one would cope with them—leaves defensive pessimists better able to deal with adversity—and routine matters as well. Careful anticipation and planning often result in action that helps to avoid the consequences one fears. The process can help people who are anxious to feel more in control, and it builds hope.

As noted previously, research suggests that if something interferes with or prevents anticipatory mental activity, sometimes things go *less* well. What might interrupt one's natural inclination to "worry"? In a laboratory experiment, it may be the conditions or experimenter's instructions. In "real life," it is usually the commonsense advice: "Don't worry" or "Relax."

The research findings described here (about how many defensive pessimists actually do worse when they *don't* worry) probably would not surprise many defensive pessimists. But these results *have* been a surprise to many people, both in the general public and in academia. After all, it seems to be "common sense" to assume that "worry is bad; relaxation is good." Contemporary culture (at least in the USA) and many voices in the world of psychology and psychotherapy support optimism and positive thinking. In an interesting comparison, Norem commented that defensive pessimism may be like left-handedness. For years, some parents and teachers tried to train left-handed children to change the dominant hand. Now we know that trying to change handedness is both ineffective and unnecessary. In the same way, defensive pessimists simply do things differently. Norem wrote, "They do not need to be *cured* (italics added) of their defensive pessimism" (p. 215). Instead, defensive pessimism, and recognizing and using it, may be ingredients of the solution.

What is the opposite of a defensive pessimist? Norem used the term "strategic optimist" to describe people who usually don't think too much about what may go wrong. In general, their dispositions are not very anxious, and focusing away from possible problems keeps their anxiety low. These people are not particularly "flaky." They generally function well and are adequately prepared for what they have to do. In addition, like defensive pessimists, they are not particularly depressed.

People can be strategic optimists most of the time—and at the same time, in specific areas, they do worry. Norem gave an example of a man who was a strategic optimist in terms of his approach to his work and things such as getting to appointments and airports on time. But when he thought about his adolescent daughter dating, his process was more like that of the defensive pessimist.

In the same way, people who are defensive pessimists most of the time may have areas where they are more like strategic optimists. Norem described a woman who used the defensive pessimism style when thinking about how a dinner party would go, how her work presentation would be received, and whether she would arrive at the airport on time. However, when it came to finances, she was uncharacteristically unconcerned—almost too nonchalant.

It is intriguing to note that in Norem's example, the two people described here were married to each other! It is fascinating to consider the interpersonal "systems" implications of this. When one's wife reliably worries about getting to the airport on time, one doesn't have to do the worrying oneself.

It is interesting to imagine how this couple might use the exercise in Topic Four of solution focused anxiety management that invites consideration of the pros and cons of a desired change. Let us imagine that the wife is the primary class member, with a desire to be less anxious about things like airport punctuality, and her husband is there as a significant other. Both do the Pros–Cons exercise, listing the positive things it would bring to their lives if she were less anxious, the challenges they might face, and how they might deal with those challenges.

The wife might write the following: "Pros of me being less anxious: I could relax a little. The trip would be more fun. Less tension with my husband. Cons: We might miss the plane. And I couldn't blame it all on him!"

Her husband's notes might say this: "Pros of my wife being less anxious: She'll be more pleasant to be around. We wouldn't have to get there three hours early! Cons: I might have to watch the time before we leave the house. I couldn't just count on her to do it."

It is interesting to speculate about what they might talk about on the way home from the class. Or they might not talk directly about it at all, but they might share appropriate caution in a different way the next time they are leaving for the airport.

Within major approaches to psychotherapy—including the solution-focused model emphasized throughout this book—there is encouragement to notice and build on the positive. Solution-focused practice highlights those occasions when the problem is absent or less problematic. Is this perspective incompatible with defensive pessimism? It is not. Sometimes, as discussed throughout this approach, the counterintuitive is an ingredient of the solution, and one size definitely does not fit all.

Sometimes, in solution focused anxiety management, there may be opportunities to invite people to do more of what they do in other areas of their lives. When working with a client who feels "too worried" about some things and "too casual" about others, the therapist might wonder aloud (only partly in jest) if the client might use a little more of his or her "other" style in a particular situation.

Valuing appropriate caution, or defensive pessimism, and incorporating it into one's view of the self are processes that sometimes occur during solution focused anxiety management. As people do this, they may reflect on the fact that what works for them is a "minority position." In Norem's words, people may prefer not to "'do' defensive pessimism out loud in front of other people" (p. 193). She added that people may decide that it works better to *privately* anticipate problems, ways of preventing them from happening, and strategies for managing them if they do come up. As in so many other ways, choice is an ingredient of solution focused anxiety management.

PREFERENCE FOR THE ROUTINE: A STYLE, NOT PSYCHOPATHOLOGY

Some people who request help with anxiety are cautious about "change." They often describe a preference for order, predictability, and the routine. Sometimes they have received diagnoses of "obsessive compulsive personality disorder" or have been described as having "features" of that diagnosis, but that is not always the case. Like defensive pessimism, a preference for order is not necessarily a problem in one's life. It may simply be a style.

Comfort with the familiar is actually a common, normal phenomenon. Even when one actively initiates a change (as in acquiring a new car or cell phone), learning to use the new features can feel stressful as well as "good" for many people. Change that has not been actively sought out can be even more difficult. Some readers of this book may have had the experience of transitioning to electronic medical record keeping in their workplaces. Sometimes professionals resign to avoid dealing with a very new system. The author recalls that when this change came to her department, an Information Technology presentation on the transition included this sentence: "The only person who likes change is a wet baby." Everyone nodded and laughed. The story of how that sentence was presented has been repeated in many therapy sessions when uninvited change has entered clients' workplaces or lives. At the session after this story was told, one client said, "They told me I might have to cross-train on a new machine at work." He said he told his co-worker the "wet baby story," and both of them decided that they were going to be stubborn enough not to let that change rob them of their good jobs.

The reader may recall the discussion in Topic One of the class about how many characteristics appear to be distributed on a bell-shaped curve. Like autonomic reactivity, preference for change or stability may also have this kind of distribution. Some people thrive on change! In their lives, the more change, the better. They may seek out activities (and relationships) in which there is constant change, and they may thrive on thrill or risk. At the other end of the continuum are those who seek out a high degree of freedom from risk, thrill, or change.

Sometimes the author compares the continuum described here to preferences for the different phases in the development of a business or a project. Some people love the "start-up" phase: creating the idea, securing the funding, getting things moving. The excitement of doing something new energizes them. The "maintenance" phase, with its daily tasks and routine, is harder for them. People often quickly recognize where they are on this continuum, and many people who come for help with anxiety are "maintenance people" in multiple areas of their lives.

Both change and routine are, of course, parts of everyone's life, and regardless of one's preference, everyone deals with both. For change-seekers, routine may be more challenging, and it might feel boring. These people may sometimes need to "exercise their routine-tolerance muscles." In the same way, people who prefer the familiar may find the inevitable changes of life challenging. For them, psychological "exercise of their flexibility tolerance muscles" may be an ingredient of the solution.

For people who are cautious about change, normalizing that stance is sometimes valuable. The author sometimes compares the process to learning to swim. Some people master kicking with the legs right away, whereas for others, the arm stroke is easier. The swimmer eventually learns to do both, even when one skill takes some additional effort or practice.

Viewing one's preference for maintenance and caution as a normal variation of style and preference rather than as pathology is freeing for many people. They appreciate that their style has advantages in many situations, and they recognize that they can often choose activities that fit what they do best. When they must face change, they recognize that it is okay to "not like it." "Not liking it" doesn't mean "not doing it." They recognize that they absolutely know how to tolerate discomfort, often by using the strengths they use in so many other areas of their lives.

Sometimes people use their maintenance skills to create regular practice in seeking out novelty and practicing flexibility! They use the tools of solution focused anxiety management to view change as an opportunity to practice.

People who are cautious in some areas of their lives can also be tremendously courageous in other areas. And sometimes they love novelty and excitement! A client like this was described by Quick (2001). Marge was growing her skills in social situations. She felt self-conscious about her hearing impairment and hesitated to speak up to people whom she considered to be more accomplished, attractive, and self-assured than she was. Marge used a courage ladder to grow her courage in interacting with other people and networking in her business. Her "baby steps" grew to some wonderful friendships. When her friends talked about how much they loved activities like yoga, Marge tried to convince herself that these interested her, too. But for Marge, yoga was boring. Travel to exotic destinations was what she wanted to do to celebrate her fiftieth birthday. And her secret dream was to go sky diving! As her courage and confidence grew, Marge found her voice and made choices that fit for her. As with everything else in solution focused anxiety management, "one size does not fit all."

CASE EXAMPLE: APPROPRIATE CAUTION IN OBSESSIVE COMPULSIVE DISORDER

Bill, a 56-year-old White man, had just completed the solution focused anxiety management class and requested an individual session to get more ideas for dealing with his "OCD." He said that he had liked the class, especially the part in Topic Two about "exposure and response prevention." He liked the idea of getting some additional coaching and discovering some additional tools.

Bill described himself as a person with many "quirks," which included germs, "checking," the number six, and needing to carry a special little stone in his right pants pocket. He was divorced and lived alone. Bill worked, mostly from home, as a computer consultant, and he also did computer graphic art. Bill said that his quirks amused the people in his life (who included his girlfriend, his adult son, a couple of work friends, and his mom), but they did not really interfere with his functioning. Bill noted that he really appreciated the message from the class that "having OCD quirks doesn't have to be a deal breaker." This message confirmed something that, on some level, he already knew.

This is an example of how "symptoms" may be "diagnosable" but not necessarily a problem. Continuing to perform those behaviors in a way that does not turn them into a problem is sometimes one component of solution focused anxiety management.

What *did* disturb Bill was his "checking." He said, "It takes me forever to get out of the house. Now that's a problem." The checking bothered Bill's girlfriend a little, but it wasn't as bad when she (or anyone else) was with him. He was rarely late to appointments (with the girlfriend or anyone else); he had never missed a plane. The checking was a problem for Bill because, in his words, "it wastes time—time that I don't have." Especially when he was leaving the house alone, to go shopping or to the gym or some other place that didn't have a clear time frame, he checked door and window locks, the stove, the computer, the sound system, and the heating/air conditioning controls, to make sure that everything was exactly as it should be. Bill guessed that this usually took about half an hour, and since Bill left the house several times a day, the "wasted time" added up. But he "couldn't help" checking.

What did Bill think might happen if he didn't check things completely? He worried about an electrical fire, the possibility of burglars getting in, and damage to his expensive computers, monitors, and sound system. He had always been a careful and conscientious person. As a child, he had collected coins and kept them in a small locked safe. Bill had spent a lot of time with his hobby and had been very proud of his extensive collection. It had hurt his feelings when his mom and brother made fun of his little safe, although he felt that his dad understood. Bill said, "I think Dad was a little like me." Bill said that one day after his brother teased him, he gave the combination lock on his safe six extra twirls before he entered the combination. Somehow, that helped him to feel more secure. He did it again the next night, and pretty soon, it was a habit.

The therapist agreed that some people are more careful than others, and that care and caution can be important strengths. Bill agreed that his careful style was definitely an asset in his work. The therapist asked if Bill still had his precious coin collection. He did. The little safe he had as a boy was still in his bedroom closet. The therapist asked what the rarest coin was. (It was a precious Indian head penny.) The therapist commented that something like that is worth protecting.

Bill remembered that Topic Two encourages "delaying" the compulsive behavior a little bit at a time and then "doing it differently." "But I need some more ideas here," he said. "I'm already delaying getting out of the house long enough. If I 'delay' it further, then the wasted time will just get longer."

The therapist agreed. This was a place where "doing something different" with the checking might be more helpful. "You mean like the lady they talked about in the class who stuck her tongue out at the stove?" Bill asked. He had thought that this was a novel idea and had tried it, but it hadn't felt particularly helpful.

As noted throughout this book, nothing works for everyone....

For Bill, it seemed as though the time expenditure was the most important piece to eventually decrease. The therapist and Bill brainstormed ways he might create a courage ladder for his checking. One possibility was to gradually decrease the number of minutes spent checking. Because his estimate of about half an hour each time was just that (an estimate), Bill would first need to know just how long he spends checking now. He was interested in doing this as a first step, and he liked the idea of calling it a "baseline." So that it truly would be a baseline, the therapist cautioned Bill against trying to shorten the process yet. Nor would he change anything else about his checking while he was gathering this information.

A fascinating phenomenon occurs when one gathers baseline data because the very act of observing something becomes a way of "doing something different." So it was not surprising that when Bill returned, he described something interesting. The first time that he timed himself, he discovered that it took 45 minutes to check everything. The next time, checking lasted just 22 minutes. Bill remembered having this reaction: "I don't need to go check the fuse box. I just checked it this morning." The next time he left the house, he sternly told himself, "Remember, you're supposed to be getting a baseline." He tried to remember to check everything. The time seemed interminable, and Bill found himself getting bored. This surprised him.

When a meeting or appointment was the destination, Bill sometimes didn't check at all. "How do you do that?" the therapist asked. Bill was not sure.

Bill and the therapist brainstormed what a courage ladder for checking might look like. Bill might try to make his checking time shorter, but that raised the question of "Shorter than what?" since sometimes he didn't check at all.

The therapist wondered aloud whether they might try to build on the variability in the checking that already existed. "Sometimes people do something once, or maybe a few times, and pretty soon it gets to be a habit," the therapist said. "And one way to change a habit is to 'mess with it.' Like, with your safe, do you still do the six extra twirls on the combination lock?" (Yes. It was a different lock, but that habit had continued for over 40 years.) "So if you were going to 'mess with' that habit—and I'm not saying you should or would want to; this is just an example—you might sometimes twirl it four times, and sometimes seven. Or sometimes you might twirl it with the other hand."

The therapist also asked how Bill coped with uncertainty and risk in other situations. Bill flew in airplanes. He had investments, some of them in equities. He had files on a flash drive, which could be stolen. Bill described how he handled all of these things. He had a preference for a particular airline. He spread his investments among various categories and regularly reviewed his portfolio. He backed up all his files on a disk drive at home and on his company's server. Bill added that he had homeowner's insurance, DVDs of all of his graphic art files at his girlfriend's house, and electronic files for his precious vinyl record collection.

The therapist invited Bill to experiment with introducing some variability into his checking, without jeopardizing the safety of his house or belongings. He might do so playfully, and he might notice what he discovered.

At the next session, Bill described sometimes going back and checking that the master switch on his sound system was off. Sometimes he checked for less time, and sometimes for more. Once, when he found himself worrying after he left the house, he went back and checked to see if the door was locked. (It was.) On another day, he just "sucked it up." One day he asked his girlfriend to check the bedroom window. The therapist and Bill continued to discuss the fact that "stuff happens" (whether you check or not), and that it was important to continue to be careful.

Over the next month, Bill discovered that getting out of the house wasn't so much of a problem. Now he requested coaching on how he might make a courage ladder for germs. He said, "I know I told you before that it wasn't a big deal, but it's getting to be cold and flu season, and I want to be careful without getting crazy about it."

The therapist asked Bill what he already knew about coping with germs. Bill actually knew quite a bit. Before his dad's death, he had regularly visited Dad in the hospital and the nursing home. Bill often attended business meetings with people who had a cold or a cough. "How do you do that?" the therapist asked.

"I don't know," Bill said. "I just do it."

Bill and the therapist made a small courage ladder for things they could do in the clinic right now. They could walk down the hall and touch various door handles. They could touch dollar bills. They could touch the doors to the restrooms. Together, Bill and the therapist took that walk and did all those things. The final stop was the clinic kitchen, and both of them washed their hands.

Back in the therapist's office, Bill said, "I notice you guys have those hand sanitizer dispensers all over the place. For years I griped that everything was unsanitary and wished that everyone else would be more careful. I would take antiseptic wipes on the plane, wipe the keyboard on a public computer. It used to be my special thing, and now everybody does it: wipes in grocery stores, hand sanitizer at the bank. It's funny, in a way I'm glad there's more awareness, but I sort of miss it being my special thing. It's weird, isn't it?"

Bill made a few more appointments from time to time over the next year to address some other issues in his life. One day the therapist was recovering from a cold on a day when Bill was scheduled to come in. The therapist considered calling Bill ahead of time, offering to reschedule. Immediately realizing that this was not something being offered to other appointments that day, the therapist chose not to do so. But the therapist did tell Bill right away. "If you would rather not meet today, that's okay. I absolutely understand."

"Oh, that's okay," Bill said. "Everywhere I go this week someone has a cold." The session proceeded as it always did. When it was time to stop, the therapist said, "Well, you have an opportunity to practice some appropriate caution as you go out of here today. We will let *me* be the one to touch the door handle as we go out." Bill laughed. "Okay," he said. "And I hope you feel better."

CASE EXAMPLE: "OCD HOARDING"

The following case example illustrates the importance of tailoring treatment to the individual and including appropriate caution as an important ingredient of the solution. Treatment for "OCD hoarding" often encourages people to "get rid of things a little at a time." In this case, a solution-focused approach led to identification of some concerns—and wonderful strengths—that the "standard recommendations" for this complaint might well have overlooked.

Delilah, a 77-year-old, divorced African American woman, a retired cook, called for help with her "OCD hoarding." She lived alone in a small house and wanted to "work on self-discipline." Delilah described having "stuff" on her dining room table, on the chairs, and on the floor. She complained that she couldn't sit at the table. "I have to eat at the counter in the kitchen. I can't have anyone over. It's too embarrassing." Delilah said that this had been a problem for at least five years. She had told herself to "just do a little every day" for ages. But she was not making any progress.

Getting rid of things a little at a time is basically a courage ladder approach, which is often recommended, and often quite successful, with this kind of concern. In Delilah's case (at least, used on its own, on her own), it was not working well enough. This immediately suggested to the therapist the importance of looking for ways of doing something different.

Why had Delilah called now? She was not sure. She said, "I just looked around that dining room one day, and thought, 'Lordy, this is getting worse. Someone is going to call the Health Department on me. And they are going to come in and condemn my property. Like they did with that lady who kept all those cats. Now I don't have any cats. But it sure is a mess in here.'"

The therapist asked about Delilah's best hopes from coming here. "To get rid of the clutter in my house," Delilah responded. What would let her know that those hopes had been met? "Starting to rid of it. Sorting through it," Delilah answered. What pieces of this were already starting to happen? Delilah was already going through some of the papers. She had found some old photos and had sent them to her ex-husband in Louisiana.

The therapist asked Delilah to tell her some interesting things about her life that had nothing to do with the problem. Delilah's face lit up. She told the therapist about moving to California when her ex-husband was in the Navy. "I was so excited about seeing the Pacific Ocean," she said. She and her ex-husband had now been divorced for many years, but they were still in contact. They had no children. The most important people in Delilah's life these days were two special friends, Josie and Trudy. Josie took Delilah shopping every week.

Delilah continued, "I didn't always have all this stuff. When I worked at the restaurant, my kitchen was so organized. And I loved photography. Not the new digital kind. The real film kind. I don't do it any more. But I still have some pictures I took on the wall. One is of a whale. I took that picture on a boat trip. That whale, it was just shining in the sun. Makes me smile every time I look at it." Delilah paused. "Maybe I'll get me the new digital kind of camera some day. But I have to get me a new computer first. My old one got viruses and stuff and I had to get rid of it. And I don't have no money for a new one."

The therapist asked Delilah the miracle question. Delilah smiled. "Well, I'd probably get up about nine o'clock. Look forward to the day: It's a new day." She would go through some of the papers on the dining room table. "I'll find what I'm looking for. And I might call some people. Maybe the bank people."

Delilah explained that she was trying to decide whether or not to get a reverse mortgage on her house. "See, then I'd have money, to buy a computer, a digital camera. Maybe I'll even get me a little car. I won't be focusing inward as much. That would bring a sense of balance to my life."

Were any pieces of Delilah's miracle starting to happen? "Well, I'm making some actual steps to that reverse mortgage. I got some papers last week. But you have to be careful about stuff like that. Real careful."

Delilah had been thinking about this idea for a long time. But she was taking her time. She didn't want to rush into it. She knew that there were dishonest people out there. "Now, I don't want you to think I'm crazy for saying this, but some of them probably are licking their chops to take advantage of some little old Black lady who don't know what she's doing."

The therapist agreed. Being cautious and taking her time were strengths, definitely things for Delilah to continue. "So how can you check this out? What can help you know when it's time to take the next step?"

Delilah thought for a minute. "Well, my ex-husband has a good head on his shoulders," she said. "He's back in Louisiana. But we talk. He knows I'm thinking about it. I think I should talk to him some more."

"What's the most important question you should be asking him right now?" the therapist asked.

Delilah answered, "Probably what it means for those old property taxes. Bank gonna pay 'em, or me? They sure do cost a lot. And twice a year, they do it." Delilah thought that the reverse mortgage holder would pay them, but she wasn't sure. As she thought about it more, she decided that she might ask the bank person about that, too.

The therapist asked Delilah, "So, would I be more helpful if I gave you a little nudge to ask some of those good questions and to keep looking for those papers and maybe do some other good things for yourself? Or would it be more useful if I suggested that you take all the time you need? Or a little of both, maybe?"

Delilah chuckled. "Well, I sure do need that nudge. But I guess I don't mind taking my time, too. Like my mama always said, 'That's one thing 'bout you, honey child, you do it when you is good and ready.'"

As the session ended, the therapist told Delilah that it seemed as though a whole lot of pieces of the miracle she had described were starting to happen. Delilah was making calls. She was starting to go through her papers. She was doing some careful thinking and had come up with some excellent questions and ideas. She had made and kept the appointment today. And she knew she needed to be careful. The therapist encouraged Delilah to keep doing all those things and to be curious about what else she might need to consider during the reverse mortgage process. She might remember that her mama was a wise woman, who understood that Delilah knew, deep inside, when the time was right to do something.

What did Delilah most want to remember from the conversation? "You can't be too careful with those reverse mortgage people."

Delilah called the therapist the next day. "You remember how you told me to keep thinking? Well, this came to me like a big old bolt out of the blue: Someone's gonna have to appraise this house, and that means they're gonna come inside and look at it. That'll get me off my rear end for sure. I just thought you'd be interested in knowing that I figured it out."

Delilah's realization illustrates how life issues—in this case, a developmental task of older adulthood—are an integral part of solution focused anxiety management.

Delilah returned two weeks later. She had made her phone calls, and her ex-husband had encouraged her to talk to several banks, not just one. A huge FedEx envelope had arrived from Chicago. But Delilah was feeling discouraged. "I can't understand all that legal mumbo jumbo. I ain't smart enough to know what all those big words mean. What if that's just bank talk for 'take that old lady's house away from her'?" Delilah remembered how her father used to call her "Dumbo." "I never did so great in school. Never did learn all those state capitals."

The therapist asked Delilah if she could tell her a little story about doing not so well in school. (Yes.) "So this is the little joke or story: What do you call the person who graduated at the bottom of her class in medical school?"

"Dumbo. Like my pappy used to call me."

The therapist shook her head. Face deadpan, the therapist said, "Doctor."

Delilah thought about it for a minute. She started to laugh.

The therapist asked Delilah who might help her translate all that legal talk into words that made sense to "people like you and me." Delilah thought about it. "Well, my friend Josie, her son sells real estate. I bet he'd know," she said.

By the time of her next appointment a few weeks later, Delilah had done many things. She had talked to Josie's son and to two people at church who had gotten reverse mortgages. One of the church friends had suggested talking to Elder Legal Services. By now Delilah had information from four brokers. She chuckled, "One of them jumped the gun. Oh, he was so sure I was going to go with him. I don't think so!"

Delilah thought she knew which broker she might go with. She said, "This one is a female. She's registered in four states. The folks from church used her. She told me what that old mumbo jumbo said and wrote it down for me. And you know what else she did? She wrote down all my questions and faxed them to the lawyer at that elder services place."

"The amount of stuff you've done is amazing," the therapist said. "How did you decide to do so much so quickly?"

Delilah laughed. "Because my back is up against the wall. Those rules, they're gonna change in January. Josie's son told me that. I asked my ex-husband and the legal services man, and they all said that's true. I'm no Dumbo. I'm going to get this done."

Delilah had not come to therapy with the specific goal of altering the "Dumbo" perception of herself, something that she had carried for more than 70 years. This was an additional positive outcome. In solution focused anxiety management, one good thing often leads to another.

Delilah knew that soon it would be time for the home appraiser to visit. In fact, the appointment was scheduled for next Tuesday. "I know they have to see that the house is worth what they give you. And they have to believe you will keep it up. So I got to do the clutter now. My auntie, she had clutter too. She was a hoarder, worse than me. Maybe that's where I get it from. Now, Auntie, she didn't get a chance to pack up any of her clutter before she had to move out of her house. Her things ended up in a warehouse and were sold."

The therapist asked how Delilah's situation was different from Auntie's. Delilah smiled with pride. "I get to keep my precious belongings," she said.

Thinking aloud, the therapist commented that "precious belongings" seemed to have a very different feel from "clutter."

As discussed in Chapter 1, the use of language, the co-construction of meaning, and highlighting of strength-based client words are important concepts in contemporary solution-focused thinking.

The therapist continued, "So how does one take care of precious belongings?"

Delilah knew how to do that: "You organize them. You put labels on them. I already started. I got a bunch of boxes at Staples, with labels: home mortgage information, art, bills, letters. And I need some help! Trudy and Josie and me, and Trudy's niece and Josie's daughter-in-law, we're doing it all day Saturday. With ham biscuits and butter beans and bread pudding for dinner when we're done. Everything gonna be ready ahead of time, just like I used to do at the restaurant. We'll be so tired at the end of that day that I won't want to lift a finger."

As noted throughout this book, the most elegant solutions come from the client, not the therapist.

Delilah did everything she had planned. She cooked up a storm all week. On Saturday, they packed and moved the boxes into the bedroom. They feasted and laughed together. Delilah rested on Sunday and Monday: "I didn't lift a finger." The appraiser was scheduled to come on Tuesday at eleven. On Monday evening, Delilah set her alarm clock for three a.m. She cleaned from four to nine and then took a long bath.

When Delilah came for her next appointment, she was proud and relieved. The appraisal was over. But she was also a little disappointed, because the final amount she would get was about $10,000 lower than she had anticipated. "So now I have to ask myself: Do I really want to do this? If I do, I don't have time to fool around."

The therapist asked Delilah what would help her most now. How might she use her resources; her friends and supports; her organizational skills, planning, and good thinking; and her appropriate caution to do what was right for her? The therapist and Delilah talked about "You can—and you don't have to."

Delilah talked to her ex-husband, Josie, and the Elder Legal Services attorney. She prayed. She talked to her deceased mama. She told the therapist, "I remember you told me a little while back that my mama was a wise woman. And when I talked to Mama, up there in heaven, you know what Mama said? 'Girl, you never listened to me before? So what makes you think you is gonna listen to me now?'" Delilah laughed. "So that's when I knew: 'Time is right. Do it.'"

CASE EXAMPLE: "I'VE ALWAYS BEEN A WORRIER"

"I'm like a poster child for being a worrier," Marcela said cheerfully. "All my life I've been a scaredy cat. '*No seas miedosa.*' People have been saying that to me as long as I can remember. My doctor told me I must have had 'generalized anxiety disorder' since I was a baby. And it's getting worse."

Marcela, a 24-year-old Hispanic woman, lived with her partner, Ana, and her dog. She worked at a call center for a large company. She liked the fact that her work was over the phone because she didn't have to interact with customers in person. "When you're as *gorda* as I am—no, Ana says

I have to say 'a big girl, not *gorda*'—it's just easier that way." Marcela was self-conscious about her size. She also worried about earthquakes, terrorism, and her dad's diabetes.

But none of that was the reason Marcela was here now. "I'm supposed to get my wisdom teeth out next month," she explained. "And I know it's not supposed to be a big deal, but for me it's huge."

The therapist asked about Marcela's best hopes from coming here. Marcela did not answer the question. Instead, she continued, almost nonstop, "It's not always a simple thing. It can hurt. A lot. And I'm not good with pain. And there's my size. What if they don't give me enough anesthetic for my 250 pounds, and they think I'm out, but I'm really not? But I'm out enough that I can't let them know? And it can mess up your sinuses. You can get an infection. I could have a horrible reaction to it. I could get a hemorrhage. I read about a man who had brain damage from the anesthetic. What if I lose feeling in my lip? The Internet said all those things can happen. What if I'm not where I think I am in my menstrual cycle? If you have less estrogen, you're more likely to get dry socket problems. I have no idea what a dry socket problem is, but obviously it's not good! And for afterwards, the dentist said he could give me a prescription for Vicodin. But that can make you throw up. And what if I get addicted?"

The therapist agreed that it sounded very scary to think about all those things that could happen. "Not everyone who has oral surgery does such careful research," the therapist told Marcela. "But I'm curious. If coming here gets you ready for the surgery, in just the way you hope it will, how will you know?"

"I don't know." Marcela answered. "When I told my dentist all that, he said, 'Maybe you should talk to someone.' Maybe he thought you could make me brave."

The therapist suspected that Marcela already knew some important things about bravery. To discover some clues about what these might be, she asked Marcela to tell her some special things about herself. Marcela described how she had done puppy rescue. Her little dog was very special to her. The therapist discovered that Marcela took her dog to the vet faithfully. She wouldn't think of skipping dog care appointments, even when she had to watch her dog get a shot.

Marcela said that almost as far back as she could remember, she had known that she was gay. That wasn't easy, especially for a girl growing up in a traditional Hispanic family. Marcela had come out to her parents when she was 15. "I knew I wanted to dance with girls at my *quinceañera*. I knew

I probably wouldn't, out of respect, because my *abuelos* (grandparents) would be there, but I wanted my mom to know. I think my mother suspected that I was a *lesbiana*. But I wanted to tell her myself. It's not something I'm ashamed of. It's just part of who I am."

The therapist was struck by the strength and courage of a young girl who knew so clearly what felt right for her. Coming out to traditional Hispanic, Catholic parents is not an easy thing to do, and the therapist told Marcela that. The therapist wondered if there had been some bravery in Marcela's decision and interaction.

"You're right, it wasn't easy, and it wasn't comfortable," Marcela said. "My mom cried, and my dad wouldn't look me in the eye for a week. But they are amazing. They totally accept it now. They love Ana. But I never thought of my telling them as something 'brave.' I mean, I'm the scaredest person I know. It was just something I had to do."

The therapist and Marcela talked about how Marcela had not needed to be "brave" to be able to do something she wanted to do. The therapist added, "I think you already know this, but you always have the right to cancel or postpone your surgery."

"Oh, I know. But I wouldn't do that," Marcela responded quickly. "It's the Friday before Presidents' Day weekend, and I have Monday off. I got that day scheduled weeks ago. That way I have an extra day to recover without taking extra time off. And I also know from the Internet that if it has to be done, it's way better to do it before you're thirty."

Marcela was making it clear that she had absolutely no intention of canceling the wisdom teeth extraction. The timing of the surgery, the careful preparation, researching what might go wrong, worrying aloud: These were all legitimate—and for Marcela, valuable—parts of her preparation. Being cautious was just part of what Marcela did. It was not going to stop her from having the surgery, and it did not have to be a problem. Validating this—something that Marcela already knew—was the most important component of Marcela's therapy.

DISCUSSION OF APPROPRIATE CAUTION IN THE SOLUTION FOCUSED ANXIETY MANAGEMENT CLASS

Many of the things discussed with Bill, Delilah, and Marcela often emerge during the discussion time in all four sessions of the solution focused anxiety management class. In Topic One, when the concept of the bell-shaped curve is introduced, there may be an opportunity to discuss the fact that caution often accompanies a naturally higher level of autonomic reactivity. Topic

Two introduces the concept of defensive pessimism and the notion that anxiety can be "signal" as well as "noise." In response to that information, participants may reflect on how caution can be valuable. In Topic Three, there is a focus on acceptance, both of reality (including the reality that "bad things" can and do happen) and of one's feelings about that reality. The notion that one does not have to wait to eliminate careful thinking about risks often emerges in the discussion. And Topic Four, with its discussion of the legitimacy of "Cons," "Ambivalence 101," and "You can—and you don't have to," often invites conversations about appropriate caution and choice.

As they hear other people's questions, participants often notice that many people mention caution, maybe in an area similar to one's own concern, and maybe in a different area. They often observe "perfectly normal-looking people" who describe themselves as "scaredy cats." They hear people describe how "of course" they have become more vigilant since an auto accident. People discover that careful preparation and anticipation of how to manage an unwanted outcome are described as strengths, not liabilities. Participants hear others' creative strategies for preparing for custody hearings, shots, financial setbacks, and many other challenges. And over and over again, they hear that one does not have to wait for caution to disappear to be able to do new and sometimes scary things.

CHAPTER 9

Perspectives from the Solution-focused Community

At the time this book was being prepared, the author was looking forward to attending the 2011 Solution Focused Brief Therapy Association [SFBTA] Conference on solution-focused practices. This annual conference provides an opportunity to learn about cutting-edge developments in solution-focused research and practice and to network with solution-focused therapists from around the world. This conference would provide an opportunity to brainstorm with solution-focused colleagues and benefit from their wisdom and experience in working with clients who describe anxiety. Seven of the presenters at the conference graciously agreed to participate in brief interviews. There was simply not enough time to interview everyone! Other solution-focused therapists kindly agreed to respond to the author's written questions. This chapter shares these therapists' valuable perspectives.

The following written request was given to all of these colleagues. During the interviews, some questions from the form were asked, and others emerged from the dialogue and the specific interests and expertise of each therapist.

A Request for Your Thoughts on Solution-Focused Treatment of Anxiety

Tell me about a way of transforming anxiety (phobia, worry, obsessive compulsive symptoms, intrusive thoughts, panic) to courage, comfort, or choice that you have seen a client discover. This might be something you discovered was already happening, or it might be something that emerged during a session during collaborative conversation.

What strengths and resources, internal and external, helped that person most? How did you invite him or her to tap those and to get through the hardest times?

Tools from other modalities often suggest procedures such as exposure (to feared situations and sensations), changing thoughts, taking action even in the presence of discomfort, relaxation, and mindfulness. Where have you discovered that clients come up with variations on these on their own?

Do you ever actively invite clients to use these tools?

http://dx.doi.org/10.1016/B978-0-12-394421-4.00009-7

If so, which?

What lets you know that the time is right to do so?

And if you use these tools, how do you do so in a way that remains consistent with a solution-focused spirit of leading from behind and inviting clients to discover their own solutions?

What else have your clients taught you about transforming anxiety to courage, comfort, and choice?

INTERVIEW WITH JOEL SIMON, LCSW

Joel has been a solution-focused practitioner, trainer, presenter, and consultant since 1992. He trained with de Shazer and Berg at the Brief Family Therapy Center on multiple occasions and has also received advanced training in Ericksonian hypnotherapy. Joel is a founding member of SFBTA, and he has authored several books (including *Solution-focused Brief Practice with Long-Term Clients in Mental Health Services: I Am More Than My Label,* co-authored with Thorana Nelson) and articles on solution-focused topics.

Ellen: I really appreciate your taking your time to share your thoughts with me. How do you respond to a client who tells you he or she has "an anxiety disorder"?

Joel: I do a solution-focused interview and ask what it will look like when the anxiety is no longer a problem.

Ellen: And if the response is "I won't be anxious any more"?

Joel: Then I know I haven't contextualized the question.

Joel described a client who had been in therapy for seven years. This young man called himself "a person with panic attacks." This client had reified the problem, as if to say "I am my disease." Although the young man was bright and had attended a prestigious college, he was now working as a security guard. He had no relationships. He had tried to return to school to study computers, but he could not tolerate being in a classroom.

The young man responded to Joel's questions about his vision for a better future by describing a time when the panic attacks would not be a problem. He also noted that he would be treating his mother better.

Joel asked his client, "When was your last panic attack?" The answer was, "Ten years ago." Joel asked, "At what point do you no longer call yourself a person with panic attacks?"

The young man thought about this. And gradually he made some changes. He began to participate in martial arts. He made figurines. He got a dog. He realized, "I'm more than my panic."

Ellen: Do you ever notice that clients come up with, on their own, some of the tools and techniques used by other models?

Joel agreed that often they did. But he does not spontaneously suggest other methods when the idea does not come from the client first. Joel described the risk that therapy can make a theory out of what worked for one person and apply it to everyone who has a particular problem. He remembered Milton Erickson's perspective: "I have a different therapy for every client." If the therapist suggests something, Joel cautioned, "It becomes my idea, not theirs."

What Joel consistently does with people who describe anxiety is the same thing that he does with every client: He asks what they want and elicits individualized descriptions of a better future.

Joel added that working with people who struggle with anxiety is made more complicated by the fact that there may be a physiological component, something that one cannot fully change. Clients may talk about that fact. If that is the case, Joel may challenge the client: "So if it can't change, and you don't think things can be different, then why are you here?" Joel may tell his clients something that Steve de Shazer often said. That message might go something like this: "There are no guarantees that this will be helpful. But I expect to do my best, and I assume that you will, too."

Joel described a woman who viewed herself as having "panic disorder and OCD" (labels that were the client's, not the therapist's). When working with someone like her, Joel said, "You look for the small stuff." In response to Joel's approach, the woman has taken a step: She took a poster from her wall and moved it to a different location. Although this would be a small thing for many people, it was a significant change for her. She told Joel that people were beginning to notice (her positive changes).

Ellen: What would this woman say you had done that was most helpful?

Joel: Looked for the small stuff.

He added that this woman would probably say that he did not accept her diagnosis as being relevant. She sometimes told him, "You don't believe I have OCD." Joel would agree: "I'm not interested in people's diagnosis." Even if the "label" was her own, this woman was not her diagnosis or her label.

Ellen: Joel, thank you so much. I really appreciate your taking this time and sharing your thoughts with me.

INTERVIEW WITH LINDA METCALF, PHD, LMFT

Linda is a professor of education at Texas Wesleyan University in Fort Worth, Texas, and she also maintains a private practice. She is the author of ten books on solution-focused practice, and she has presented to trainees in more than ten countries.

Ellen: How do you respond to a client who tells you he or she has "an anxiety disorder"?

Linda: I ask, "How will you know when it's not a problem?" If I hear, "I'm anxious because I'm getting married, or have a new job," I say, "Makes sense to me. How have you gotten through before?"

If a client uses a diagnostic label, Linda asks the client what he or she would like to call the area for change. She noted that she is drawing from her exposure to narrative therapy here. Linda might ask if the problem (whatever it is to be called) is keeping the client trapped or away from something he or she would like to be doing, and if so, what it will look like when that is no longer happening.

Linda described a 22-year-old who came to see her. The young woman had had two abortions in the past year and now was pregnant again. The woman was single, and she felt anxious about the need to make a decision very soon, either to terminate the pregnancy or to do something else. Linda asked, "If a miracle happened, what would be going on?"

The woman replied, "I would be in a stable place in my life. I'd have a house with a white picket fence. I'd know I could provide a stable environment for my child." Linda described how the dialogue continued:

Linda: Tell me what you do.

Client: I'm a personal trainer.

Linda: Are you good at your work as a trainer?

Client: Yes.

Linda: Are you stable in your work?

Again the answer was yes. The woman had opened a business in the city recently, and it was doing well.

Linda: It sounds like what you're telling me you need is what you're already doing.

Linda made this suggestion: "I want you to watch for things that tell you that you have that white picket fence."

The next week the woman came back and told Linda that she had made her decision. She said, "After I left here, I thought: 'Maybe I do have what it takes.' I told my parents I was pregnant. And they said, 'Great! You can live here.' I told my boyfriend—and he proposed." The client decided to continue her pregnancy.

Five years later a man came to Linda's office. He identified himself as the husband of the woman she had treated five years earlier. He said, "I want to thank you for my son. And I have a daughter, too."

Ellen: Do you ever notice that clients come up with, on their own, some of the tools and techniques used by other models, like relaxation, desensitization, changing one's thinking?

Linda: Not relaxation. I do ask, "What have you done before to shrink your anxiety?" I hear about listening to music, writing, going to the gym at 4 a.m.

Linda does not teach specific relaxation techniques

Ellen: What about encouraging clients to do things a little at a time?

Linda: Sometimes. Calling a parent, checking out a university. I encourage people to go very slowly. I might also ask, "Who will be around? Where will you do it? Can you tell me one person you can walk with?" Things that will help you to take the first step.

Then, after that step has been taken, Linda will often ask, "How did you make the first step?"

Ellen: How do you help people to discover how they already tolerate discomfort?

Linda: I might ask, "How long does that anxiety last?" "So, we know, your heart will beat rapidly, but we also know that it will end after five minutes."

Linda used this with a mom who was anxious about her child's fussing at bedtime. She told the woman, "We can count on it being there for five minutes, being uncomfortable for five minutes." The mom said this to her child, something like this, "Okay, I guess you are going to fuss for five minutes." The fussing actually stopped a bit sooner.

Linda: It's finding a way to cooperate with the anxiety.

Ellen: What have you found helpful with people who describe themselves as having OCD?

Linda: "It seems you're a cautious person. You like things just right. How does that help you?" Usually people talk about how it gives them a sense of control. "What else? Sounds like what you do is pretty helpful to you."

If the person wants to change something, Linda might ask, "What could you begin to do on a small scale that would still let you maintain control?"

Ellen: What lets you know the time is right to ask about this?

Linda: When someone is very distressed about it, or overwhelmed about it.

Ellen: What else have your clients taught you about what is helpful when people feel anxious?

Linda: When I can normalize and let them know it's okay to be anxious sometimes. They say, "Oh, really? Is it?" "You're a human being going through this situation. Makes sense to me."

Ellen: Linda, thank you so much. This was so helpful. Thank you for sharing all this with me.

INTERVIEW WITH JAY MCKEEL, MS

Jay is a therapist in private practice in Laurel, Maryland. He also conducts training and supervision in solution-focused practice. Jay has written extensively about process research in solution-focused brief therapy.

Ellen: What ways of transforming anxiety to courage, comfort, or choice have you seen clients discover?

Jay: What a wonderful way to say it. I don't think in terms of anxiety or depression. I'm going to look at what *your* anxiety is. So I'm never working with "anxiety"; I'm working with the person, what she wants to be different, past successes, her courage. For me, I don't start with "This is anxiety." It's this is "Jane."

Ellen: Can you share an example?

Jay: I'm thinking of one person. She was quite beautiful. In fact, she had been Miss *(name of state)*. All her life, a lot of how the world had responded to her was in terms of her beauty. When I was seeing her, she had just turned 30. She had been engaged and had discovered that her fiancé was having an affair. She decided to leave him. She had moved away from her home and felt anxious and insecure.

When we talked about what she found useful, she talked about journaling. But what she journaled about was her despair and her weakness. So we added something to it. At the end of each day, she would journal about something she had done that she was proud of. We called it her "pride journal." This task assumed she was doing some things she was proud of.

Ellen: How did you decide to use the word "pride"?

Jay: Her focus had always been on her appearance. That was what she had always been proud of. Even though she had a new job and was named "rookie of the year," she didn't feel like she was getting validation. It was a switch for her to feel proud of other things she was doing.

Ellen: Tools from other approaches sometimes suggest things like graduated exposure, relaxation, and other things. Do you ever notice that people are doing these things on their own?

Jay: When I ask for exceptions, I might find some. I sometimes think I should teach people to do relaxation, and I don't think I ever have! When I ask what people have done that has helped them to feel better, they most often talk about exercise. They say, "Exercise helps me. But I don't go to the gym very much." I remind them to do more of what works.

Ellen: Do you ever suggest any variations of interoceptive exposure, or bringing on and getting desensitized to the sensations of anxiety?

Jay: Sometimes I ask people to schedule their anxiety. Instead of trying to get *(intrusive thoughts)* out of their mind, we might talk about delaying the anxious thoughts, the compulsive thinking, to "your anxiety time." During that time they can be as irrational or crazy as they want to be.

Ellen: What lets you know that the time is right to suggest that kind of tool?

Jay: When they are asking for help with this. I tell them that other people have found this helpful and see if they want to try it.

Ellen: What else have people who struggle with anxiety taught you?

Jay: One thing they say that I don't fully understand is "Time will take care of this." I wonder what they know that Jay doesn't know.

Ellen: What else have you learned from these clients?

Jay: If you want to talk about anxiety, someone might say that the "rational" thing might be to ask how it started. From a solution-focused perspective, I'm more interested in finding our how it *ended*. You get things like: "I had to go to work" or "My mom called me" or "I took a shower." Then you can talk about: "Maybe you can do that sooner." It's easier to do that when the intensity of your anxiety is at a three rather than at a ten *(on a scale where zero is no anxiety and ten is severe anxiety)*.

Ellen: I know you've looked at the common factors perspective in solution-focused therapy. How does that fit with what we're talking about?

Jay: There are things across models that work. One of the things is a relationship where people can feel safe, talking about their weaknesses in a safe place. It reminds me not to be "solution-forced"[1] or to make it seem like we can't talk about the anxiety; we can't talk about the problem. Once you do that, and people feel comfortable, then you can also look at exceptions to the problem. You help people to observe past successes and build an expectation of more success.

Ellen: What about the literature that talks about the 15% *(of change in therapy)* that is accounted for by specific models?

Jay: I don't buy the "pie chart" view. That's older thinking. The factors are all interrelated. But if I borrow a task from another model, or if I invent a task myself, I put a strength-based twist on it. It's not about weakness, but about strength. I'm more devoted to my client than to the model.

Ellen: Jay, thank you so much. I really appreciate your perspective.

INTERVIEW WITH FRANK THOMAS, PHD, LMFT

Frank has been practicing solution-focused therapy and supervision since the 1980s and has written and presented extensively on solution-focused practice. He is professor of counseling at Texas Christian University in Fort Worth, Texas. As the archivist for the SFBTA, he preserves the legacy of the Brief Family Therapy Center.

Ellen: I'm interested in continuing yesterday's conversation about Aikido as a metaphor for solution-focused practice, and how you might use that when clients talk about panic, intrusive thoughts, or fear. *(This interview was conducted the day after Frank had facilitated a workshop on "Aikido and difficult therapy situations.")*

Frank: That would be something to be developed. I think about (Milton) Erickson's principles of matched breathing. *(This refers to the phenomenon that occurs when two people are having a conversation and*

[1] See Nylund and Corsiglia (1994) in References.

are looking at each other: They tend to begin to breathe together. As the client's breathing becomes more rapid and shallow, the therapist's breathing is likely to follow.) I recognize I need to slow my breathing down, and they match me. With little kids, you make them notice your breathing. *(He models this, face to face, with eye contact, slower breathing, and then a smile.)* Kids immediately take a deep breath.

Frank commented that school counselors often describe this as one of their most helpful and commonly used interventions: They teach relaxation to kids, who learn to create control. Kids say, "I did this before a test, and it worked."

Frank noted that he generally begins conversations with clients by trying to discover if there are exceptions to the anxiety. But he said, "If there are no exceptions, and the client is asking 'Can you help me with this?' I'm going to say, 'Would you be willing to try something?'"

Frank continued, "The client is the expert on the client's life, but you might be the expert on some other things." Frank does not believe that it is always sufficient to assume, or to say, that people have the answer within, "because sometimes they don't.... Like Bill O'Hanlon[2] said, 'You can do A, B, or C, or none of the above.' It's an invitation."

For example, with clients who have migraines, Frank might say, "I'm going to email you a link to a site through Rutgers Medical School." For people who have medical problems, he might let them know that tension increases pain: "It's less painful if you relax. That happens with anxiety, too. People learn they have some control." Frank often teaches breathing and relaxation exercises, and clients create their own versions of them.

Ellen: How do you approach people who want help with panic?

Frank: I try to understand why they call it that. I don't want to jump into finding exceptions until I know what it feels like for them. A lot of people have some kind of metaphor, like a balloon inside, feeling like "I can't get the air out," or "It's like I swallowed an apple." I ask them, "What have you told people about it? And how do they respond when you describe it?" Usually other people tell them something like "Calm down." And the person feels like, "You just don't understand how bad this is."

[2] See O'Hanlon (2003) in References.

> I say something like, "That sounds horrible. I can see why you want to run out of the room screaming." After I let them know it sounds horrible, I say, "Can I ask you some questions about it? I'm curious if there have been times it doesn't happen just the same way. Maybe a time when you've been able to keep it from getting worse? Or a time when you thought it would happen and it didn't?" Asking about the exceptions is the intervention.

Frank noted that if he gets a "Yes, but …" response, that may mean that he has not heard the person or the metaphor accurately.

If Frank notices that his client's anxiety appears to be escalating at any point during the session, he may ask something like the following: "Is it helpful to talk about this?" or "Is this going to escalate into something you can't control? Because I don't want that to happen." If the client thinks that anxiety is escalating, Frank may suggest doing something different. He might invite the client to think about something that helped in the past when anxiety was "amping up." He may return to matching and slowing breathing.

Ellen: Some approaches deliberately encourage clients to bring on anxiety so they can practice riding through it. Do you ever do anything like that?

Frank: Bring it on? No, no more than I would induce a grand mal seizure. I don't need to see it.

Ellen: Do you use any variation of exposure techniques?

Frank: Rarely. Mostly when they've done it themselves.

Frank noted that he looks at the exact context where anxiety occurs. He does use scaling questions. When Frank looks at what works for clients, he considers whether the solution was purposeful or spontaneous. He said, "If it's purposeful, then do more of it. If it's spontaneous, notice it, like Walter and Peller[3] talked about."

When asked about what helps most with anxiety, some people quickly respond, "My medicine." Frank talked about the client who might say, "As

[3] See Walter and Peller (1992) in References.

long as I've got my Xanax, I'm good." Frank might ask such a client, "What percent of your anxiety can you diminish?" *(as opposed to the percent that is diminished by the medication).* Clients respond with a percentage, which, in Frank's experience, is rarely less than 25%. Once the percentage has been given, Frank asks, "Would it be okay if we talk about that part?" Clients generally agree to do so. After they are doing something different, they often report that "the medicine works better." Frank noted that he does not attempt to challenge that perspective.

Ellen: What strengths have you noticed among people who describe a lot of anxiety?

Frank: They have a lot of awareness of physical sensations, how their bodies feel in the moment. That's very different from what you see in depression. They are quick learners, and they can pay wonderful attention to detail. They already have the skill of noticing. They recognize when their anxiety amps up. I want them to pay attention to other times, when the outcome is different. I want them to notice what they did to bring that about.

Ellen: What other strengths have you observed?

Frank: They are socially sensitive. They are empathic. When they see that other people are anxious, they respond to that, like when multiple people start fainting in a room. So I want them to refocus, to notice people who are calm.

Ellen: Frank, thank you so much. This is really helpful.

INTERVIEW WITH HEATHER FISKE, PHD

Heather is a psychologist with more than 35 years of clinical experience. Currently, she is in private practice, and she coordinates a postgraduate training program on solution-focused practice at the University of Toronto and trains providers who work with homeless people. She is the author of *Hope in Action: Solution-focused Conversations about Suicide.*

Ellen: What have you discovered that best transforms anxiety into courage, comfort, or choice for your clients?

Heather: It's different for every person. I do the standard solution-focused stuff. I look for the exceptions. Naming is important, how it fits for them. For some people, it's useful to have a diagnosis. That says it's something treatable. For other people, it's more helpful to call it stress and worry. I use some of the "state-changing" tools, like relaxation and hypnosis. And I like 54321. *(See Chapter 3 for a description of this tool.)* But I don't start with those. I start with what people are already doing that's working. I use the other things when people need more. And even then, they've got their own stuff that can be built on.

Heather noted that if she introduces some kind of state-changing technique, this is done in the context of a message something like this: "There are thousands of these tools out there. You're the expert. If the one I'm showing you seems like it might be useful, you can go home and try it out. And if it is a good fit, that's great. And if it's not a good fit, that's great too, because it gives us clues as to what might work better." Heather continued, "Then sometimes they come back and say, 'I tried that thing you gave me, and I have one I like better.'"

Heather noted that she is cautious about introducing guided imagery or relaxation techniques that suggest tensing and relaxing specific parts of the body. Her work with people who have experienced trauma has led her to recognize that it may be difficult to predict in advance the kind of imagery or focus on body parts that might *increase* anxiety rather than decrease it. She prefers to invite people to create "self-guided imagery." Heather might tell her client that there are many things one can do to change one's state, and she invites them to remember—or to create—what works for them.

One of Heather's clients who experienced anxiety during her pregnancy remembered how she had helped herself to fall asleep as a little girl with the image of a "dream house." As a child, she had pictured herself going from room to room, and that helped her to fall asleep. Now, as an adult, her mind could go from room to room in her own house, imagining how she would paint each room.

Heather described another image that had worked for a musician who had terrible anxiety. Unable to drive, he had to take the train or bus to get to work. His imagery was to imagine that he was reading a musical score and conducting an orchestra. Picturing that helped him to get through the most difficult times.

To help people to develop self-guided imagery, Heather begins with what the client describes as the "instead" feelings—that is, what will be present instead of the anxiety. Through collaborative conversation, she and the client develop "custom" guided imagery. In the most detailed versions of this, Heather might take notes as the client describes sensory details: what was seen, heard, felt, etc. The content of this "script" might be printed out for the client to take home, and the client might be invited to experiment with using it. The expectation might be that more images and sensory data may be evoked. At the next session, Heather might ask "what else" might be added, and the script is refined. Heather noted that she typically does not read the script to the client; instead, she encourages the client to do the reading.

Does Heather ever suggest some of the techniques used by other approaches (such as graduated exposure or changing one's thoughts)? Heather noted that when people talk about how they get through periods of panic or intense anxiety, they sometimes say, "I tell myself I've done this before." Heather said, "I tell them: You've done the self-talk thing before. There's this whole area of psychology that talks about what you've figured out for yourself! I wonder if there's more of that that would be useful for you to hear about?" If so, she might share information about some technique. Some of her clients have been interested in learning "thought stopping."

Heather: They'll tell you what they think might be useful. Or they tell you about the piece that wouldn't work for them, and that's useful. You put a solution-focused frame around it by asking about the parts that would be useful.

Ellen: What have your clients taught you about what works to transform their anxiety to courage, comfort, choice—or whatever they want instead of the anxiety?

Heather: I suppose how absolutely possible it is. It seems like this huge, impossible thing—and people do it every day.

Heather has been struck by the phenomenon of "vicarious resiliency," described by Hernández, Gangsei, and Engstrom (2007). Addressing therapists, Hernández et al. asked something like this: What challenges have you seen your clients overcome? What has that elicited in you that you want to nurture and expand? These questions presuppose that it is not just trauma that we (both clients and therapists) learn from observing others. Other people's resilience may be "contagious" (this word is the author's) as well. Heather notes that she might change the wording of this inquiry to eliminate specific references to "challenges." Her version might invite others to notice—and absorb—the strength and courage shown by others.

Ellen: Heather, thank you so much. I really appreciate your perspective and your sharing it with me.

INTERVIEW WITH ELLIOTT CONNIE, MA, LPC

Elliott is a solution-focused therapist in Keller, Texas, who works with individuals, couples, and groups. He conducts numerous trainings and presentations. Elliott is the co-editor (with Linda Metcalf) of *The Art of Solution Focused Therapy.*

Ellen: In your work with clients who want help with anxiety, I'm interested in what you've seen them do so that it isn't a problem any more.

Elliott: It's funny that you should be asking that, because the week before the conference I just had a first session with an adolescent who had some pretty severe anxiety. I asked him what he'd rather be feeling. He said he'd rather be relaxed. I asked him when he already was relaxed. And the client said, "I seem to relax at wrestling practice, and at home when I watch TV."

Elliott asked his client to make a list of 25 skills, traits, and characteristics that he already uses to create relaxation. He also asked the young man if he could write these on note cards as the client mentioned them. (Elliott commented that he typically keeps a pile of blank note cards readily available for such occasions.) At the end of the session, the client asked if he could take the stack of note cards with him. Of course, the answer was yes. Elliott asked his client what he was going to do with the cards. The client replied that he planned to read them and remind himself of his strengths.

The next week, the client returned and said that he had not felt anxious. Elliott asked him how he had done this. The boy responded that he had read the note cards.

Elliott: What this illustrates is that when anxiety, like any other problem, is treated in a solution-focused way, you ask what the person wants instead.

Ellen: What were some of the things that were on his note cards?

Elliott: That he was funny, a good person, compassionate, smart, loving.

Elliott added that when the boy's mom came in to pay the bill, the boy spontaneously "bragged about" the note cards, telling the mom how cool they were.

Elliott: I was originally taught to use CBT for anxiety. And one of my biggest concerns was that if I taught you a technique that, in my assessment, was highly likely to work, I'd also have to teach you to remember to do it in the moment when you're anxious.

Elliott's experience was that clients did not typically use such techniques, things that came from the therapist, not the client. He asked his clients if they had tried what he had taught them, and they often responded that they had not thought of these tools when actually anxious.

Elliott: This kid decided, of his own free will, to take out the note cards.

Ellen: Do you use variations of the miracle question with clients who want help with anxiety?

Elliott: Yes, typically with every client.

Ellen: Is there any particular wording you use?

Elliott: What I do is pretty much what I do with every client. I don't use the name of the problem or the word "miracle." I ask about the client's best hopes. And if they talk about anxiety, I ask what they would rather have instead. If they say "Relaxation," I will ask, "So, if you woke up tomorrow morning and had relaxation …" I find out what that would be like.

Ellen: I'm interested in how you deal with anxiety in couples, when one partner is more anxious. *(This question was asked because of Elliott's interest and expertise in solution-focused work with couples.)*

Elliott responded that his experience is that partners tend to "match" each other, including in level of anxiety (or relaxation). His assistant is typically the one who receives the information about "problems," and Elliott often works without using that information. In those situations in which one partner is more of a "worrier" than the other, he assumes that this is the way it has always been for this couple, and that there was a time when any difference between their styles was not a problem. He gathers information about how they created their relationship and builds on that.

Ellen: What else have your clients taught you about transforming anxiety to courage, comfort, and choice?

Elliott: They've taught me that their ideas are so much better than mine. And the unbelievable power that comes from their taking the credit for their exceptions. I'll always tap back into that. It's one of my favorite things to do.

It's really important to me that people understand that solution-focused therapy can impact anxiety. But we do that the same way we do anything else: by tapping people on the shoulder and inviting them to do something different.

Ellen: Elliott, thank you so much. I really appreciate your sharing all this with me.

INTERVIEW WITH YVONNE DOLAN, MA

Yvonne is one of the founders of SFBTA and conducts training in solution-focused practice all over the world. She is the co-author of *More than Miracles: The State of the Art of Solution focused Brief Therapy.* Yvonne has been a psychotherapist for more than 30 years and describes her work as an integration of solution focused therapy and Ericksonian hypnotherapy.

Ellen: Yesterday you said that you like to work with anxiety. How exactly did you put it?

Yvonne: I enjoy working with people who want help with anxiety. And I thought of some solution-focused strategies I use. One is that I draw a scale. It's sort of an unusual scale. On one end, they're so relaxed they're asleep, and on the other they're so anxious that they're frazzled. *(Draws following scale)*

Figure 9.1 Yvonne Dolan's "Alertness–Relaxation" Scale.

Yvonne went on to explain how she tells clients that most people have an area that is their comfort zone. She invites them to indicate an area of the scale, like this. *(Adds comfort zone to scale)*

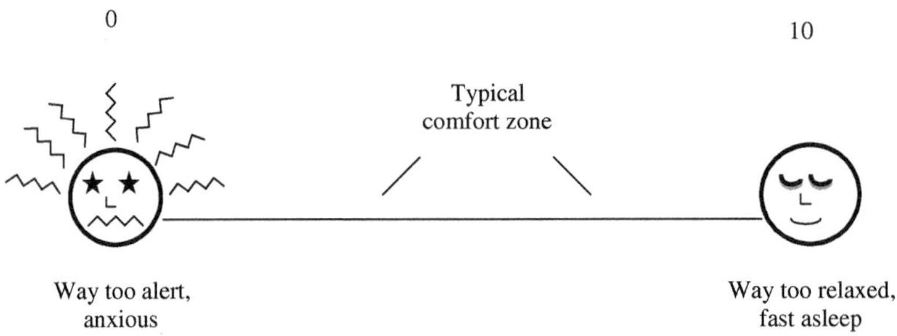

Figure 9.2 Yvonne Dolan's "Alertness–Relaxation" Scale, with comfort zone.

Then she asks them to mark on the scale where they are now.

Yvonne: Then I ask them to think of a time when they were more in their comfort zone and what that was like—what they were doing, and where they were, and in thinking about it, where in their body they experience the memory of that good feeling. "Stay with that for a moment and notice what it's like to be connected to that good feeling. Sometimes people tell me it's useful to connect the feeling in that part of the body to the number on the scale. So, let's suppose you go down to a zero, what would help you connect with that good feeling?" So you look for an exception. This is one I use all the time.

Then there is Betty Alice Erickson's 54321.

Yvonne described this technique, which involves asking the client to name five things he or she is seeing, hearing, and feeling. Then the client names four in each category, then three, and so on. *(As noted earlier in this chapter, one version of 54321 is described in Chapter 3.)*

Yvonne noted that she uses this method less frequently. She is most likely to introduce it when anxiety is accompanied by waking and the client is having trouble getting back to sleep. She asks what has helped in the past, and if the client is interested in learning something new, she may introduce this method. She noted that she is careful to say that many people find this technique helpful, and if the client likes, she can describe it. People are invited to experiment and discover what else might be helpful for them.

Yvonne commented that she finds it helpful for many clients to get up and "move" during a session. Scaling provides an opportunity to invite physical movement.

Yvonne: I often, if I can, draw the scale on the board, and the client gets up to do the scale. I'm convinced, anecdotally, that there's something in evaluating the scaling question that counterbalances emotion. And I'm transparent about that with my client: "Would you mind answering this question? It helps me to understand better. And, I don't know why, but often people find it useful if they stand up and write it, perhaps because it activates a different part of the brain."

Yvonne described another tool that she sometimes offers to people who want help with intrusive thoughts.

Yvonne: This is an old technique from BFTC. It's sort of a pattern interruption: "Write, read, and burn," or tear up in little pieces. *(This is a variation of the "Write, read, and shred" tool introduced in Topic Two of the solution focused anxiety management class.)* Something I add now is the message they want to replace it [the intrusive thoughts]: "And if this thought were gone, what would you be thinking about instead?" The thought comes from them. *(The client is now invited to write that thought on a different piece of paper.)* And it may be more effective to write it first with the dominant hand and then with the non-dominant hand.

Yvonne added that clients often keep this second piece of paper, perhaps in a pocket. Then, when the intrusive thought returns, they can touch that paper. Or they might write the "instead" thought again, again first with the dominant hand and then with the non-dominant hand.

Ellen: What have your clients who have struggled with anxiety taught you?

Yvonne: People seem to reach a turning point. They reach a realization that no matter how terrible the anxiety is, it will not last forever.

Ellen: What helps them most to realize that?

Yvonne: They recall a time when they were calmer. 54321 helps. And it's important that therapists remain calm, and breathe. I also find it useful to give people information about the nature of anxiety, how adrenaline peaks and it takes some time to come down, and other things you can do for it.

Ellen: It's so interesting to hear that, since the book that this interview will be part of presents some of that information. I'm interested in your thoughts about how that kind of information fits with solution-focused practice.

Yvonne: During the year before Steve (de Shazer) and Insoo (Kim Berg) died, when we were working on *More Than Miracles,* there was also discussion about writing a book about treatments for different conditions, presenting the information in a solution-focused frame. Insoo said, "Why would you withhold information from people?"

Yvonne explained more about how the process would work. Therapists would still begin by identifying clients' own solutions and exceptions to their problem. In addition, if there were tools that were often helpful for that problem, therapists could ask clients if they wanted to hear about them.

Yvonne: The consensus was that it would be immoral to withhold knowledge if you know about something that might be helpful to someone. As my friend Luc Isebaert says, "Just because someone doesn't spontaneously think of insulin doesn't mean you wouldn't suggest it to them." *(Luc is a Belgian psychiatrist who developed important solution-focused methods for the treatment of alcohol abuse.)* Unfortunately, any new approach often is defined more rigidly than it was intended to be. Or perhaps it is misconstrued. The founders were much more flexible about psychoeducation than many of their protégées interpreted it.

Ellen: Yvonne, thank you so much. I really appreciate our conversation and your sharing all this with me.

INPUT FROM OTHER SOLUTION-FOCUSED COLLEAGUES

As noted previously, there was simply not enough time to interview all of the wise solution-focused therapists at the conference! Several colleagues graciously provided written responses to the author's short questionnaire.

Comments from Terry Willey, MFT

Terry is a psychotherapist with more than 30 years of clinical experience. He practices at the Kern County Mental Health Department, where he has supervised the Kern UCLA Residency Program, the Mini Clinic Brief Therapy Team, and the Behavioral Medicine Clinic. Terry has received the Jimmy Parris Mental Health Professional of the Year award from Kern County Mental Health and the National Alliance on Mental Illness.

Tell me about a way of transforming anxiety (phobia, worry, obsessive compulsive symptoms, intrusive thoughts, panic) to courage, comfort or choice that you have seen a client discover. This might be something you discovered was already happening, or it might be something that emerged during a session during collaborative conversation.

I've had a lot of success with exposure, response prevention, and systematic desensitization. The fear hierarchy is their language focusing on what they want to achieve. As they reach new heights, they quickly gain confidence. Looking at the miracle gives them a point to leap forward.

What strengths and resources, internal and external, helped that person most? How did you invite him or her to tap those and to get through the hardest times?

Regardless of the strength of the fear, the strength of the person is greater. Each success moves them forward, and if you get stuck, you look for smaller steps.

Tools from other modalities often suggest procedures such as exposure (to feared situations and sensations), changing thoughts, taking action even in the presence of discomfort, relaxation, and mindfulness. Where have you discovered that clients come up with variations on these on their own?

Clients break their fears into smaller steps.

Do you ever actively invite clients to use these tools?

Yes.

If so, which?

Goal lists.

And if you use these tools, how do you do so in a way that remains consistent with a solution-focused spirit of leading from behind and inviting clients to discover their own solutions?

It's the client's list of goals, and accessing their strengths achieves the goals.

What else have your clients taught you about transforming anxiety to courage, comfort, and choice?

Their strengths move the treatment—I just provide the frame.

Comments from Bruce Gorden, MFT

Bruce is a psychotherapist and has been designated an Approved Supervisor by the American Association of Marriage and Family Therapists. He practices at Harmonious Solutions in San Diego, where he helps couples, families, and individuals solve problems with chemical dependence, family violence, sexual assault, depression, and anxiety. Bruce has extensive expertise with a culturally diverse population.

Tell me about a way of transforming anxiety to courage, comfort, or choice that you have seen a client discover.

So, over the years, people I have talked with displayed a range of abilities that were helpful to them in changing their relationship with "anxiety, fear, phobia, rituals, etc." I ask, "What have you done already to cope?" And then I say, "Let's brainstorm on stuff that you haven't yet done or thought of."

Some examples: While discussing cases, a colleague mentioned he had intrusive thoughts. He described them, and I said, "Wow, they sound like Steven King books!" He decided he should write short stories of that genre, and the thoughts ceased to be troublesome and turned into stories!

A high school student I worked with at San Diego High in the classroom was unable to concentrate on his studies because of troubling memories. When he was two years old a SWAT team broke into his home and put a shotgun to his mother's head and led her away. He was talking with me about gangs trying to recruit him. I asked him how he dealt with them. He said, "I told them to haul ass." The "memory problem" he mentioned in passing. I asked, "How long have these memories been stealing time from you?" He never mentioned them again. So I asked later what had come of them. He said, "I told them to haul ass." This, I think, was collateral healing for him, his application of a solution he had used in another area.

What strengths and resources, internal and external, have helped people most? How do you invite people to tap those strengths and to get through the hardest times?

The internal resources are curiosity, creativity, willingness to try new things. And courage, gobs of that. I find that people living with these types of problems live courageously every day. Some wake up feeling fearful, on the verge of panic, and they manage to get up and do what needs to be done in spite of it—or with it or because of it.

Tools from other modalities often suggest other procedures. Where have you discovered that clients come up with variations on these on their own?

Again, my ideas came from people living with. One cool one was a client who came in asking for help with a sort of "free floating anxiety" (what his previous therapist said it was). Well, he had a workbook on anxiety and said it was helpful. I said research showed those who worked through the workbooks benefited from the exercises. So, he chose the ones he thought he could follow through on. For him, one was learning to breathe normally during a difficult period of time. That involved purposely entering an anxiety/fearful situation, and practice, and then scaling his progress. He also visualized family of origin sensitizing events, and he practiced cleansing breaths. He also went downtown, on Harbor Boulevard, to a hotel that has a glass elevator. Riding it up and down provoked certain feelings and gave him an opportunity to feel the feeling he preferred to avoid.

Do you ever actively invite clients to use these tools? If so, which?

When we brainstorm together. Or when I ask, "What have your friends suggested?" My invitation is, "Do you think that might work?"

What lets you know that the time is right to introduce these tools?

The conversation seems to invite me to invite them. Or an idea comes to mind that someone else has tried. I define brainstorming as throwing ideas out, without evaluating them. I participate in the process, sometimes just to get it going.

And if you use these tools, how do you do so in a way that remains consistent with a solution-focused spirit of leading from behind and inviting clients to discover their own solutions?

I remain "collaborative" and wonder with people what might be helpful.

What else have your clients taught you about transforming anxiety to courage, comfort, and choice?

Just their willingness to confront the problem by first asking for help. The fear some people must cope with is oftentimes "bigger" than they are. When I attend to how they have coped over the years, it becomes evident that they have done a lot in the face of a lot. And I stay genuinely curious for a long time about how they were able to do activities of daily living. I ask about tiny things done each day. So they eventually tell me rather amazing deeds done.

Comments from Ross Kremsdorf, PhD

Tell me about a way of transforming anxiety to courage, comfort, or choice that you have seen a client discover.

Diana came to treatment because her fears and anxiety had progressively limited the positive activities she wanted to do and kept her from accomplishing her long-term goals. She was fearful of driving out of her area to obtain the benefits of a nearby larger city and felt hopeless about ever accomplishing one of her life goals (to visit Washington, DC). This resulted in increased depression that further reduced her motivation to take positive steps on her own.

In treatment, conversations progressively focused less on her limitations and more on her goals, with an initial focus on her miracle picture. Despite being initially hopeless about achieving her longer-term goals, she gradually spent more time in future-focused conversation. She was "willing to give it a try" because, as she told me later, she saw that I believed in these possibilities.

We focused on the positive aspects of anxiety and the great benefits if she could channel this energy into a positive plan for change. Diana commented that she realized that she had to learn to live with some level of anxiety because without it she might not have the energy to accomplish anything.

We moved from her miracle picture to a variety of goal steps/solutions that might help her move forward, and we discussed the most realistic and potentially beneficial actions to take first. Despite feeling hopeless, she was willing to define and take small steps in these areas, and this led to the collaborative development of what might traditionally be seen as developing a hierarchy of steps that might move her on the path to her goals.

She commented that each step down the path of graduated solutions increased her confidence as she experienced success, and this increased her willingness to take the next step. If a step was too large, we would break it down into even smaller movements forward. Some of these steps required

Diana to bolster her relaxation skills, and she asked for some instruction on developing these skills. In her case, she found simple breathing exercises most helpful, and we collaboratively developed a short relaxation self-study program, which we continued to follow throughout treatment.

As Diana progressed in her self-rating of progress toward her goals, she spontaneously began to believe she could move even faster than she had originally considered, and she began taking larger steps without the fear of a complete relapse. For instance, she encouraged her husband to escort her as she drove down a narrow and windy mountain road to reach the neighboring city, telling herself that the worst that could happen would be to pull over and let him drive.

She also began planning those specific steps she would have to take to visit Washington, DC. She still found the thought of making such a major trip on an airplane somewhat terrifying, but she now believed it might be possible.

At this point, I moved to another area, and we terminated treatment, as Diana felt she could continue on her own. Almost two years later I ran into Diana. She was excited to tell me that she had made her cross-county trip and now was functioning quite effectively, despite momentarily having feelings of anxiety that she was better able to overcome.

Background note from Ross: I was CBT oriented for many years and worked extensively with anxiety disorders and stress management programs. In addition, I became certified as a Biofeedback Therapist. Through trial and error, I found that such structured programs often were not individualized enough to meet the needs of many of my clients, and this required me to modify many of these interventions to connect with the client's frame of reference (consistent with my early Rogerian background). My later exposure to the solution-focused model provided principles that appear to better engage my clients in the treatment planning process, and the interventions that resulted were much more congruent with what would be helpful for each individual to reduce anxiety and build a better life. While there are instances in which the client and I have utilized traditional anxiety methods, these are planned and used in a more individualized manner that "fits" for the client.

Using tools from other modalities: I don't actively invite clients to use these tools as the first step in the therapeutic process but only after we have explored "exceptions" and worked with those first and the client does not yet believe she/he has sufficiently accomplished her/his treatment goal (i.e., in discussion of a self-rating on the scaling questions).

Even then, I attempt to remain consistent with the solution-focused spirit by following a process that moves from using the client's own strengths first. Then we collaboratively consider "doing something different" if more change is desired. My approach to incorporating traditional tools within solution-focused practice can be roughly outlined as follows:

I work initially with "exceptions" and other client strengths, resources, and coping skills in designing small steps that will both reduce anxiety and increase the probability of achieving that individual's miracle picture.

If the client does not yet believe she/he has sufficiently accomplished her/his treatment goals within a reasonable period of time, or if the client requests more specific/traditional anxiety reduction skills, my solution-focused approach steps tend to be:

Focusing on those traditional tools that (in order of priority):

a. The client specifically suggests; or that
b. Fit what the client says they want to accomplish or techniques they might wish to try; or
c. If the client can't think of anything else, we start a discussion on the benefits of attempting to do something different, including asking:
    i. What the client thinks might be something "different" to try;
    ii. Anything they have tried that worked even a little (exceptions);
    iii. What other trusted people have suggested;
    iv. If the client is willing to experiment.

If the client is willing to experiment, either with his/her options, or with options I might suggest based on their own strengths, I attempt to develop a collaborative conjoint "small steps" plan with some of the following elements:

a. Determine what might be the first thing to try/experiment/pilot;
b. Ask the client what small step the client might be willing to try (i.e., what would they be willing to do that might move them up one notch on the scaling question scale);
c. Determine if the client desires any additional skill development in the area chosen (e.g., learn a relaxation technique);
d. Implement the plan and monitor if successful.

Additional things that have been suggested while brainstorming with a client in the search for "doing something different" that fits for the client have included:

a. Suggesting a client read a self-help book in the area to see what she or he might find useful;

b. Suggesting the client attend a local self-help anxiety group to gather ideas from peers.

Comments from Adam Froerer, PhD

Adam is an assistant professor at Argosy University, Chicago, where he is the assistant chair for the clinical psychology master's program and the industrial and organizational psychology master's program. He has practiced solution-focused therapy with individuals, couples, and families in multiple settings. Adam has conducted process research using microanalysis and serves on SFBTA's research committee.

Tell me about a way of transforming anxiety to courage, comfort, or choice that you have seen a client discover.

I just met with a client today who is worried/anxious about her safety given that she is in a domestically violent relationship. I would consider her worry, stress, and anxiety warranted and appropriate given her situation; however, it is something she would like to change. A complicating factor for this client is that she is not yet ready to leave her relationship (although she knows that ultimately this is something she wants). Rather than focusing on how worried she is, together we turned this worry and vigilance into a strength through a scaling exercise that took the bulk of the session today.

At the beginning of the session she put herself on a "confidence that you are safe" scale at a four. We spent several minutes talking about plans she had already put into place that helped her feel somewhat safe. She mentioned these things: setting up safety plans with her co-workers, arranging to spend time with friends and family members if needed, and placing a bag with necessities in her car trunk in case she needed to leave the situation. We discussed that maybe her worry and stress were in some way helpful because they served as a signal to her that she needed to leave potentially violent situations and keep herself safe. The client agreed that this was true. She also commented that she would like to feel safer overall.

When I asked her about what would help her move to a five on her confidence scale, she commented that she would need to spend less time with her boyfriend. She commented that less time with him would allow her to relax and "not be so agitated." When I asked her what she would do instead of spending time with him, she mentioned that she would be more productive at work, she would enjoy her alone time through exercise and church attendance (rather than be on edge all the time), and that she would spend much more time with other people.

Since writing the above (this is being written three days later), the client has called me to say that she has instigated a 72-hour no contact agreement with her boyfriend, that she has spent two nights in a row out with friends, and most importantly, that she feels calm and confident. She mentioned that she might not even go back to her boyfriend.

What strengths and resources, internal and external, helped that person most? How did you invite him or her to tap those and to get through the hardest times?

Friends, meditation (listening to YouTube clips), planning ahead, and church. We discussed these things in relation to her reaching a four (on her "confidence you are safe" scale) and talked about how these things have been helpful to her.

Tools from other modalities often suggest other procedures. Where have you discovered that clients come up with variations on these on their own?

I think my clients have really benefited from relaxation and mindfulness techniques. Like I mentioned about my client above, she really likes to listen to guided imagery and meditation prompts on YouTube. When I ask clients about what has worked in the past, many have talked about these kinds of things.

Do you ever actively invite clients to use these tools?

I think the most active I get about inviting these things is saying something like, "Other people have mentioned that such and such has been helpful. Have you ever used something like this before? Or have you ever thought about these things as options for you?" Otherwise, I let my clients come up with their own helpful solutions—they know what is going to help them the best.

If so, which?

Meditation, mindfulness.

What lets you know that the time is right to do so?

Sometimes clients will ask me what I think or if I have had other people say what has helped them. In these times I will say something about these things. Otherwise, if we are talking about needing to relax, my clients usually know what will help them. Sometimes, they have to imagine that they know before they can verbalize it, but they get there in the end.

And if you use these tools, how do you do so in a way that remains consistent with a solution-focused spirit of leading from behind and inviting clients to discover their own solutions?

Like I mentioned before, I will say, "Other people have mentioned that X has been helpful; have you ever considered that?"

What else have your clients taught you about transforming anxiety to courage, comfort, and choice?

My clients have taught me that we are stronger than we sometimes give ourselves credit for. I have been amazed how much people are able to do, even if they feel unable to move in one aspect of their lives. In addition, I have learned that what I think should be overwhelming is regularly not overwhelming to my clients—they know themselves better than I could ever know them.

EMERGING THEMES AND AUTHOR COMMENTARY

As I (Ellen) reflected on the wisdom and creativity that my colleagues had graciously shared, I was aware of several common themes. One was that the same solution-focused processes, attitudes, and methods that "work" with any area for change "work" with anxiety. Several people (Joel, Jay, Elliott) directly said that treatment for anxiety is "no different from treatment for anything else." All of the respondents inquire about their clients' best hopes. When clients describe anxiety, they ask what people want instead. They assume that there are already "exceptions" to the problem: times when relaxation, courage, and other strengths have been present and/or when, for whatever reason, anxiety has not been a problem. The respondents inquire about what helped before. Many use scaling, often in creative ways (Yvonne's scale, Adam's "confidence you are safe" scale). In Ross's words, they "believe in possibility." They notice and amplify pieces of solution that are already present (Linda: "Look for signs you already have that white picket fence").

Every therapist made it clear that solutions grew from what was important to the individual client—activities, language, imagery. What amazing creativity was shown by the therapists' clients—and by the therapists who recognized and built on it! For Joel's client, making figurines and getting a dog were elements of the solution. Bruce's colleague discovered the language of Stephen King books, and one of Bruce's clients came up with the idea of telling his anxiety to "haul ass." For Heather's client, conducting a musical score was an ingredient of the solution. Elliott's client remembered and used how he had relaxed at wrestling practice.

In response to inquiry about whether they suggest techniques used in other modalities, there was a wide range of responses. Some therapists rarely do so. Joel noted that if he attempts to introduce an idea that is not the client's, "It becomes my idea, not theirs." Elliott pointed out that when he "taught techniques" (from CBT) to clients, the clients sometimes learned a technique but did not think to use it when the anxiety was greatest.

Other solution-focused therapists clearly do suggest specific techniques. Jay talked about inviting clients to schedule "worry time." Heather and Yvonne sometimes use state-changing techniques. Both specifically mentioned 54321. Frank uses matched breathing and relaxation. Adam also sometimes uses relaxation, along with meditation and mindfulness. Ross referred to graduated steps. Yvonne sometimes suggests "Write, read, and burn," and she may offer didactic information about anxiety. Terry sometimes uses exposure, response prevention, and systematic desensitization. When clients have already used self-talk, Heather sometimes asks whether they would like to hear more about using this kind of tool.

Frank and Yvonne specifically referred to the fact that although clients may be the experts on their own experience, therapists may "be the experts on some other things" (Frank's words). From this perspective, the therapist does not have to wait for clients to discover these tools on their own, and it is fully compatible with solution-focused practice to introduce such things. In fact, *not* suggesting certain tools that have been demonstrated to be effective was compared to not suggesting insulin to a diabetic just because that person has not spontaneously thought of it (Yvonne, recalling conversations with de Shazer, Berg, and Luc Isebaert).

At the same time, all of the therapists either explicitly stated or implied that how and when a technique is introduced makes a tremendous difference in whether it is solution-focused. The technique is rarely, if ever, the first step. Instead, solution-focused treatment of anxiety begins with exploration of client goals, best hopes, and exceptions.

Often clients have discovered on their own the very same principles that "experts" from other modalities would teach them! These therapists have often seen this occur (Linda's and Terry's comments about people taking small steps; Heather's observations of people who use the equivalent of "cognitive" techniques on their own). When this happens, the therapist amplifies what is already working in the client's life. When what the client is doing is not working well enough, or when the therapist believes that something additional would be useful, any information or tool is introduced in a tentative way, with a message like Frank's (from Bill O'Hanlon): "You can do A, B, C, or none of the above."

Several therapists emphasized the importance of understanding, empathy, and support. Jay commented on the importance of a therapeutic relationship where it is safe to talk about weaknesses, including anxiety. He reminds us not to allow "solution-focused" to become "solution-forced" (Nylund and Corsiglia, 1994). Similarly, Frank highlighted the importance of understanding the client's experience—and communicating that understanding—before searching for exceptions.

Other themes include normalizing anxiety. For example, Linda told her client, "Makes sense to me," when anxiety was experienced at the time of a developmental transition. There is "tweaking" of something already in a client's repertoire. For example, to highlight strength, Jay suggested the shift from a journal of weakness to a journal of "pride."

The respondents consistently recognized tremendous strengths in their clients, and all of the therapists mentioned that they have learned much about courage from the remarkable people they have treated. Frank described clients who have a great deal of awareness of physical sensations, along with social sensitivity. Bruce has seen courage, creativity, and amazing willingness to try new things. Ross and Adam highlighted their clients' appropriate caution. Adam referred to some of the amazing things people can do, even with significant anxiety and in very difficult circumstances. Heather has learned "how very possible it is." Her clients have demonstrated resilience—and have taught her about the "vicarious resilience" that therapists can absorb from our clients. Yvonne has seen that "people seem to reach a turning point. They realize that however terrible it is, the anxiety won't last forever." Elliott has learned "that their ideas are so much better than mine!"

Overall, both common themes and wonderful variations emerged from the comments. All of the respondents use and trust the basic solution-focused process and tailor treatment to client strengths and preferences. Many, but not all, add something, and the "something" that they add may be a tool that they are aware of or one that worked for previous clients. Just as all clients are not alike, "one size does not fit all" among expert solution-focused therapists who treat anxiety. These responses echo something that solution-focused therapists already know: that there are so many ways to create courage, coping, appropriate caution, and choice.

CHAPTER 10

Concluding Questions: What Creates Change in Solution Focused Anxiety Management, and How Can We Do More of It?

As illustrated by the examples throughout this book, something occurs during the solution focused anxiety management process that changes the experience and perception of anxiety. Often anxiety diminishes significantly. On other occasions, physiological arousal, caution, and avoidance may still be present, but they may be viewed very differently and may not be a problem. No longer do they interfere significantly with functioning. Instead, they may be viewed as parts of the self, sometimes parts that are valuable. Where anxiety once seemed to be, courage, coping, appropriate caution, and choice emerge instead. What might account for this transformation? This chapter offers some ideas and possibilities.

One of the core attitudes within solution-focused practice is the view of the client as the expert: on the area for change, on the goal, and on "what works." It follows from this that clients are also the experts on what it is about the solution focused anxiety management process that is most useful. The following section presents some information about these all-important client perceptions.

TAKE-HOME MESSAGES IN A SOLUTION FOCUSED ANXIETY MANAGEMENT CLASS

As presented throughout this book, solution focused anxiety management class participants complete End of Session Forms each week. These forms include narrative comments about what participants most want to remember from the session. When possible, the form is duplicated, with one copy for the participant and one for the clinical record. As noted in Chapter 2, the information on the forms provides a rich source of data for much-needed research. Although (to the author's knowledge) formal research has not yet been done, a small pilot qualitative analysis was conducted on the narrative comments on some of the forms. (Unfortunately, the numerical

Solution Focused Anxiety Management
http://dx.doi.org/10.1016/B978-0-12-394421-4.00010-3

[zero to ten] scaling question responses were not available on this sample. As a result, quantitative analyses could not be conducted. The pilot study included qualitative responses only.)

A sample of 138 written comments was available. These were completed by 60 people who attended classes over a six-month period. Responses were transcribed and clustered into categories by the author. Many forms included multiple comments, and some of the categories overlapped. Meaningful clusters of responses did appear in the data. These are described in this section, beginning with the categories with the largest numbers of comments. Sometimes individual comments were both poignant and profound, and a few examples are included.

The largest category involved "Acceptance": acceptance of a range of feelings, acceptance of anxiety, and acceptance of uncertainty. Fourteen responses fell into this category. The fact that anxiety is a normal reaction was highlighted in 11 responses. "I'm not crazy," wrote one person. "It's normal to react the way I do, so I need to be gentle with myself," said another. Accepting being a "body reactor" was mentioned 7 times. Four comments specifically referred to ambivalence and the normalcy of mixed feelings. A few of these responses suggested that this was a new idea.

The next cluster might be described as "Taking little steps and seeking out what is challenging, even with anxiety." This category included three sub-categories: "Courage ladder," "Doing things in the presence of discomfort," and "Bringing it on." Sixteen comments referred to the concept of constructing and using a courage ladder. Participants described "baby steps," "taking small steps," and "practice." Nine comments specifically mentioned that the process involves taking these steps in the presence of discomfort and anxiety. Expecting the discomfort to be there seemed to be a novel idea for some participants. The "Bring it on" category included five responses, which often included those words ("bring it on"). People referred to actively seeking out what is difficult and how different this was from avoiding it. Some of the comments referred to "the commonsense and the counterintuitive."

"Addressing life issues, even with anxiety" appeared to be the next category. There were 12 responses that mentioned this. For example, one participant wrote, "I need to decide whether to move overseas (or not)." This response suggested that this was a new awareness for this person. The life issues category appeared to overlap with a cluster that might be called "Insight," which included 5 responses. Here are some examples of comments here: "I realize I want to control everything." "My mother must have had an anxiety disorder." "I see that I never want to feel any discomfort. And that's not possible."

"Physical coping techniques" emerged in the next cluster, with a total of 16 responses. Eleven of these included the intention to use these tools. "Don't fight it; it will pass"—the message from the Claire Weekes "Wave" technique—was noted 10 times. Six comments specifically mentioned "Breathe!" or "Remember to breathe."

The next cluster of responses specifically mentioned "Assertiveness." There were 11 comments in this category. Several of these included the idea that assertiveness involves active choice. Two more responses specifically referred to the idea that "You can—and you don't have to."

Eight comments could be categorized as "Tools for worry." Six of these referred to the "Write, read, and shred" exercise. Two people referred to the idea of "transforming worry to a plan," and two others noted "discriminate signal from noise."

"Changing your thoughts" was noted seven times. "I can look at things differently, and that makes a difference" is an example from this category.

Another cluster of responses mentioned "Hope." Six people mentioned that hope grew from discovering specific methods. "There are things I can do, tools I can use to make it manageable" is an example from this category.

"Developmental stages" were highlighted in five comments. One person mentioned "Courage," and one referred to "Stubbornness." (These two responses might be included [respectively] in the clusters referring to courage ladders and doing things even with discomfort, but because the meanings may be slightly different, they are listed separately here.)

As the participant comments indicate, different components of the class stood out for different people—a finding completely consistent with the solution-focused perspective that "one size does not fit all." Class participants wanted to remember and use what resonated for each of them. At the same time, there were recurring themes. Acceptance (of discomfort, physiological reactivity, and mixed feelings), taking small, specific steps (even in the presence of anxiety), and depathologizing anxiety emerged repeatedly.

More systematic and sophisticated qualitative research is clearly needed, and, as noted in Chapter 2, this can easily be designed in settings where this class is conducted. Client responses could be analyzed by therapists who were familiar with solution focused anxiety management but who had not taught the class and did not know the participants. A larger sample could be obtained.

It would be extremely useful to contact participants at some interval after completion of the program (six months or one year later, for example). A variation of the End of Session Form could be created—perhaps a "Follow-up Form." This form could request both quantitative ratings of freedom from anxiety and subjective comments. If permission for future contact were obtained at the time of treatment, data could be collected later by telephone interview, in-person interview, mail, or email. Participants could be invited to comment on what had been most helpful and how they had gotten back on track after "slips." Analyses could compare the clusters of variables emerging at follow-up with those emerging at the end of each session. Perhaps some components of the program stand out more over time.

Quantitative data might be available from class participants, ideally at intake, at the end of solution focused anxiety management class sessions, and at follow-up. Higher (or lower) initial scores on the zero to ten scale might be associated with particular clusters of comments. Maybe people who change more (or less) focus on different parts of the material. This kind of research will provide valuable clues about how change grows in solution focused anxiety management.

SECOND-ORDER CHANGE: A POSSIBLE EXPLANATORY FACTOR

The question of what accounts for change following therapy (of any modality or orientation) has been debated in the field for some time. As discussed in Chapter 1, meta-analyses of psychotherapy research outcome studies have suggested that common factors (client variables, the therapeutic relationship [in group treatment, this includes the relationships among members as well as the relationship between each member and the therapist], and hope, or the expectancy of positive change) account for a significant proportion of the variance. In addition, specific techniques, some brief and targeted, seem to contribute to change (Lebow, 2007).

Fraser and Solovey (2007) looked at the question of "how therapy works." They asked how seemingly different treatments, or elements of treatment, become parts of a unified whole. How do the common factors described previously and various specific tools or methods interrelate and work together, producing a whole greater than the sum of its parts? These authors proposed that the unifying factor that integrates the multiple components may be *second-order change*, and they have called this the "golden thread that unifies effective treatments."

Recognizing the importance of "second-order change" grows from understanding "first-order change," "second-order change," and the difference between them. Fraser and Solovey therefore attempted to define these terms. They explained that "first-order change" is change within a system that itself remains the same. In contrast, "second-order change" changes first-order solutions (Fraser & Solovey, 2007, p. 15). Second-order solutions may appear to be counterintuitive. Referring to an essay on a Zen approach to archery, Fraser and Solovey described how focusing too directly on the bull's-eye (trying to solve the problem directly) may increase the archer's tension and the likelihood of error. In a Zen approach, the student focuses on concentration, drawing the string, and controlling the breathing. In a "second-order" approach, arriving at the goal will be the outcome of "a good process."

Sometimes first-order change is sufficient. It may be straightforward, and simple actions may produce the desired results. Repeating what has worked in the past when the situation comes up again might be viewed as a good use of first-order change in solution focused anxiety management.

But sometimes first-order change may not work well enough. In addition, as discussed in Chapter 1, well-meaning efforts to solve a problem directly sometimes make things worse. Fraser and Solovey described some categories of first-order actions that may produce this effect. These were originally described by the MRI therapists (Watzlawick, Weakland, & Fisch, 1974). Sometimes action is needed but not taken. On other occasions, action may be taken when it is not really necessary, or action may be taken at the wrong level. Like the archer described previously, people may "overpursue" the problem. They may "overintervene" in a situation that just has normal ups and downs. Or they may trivialize or ignore something that warrants attention.

Describing how change may occur in psychotherapy in general, Fraser and Solovey proposed that the following second-order shifts take place:

1. *If the first-order solution is to* go away from the problem, *then the second-order solution will have something to do with* going toward it.
2. *If the first-order solution is* to overpursue the problem, *then the second-order solution will have something to do with* stopping and reversing the pursuit.
3. *If the first-order solution is* to not attend to the problem, *then the second-order solution will involve* acknowledging the problem *and* taking necessary problem-solving action.
4. *If the first-order solution involves* making the problem overly complex, *then the second-order solution will involve* simplifying the problem …

5. *If the first-order solution is to* overintervene *with the normal ups and downs of daily living, then second-order solutions will involve* tolerating and accepting ... *unpleasantness that is a natural part of the human condition.*
6. *If the first-order solution* reads too little into the difficulty, *or* simplifies it so much as to trivialize it, *then the second-order solution will* honor the complexity of the problem. (Fraser & Solovey, 2007, pp. 272–273).

Fraser and Solovey discussed how all of this applies to anxiety. People often attempt to master anxiety by avoiding it, desperately trying to assure that anxiety does not appear at all. (This is what solution focused anxiety management refers to as attempted "anxiety elimination.") This attempt typically does not work well enough. Fraser and Solovey continued that people often fail to realize that arousal is a normal reaction to stress. People may not see that the arousal dissipates when some of the following processes occur: When people recognize the precipitant, and when they understand the physiological mechanisms of anxiety, people may view their reactions as unpleasant but normal and move beyond them (p. 118). Anxiety decreases when one does something about the situation that precipitated the anxiety or uses one's skills to cope. Anxiety diminishes when people recognize that they misinterpreted things or overreacted.

But when people worry about a normal reaction and its meaning, they do everything in their power to avoid a recurrence of that reaction. Fraser and Solovey proposed that empirically supported approaches—which may appear to be different from each other—may work by having clients do something different from avoidance. These authors therefore proposed that successful treatment of anxiety may include several seemingly different components. One set of procedures includes exposure: to scary thoughts, to feared behavior, and to unwanted sensations. Other treatments include variations on acceptance and mindfulness: allowing worries or sensations or scary thoughts to "just come" (without actively "bringing them on," as one does with deliberate exposure). When this happens, people discover that the scary things drift away on their own (again, without actively "chasing them away"). Other treatments include a group or class component. Some teach relaxation. Some invite identifying and coping with the life situations that contributed to the anxiety. Treatment offers a rationale: education about the physiology of fear and the fact that there is an evidence base supporting the fact that treatment makes a positive difference.

Solution focused anxiety management includes all of these things. Its philosophy and procedures balance acceptance and change. The message is not one of "Just get over it: Use these tools and your anxiety will be gone." Nor is the message one of "Just accept it; that's how you are and how you will be forever." Rather, acceptance leads to change, and change leads to acceptance, in a continuing positive spiral. As one accepts and tolerates emotional and physical arousal, that arousal often diminishes. In solution focused anxiety management, distress is acknowledged. Ups and downs are normalized.

In addition, solution focused anxiety management invites noticing the many places in one's life where anxiety is already "not a problem" or where it has been coped with successfully. Striving for "anxiety elimination" might be seen as a first-order attempted solution, with anxiety *management* a second-order perspective.

Solution-focused practice (in general, not just for anxiety concerns) produces second-order change in multiple ways. People often think that change comes primarily from the therapist, and solution-focused practice highlights how people solve things on their own. Solution-focused therapists know that the *client* is the most important member of the "solution design team."

As Fraser and Solovey noted, the adoption of a future position is an example of second-order change (p. 61). They pointed out that most clients come with a "past-present" orientation. Often they do not see beyond now to a better future. Looking to that future, describing it, and presupposing that pieces of that future are already starting to happen are core components of solution-focused practice. In Fraser and Solovey's words, this second-order change produces a shift from "demoralization to hope" (p. 25).

Solution focused anxiety management normalizes the ups and downs of daily life when it addresses the common issues and dilemmas that emerge during different developmental stages. By emphasizing that anxiety is common when people "hit bumps on the road of life," this approach does what Fraser and Solovey called "simplifying" what has been made "too complex." When people assume that their physical and psychological reactions to stressors are evidence of severe and complex medical and psychiatric illness, solution focused anxiety management proposes a simpler alternate explanation: One might simply be a "body reactor" or "mind reactor" (as are many other people in the room).

At the same time, there are several components of solution focused anxiety management that do what Fraser and Solovey called "honoring the complexity of the problem." This program openly acknowledges that feared consequences sometimes can occur, because life includes uncertainty and risk. Inviting reflection on both the pros and the cons of anxiety reduction communicates the message that situations are multifaceted. The change one wants can be accompanied by mixed feelings and interpersonal challenges. And acknowledging these things directly does not have to become a problem; instead, open discussion about issues and challenges often leads to creative solutions.

Fraser and Solovey also asserted that the context of the treatment and the therapeutic relationship are not separate from the intervention; rather, they *are* an intervention, or a component of an intervention (p. 82). In solution focused anxiety management, the very acts of signing up for and then coming to the class produce a shift. Simply learning that the class exists counters a common view that "my sensations and feelings are so weird and severe that no one else has had them." One client said, "Just knowing that there is a class like this and that people have been showing up for it every week for years changes things." As solution-focused therapists know, significant change often occurs before the first session. And once people attend a class, they discover the "same boat phenomenon" (even if they never share aloud specifics about their own situations). One hears the instructor and other participants describing experiences that may have seemed unique and too unusual to say aloud.

Solution focused anxiety management transforms the familiar, the many "ingredients of solution" that are already part of the client's repertoire, into courage, coping, appropriate caution, and choice. Often what is transformed is something the client may have viewed as pathological. For example, caution is transformed from something to be ashamed of and scorned to a valued attribute. Appropriate caution leads to personal choice to do something (or not do something). That choice may be "for now," with the option to choose something different at some time in the future.

Jay Lebow wrote, "Clinicians today tend to be far more focused on doing what works than on sticking rigidly to a sacrosanct model" (2007, p. 46). Solution focused anxiety management does not hesitate to combine multiple ideas and tools, some from very different models. Sometimes different components of the program may seem to work in different ways. What unifies them, however, may be the way they shift perspectives or invite the unexpected—all things which create second-order change.

SOLUTION-FOCUSED PRACTICE: A PERSPECTIVE THAT MAY LAST FOR GENERATIONS

In her keynote address at the 2011 SFBTA Conference on Solution Focused practice, *SFBT: Practice that makes a difference to the client*, Yvonne Dolan presented a videotaped interview with Matthias Varga von Kibed (a Wittgenstein scholar from the University of Munich who dialogued with Steve de Shazer about the relationship between some philosophical ideas and solution-focused therapy).

In the taped interview, von Kibed asserted the following: "There are some ideas that last for generations. I think the solution-focused perspective is one of those ideas." Dolan inquired about what allows a perspective to be so influential. Von Kibed described three crucial criteria. First, he noted that the perspective needs to be a "well-formed idea." Second, it should be a "paradigm shift." Third, it has to continue to evolve.

Dolan's keynote included video excerpts of conversations with other solution-focused therapists, from around the globe, who described some cutting-edge developments in the field. Clearly, the field is continuing to evolve, and several of the therapists described new ways for solution-focused practice to transform anxiety.

One of the colleagues interviewed was Therese Steiner, a Swiss child psychiatrist. Steiner has adapted solution-focused practice for work with African orphans whose parents died of AIDS. Using art, Steiner invited the children to draw, on outlines of a person's body, the place where the "good intentions" of the parents might be. Later, many children said that this "body mapping" helped them to remember the parent in a new way, when they most needed comfort and courage. Steiner commented on the importance of discovering, in any culture—and, one might add, for any individual—the signs and images that best support courage.

There was also an excerpt of a conversation with Paul Koek. Koek is a Belgian physician/therapist and business coach who has developed an Internet version of some brief solution-focused questions that can be used by people who, for whatever reason, prefer this format to in-person visits with a therapist. Many of the people who used this version described anxiety. One of the online questions asks "What was helpful" (for your anxiety)? For many people, the first answer was "My medicine." The next questions ask "What else?" and "What else?" The answers here tended to be simple, daily activities, such as "walking," "sitting in the garden," and "playing with my daughter." Relaxation techniques were used only 5% of the time. Koek reported that the "simple things in life" were by far the most important elements of the solution for these people. After an average participation time of five weeks, participants in this program reported 77% stress reduction.

Clearly, solution-focused practice is evolving. The solution focused anxiety management program presented in this book may be viewed as another example of evolving practice. The ideas are clear and, in von Kibed's words, "well-formed." And the many ways that solution focused anxiety management creates second-order change produce the paradigm shift von Kibed was describing.

HOW CAN WE BUILD ON WHAT WORKS?

There are a number of ways that readers of this book may be able to participate in the continuing evolution of solution focused anxiety management. As noted in earlier chapters, some readers may be planning and conducting solution focused anxiety management classes. In conjunction with this, they may have opportunities to design and conduct the kind of quantitative and qualitative research described earlier in this chapter, perhaps in combination with other kinds of program evaluation. Other readers may primarily conduct individual therapy. These therapists may use the specific methods and materials in their work; they may also use solution-focused methods and attitudes in a more general way. In their own settings, they may also have an opportunity to create intake forms that invite clients to think and write about courage, coping, and the future (in addition to the typical items on such forms about symptoms and the past). Those readers who are taking a solution focused anxiety management class or are using the approach on their own can apply the ideas in their own lives.

Other readers may be using this book in conjunction with graduate training they are receiving in any of the behavioral healthcare fields, or in medicine, dentistry, nursing, or education. These readers may be able to use these ideas in future practice or program development. In addition to applying the methods that now exist, they may create variations tailored to the unique characteristics of the populations they will serve and the settings where they will practice. This program is designed for adults, but variations can easily be created for children and adolescents. The variation described previously for the African orphans is an example of this.

Those readers who are teaching or supervising trainees or staff in agencies have the opportunity to teach and support a solution-focused approach to anxiety management. They can educate colleagues about the legitimacy of a solution-focused approach, and they might point out that a solution-focused/strategic approach has been considered one of the three primary approaches practiced today (Sperry, 2010).[1] In addition to sharing specific ideas and methods, supervisors and managers can model collaborative, solution-focused attitudes in their relationships with their colleagues and supervisees.

Some readers of this book may be treating anxiety or offering anxiety education from a perspective different from the one emphasized in this book. In some settings, therapists are required to use a pre-existing program or protocol that does not explicitly include a solution-focused component.

[1] Sperry stated that the other two are the cognitive behavioral and the psychodynamic approaches.

Therapists who are using such a program might experiment with adding solution-focused attitudes to what they are already doing. In the spirit of "baby steps," they might do so a little at a time, with curiosity about how doing so makes a difference. These therapists might discover that anxiety decreases more rapidly when one expects that clients (or students or patients) already have significant expertise in courage, coping, appropriate caution, and choice. Anticipating that people will build on what works for them might make the therapist's or teacher's job easier. Physicians and other providers who prescribe medicine for anxiety might begin to ask their patients "what else" (in addition to the medicine) decreases anxiety, and they might wonder aloud with their patients "how you help the medicine to work."

There is another part of the solution focused anxiety management perspective that may contribute to the fine-tuning and evolution of "what works." As discussed throughout this book, facing and even inviting discomfort may sound counterintuitive, but they are important ingredients of the solution. In the same way, when there are challenges to the *therapist*—for example, anxiety problems, situations, or systems that do not appear to respond to attempts to provide solution focused anxiety management—the therapist might be invited to welcome them. Just as solution focused anxiety management includes deliberate exposure to what is difficult, therapists can ask themselves (or their colleagues) our solution-focused questions. We might ask:

- What was different when, for whatever reason, this kind of situation wasn't a problem?
- Where was your caution (about this client or situation) a good thing?
- What helped you choose what to do in such a sensitive situation?
- How did you keep things from getting worse?
- What do you already know about this person's (or system's) unique ways of cooperating?
- How can that knowledge help you to tailor your approach more effectively?
- How could you change things very gradually, just a little at a time?
- When something didn't work well enough, what could you do next time that might be more helpful?
- How would your client (colleague, trainee, supervisor, manager, etc.) answer that question?

- What would a skeptic need to see that would eliminate any concerns about a solution-focused approach to anxiety management?
- What would it take to transform that skeptic into an enthusiastic advocate of a solution-focused approach?

Just as the solution focused anxiety management perspective assumes that clients have the strengths and resources within to get through difficulty, the assumption is also that therapists (and those of us who are not therapists, as well!) will tap multiple resources (within ourselves, within the professional literature and growing evidence base, within our organizations, and within the larger community). We can discover times "when the problem isn't." When something isn't working well enough, we can do something different. We can ask others what will be most helpful. We can embrace challenges; find new ways of combining what works; and discover creative, emerging solutions that transform anxiety into courage, coping, appropriate caution, and choice, in a way that works for this person, and this situation, today.

APPENDIX A

Learner Readings for Topic One: Physical Reactions and Coping Techniques

This reading covers the information presented in Topic One. This may or may not be the first handout in this series that you are reading, and that is perfectly okay. You can begin any place in the series that you like.

In this series, you are learning to celebrate and build courage. You are discovering how to ride through sensations and discomfort in a way that works for you. You are learning that anxiety doesn't have to get in the way of the things you want to do, and you are learning that anxiety certainly isn't the most interesting thing about you. Please use, adapt, and share this material in any way that works for you. By reading this short handout, *right now* you are doing a good thing for yourself and taking a step in the right direction.

Topic One discusses physical reactions and some ways of dealing with them. It includes five specific physical coping techniques. Like everything else in this class, please use this information in the way that works best for you!

PHYSICAL REACTIONS

This section reviews some physical reactions and some ways of dealing with them. When we are confronted with a stressor—and not just people, animals too—we may have certain physiological reactions. Our bodies make chemicals that produce these reactions. These reactions may seem maladaptive, but they are the body's preparation for dealing with a stressor.

People in our classes have described these reactions:

- My heart starts to pound.
- My breathing gets fast.
- I can't concentrate.
- The room starts to spin.
- I feel like I have to get out of here.
- I sweat.
- My face and neck get red and blotchy.

- My stomach starts to hurt.
- I get a headache.
- I feel weak.
- I can't swallow.
- My hands start to tingle.
- I feel like I'm going to faint.
- I can't think of anything to say.
- My voice wavers.
- I start to cry.

There are some things on the list that change in different directions for different people. Some people sleep more when they are under stress; others can't sleep. Some people can't eat; some can't stop eating.

Sometimes people feel as though they're having a heart attack or a stroke. Or they feel as though they're "losing it," or "going crazy." Sometimes people worry that they are dying. This stuff can be scary!

Everyone's body is different, and some people respond more strongly than others, in the same way that some people sunburn more easily than others. And sometimes there's a part of your body that has always been sensitive to stress. You might think of it as a physical predisposition. An example would be if someone is a "stomach reactor." Maybe that person remembers that, as a little boy, he always got low-level tummy aches before tests. Then, maybe in high school he couldn't eat before a big game. Maybe it wasn't a huge, big deal, but as he thinks back, he might recognize that his "stomach thing" was always there a little. So maybe now, as an adult, he may be having it in a more intense way.

Why might that be? Well, there are a number of possible reasons. He might be facing a stressor at a time when his resistance is already low because of fatigue or illness. Or maybe there was some recent change in his life or conflict with somebody or financial problems—or some combination of those things, because sometimes it seems as though everything happens to us at once! But, for whatever reason, or combination of reasons, he might have his stomach reaction more intensely than he ever did before.

So, all of these reactions people have described can be *normal* reactions to a stressor, and *they are not necessarily dangerous*. Now, this next point cannot be emphasized too strongly: *This is not saying that reactions like stomach pain and chest pain and dizziness can safely be ignored! All of those reactions can be dangerous.* If you have a physical symptom that concerns you, or if there is a change in a medical condition that hasn't been evaluated by a physician, then you definitely should get that checked out.

But many people who come to a solution focused anxiety management class *have* been checked out by a doctor or at the emergency room—that's actually one of the things that sometimes leads people to come to a program like this. They get examined and are told that they are okay, medically, but that's *really* hard to believe, because the reactions are still there.

So, if you have been told by your doctor that you were okay—which, of course, means at the time you were checked out, with whatever tests were done—and that your reaction was probably "anxiety," your doctor may well have been correct. *Every one* of those reactions described earlier can be a reaction that some people have when they are under stress.

There is something else about all those physical reactions that feel so scary. They are what we call *time limited*. That means that they will stop on their own. If you have come to Topic One, you may remember an exercise inviting you to make a fist and then to observe your reactions, both physical and psychological. Eventually, the muscles in your hand just let go. They do so on their own, *all by themselves*. And so will the muscles, and the nerves, everywhere in your body. All those parts that tighten up, that feel like they will stay tight forever, that fire off when you're having a huge panic attack, will let go *all by themselves.*

So, to summarize, our reactions may be normal reactions to stress. Often they are not dangerous. They are time limited—that is, they stop on their own. But when these reactions happen, sometimes even once, or maybe a few times, we human beings don't know that they're normal and not dangerous. We don't know that they are time limited and will go away on their own. Or even if we've learned it, we don't *know* it, inside. Because it's scary! We get frightened that the reactions are going to happen again, or keep going forever. The mind flashes "Danger!" When that happens, the body has its physical reaction again, but now at a higher intensity. Now the mind screams "Danger!" louder. We may start thinking, "What if I lose control?" "What if I go crazy?" "What if I make a fool of myself?" It becomes a vicious "spiral": a feeling of panic.

Claire Weekes, an Australian psychiatrist, called the original physical sensations the "first fear" and the worry about having a panic attack the "second fear." She pointed out that the physical symptoms that come with the first fear will come in a wave and diminish on their own if you just wait. Your body may flash fear from time to time, but the panic will not mount (remember the "making a fist" experiment) *if* you don't fall into the trap of "stoking the fire" of your "first fear" with more "second fear" and more adrenaline.

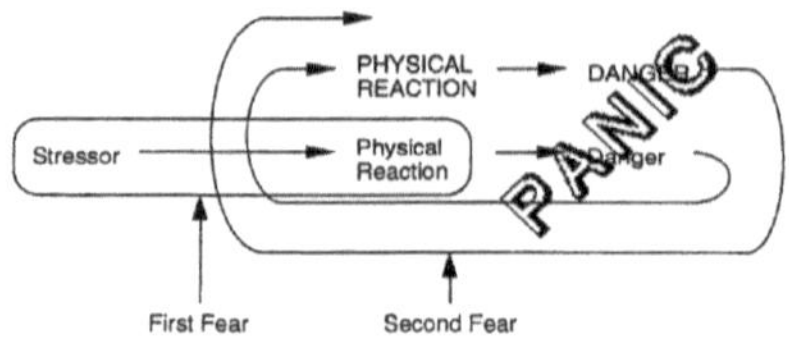

Figure A.1 Cycle of panic.

Some people's physical reactions seem to just come "out of the blue." That can be particularly frightening, because you don't know if there was a "first fear" or what it might have been. But if you can't label a precipitant, don't struggle to do so. Panic attacks that come "out of the blue" are called *spontaneous panic attacks* and are *very common*. The physical symptoms will often pass if you don't keep worrying about their happening again.

You are invited to remember the following concept: *body reactor*. Our definition of a body reactor is this: someone who tends to get a lot of the reactions described in this section. If you are a body reactor, that's a tremendously useful thing to know about yourself. In fact, some people have said that this is the most valuable concept they have taken from Topic One!

One might ask: Isn't *everyone* a body reactor? Doesn't everyone get these reactions? Well, to some extent, yes. But some of us "get" them to a greater degree than other people do. There's also a variation of body reactor that we call *mind reactor*, and that would be someone who tends to worry or obsess a lot. We talk a little more about mind reactors in the other sessions.

You can also think about being a body reactor as something that's "distributed on a bell-shaped curve." If we draw a graph of "autonomic reactivity," most people who come to this class have a "dot" somewhere near the high end.

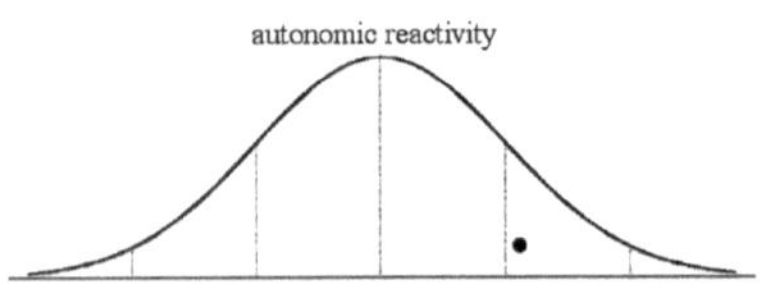

Figure A.2 Bell curve, autonomic reactivity.

Your "dot" may never be way down at the low end, but you may be able to move your functioning significantly toward the center by experimenting with some of the things in this program—and by doing other good things for yourself.

COPING TECHNIQUES

If you are a "body reactor," then the next step is to learn some *coping techniques*. There are many different coping techniques, and for each one there are probably some people who insist that "this one is the best." Our position is that there is no single best coping technique. Different things work better for different people, and in different situations. So the best plan may be to learn a whole range of strategies and to approach them in the same way you would approach the food at a smorgasbord or salad bar: You try what interests you, and you come back for more of what you like.

There are two main categories of coping techniques to learn, and we are going to call them the *physical* techniques and the *thinking* techniques. The thinking techniques are discussed in more detail in Topic Three. You may have already learned about them, or you may be learning about them soon. Of course, none of the techniques are only physical or mental. There is always some overlap. But in general, they can be grouped that way. The physical techniques are the ones that mainly emphasize things that you do with your body—your muscles, your breathing, your general level of tension in your body, etc.—and the thinking techniques are the ones that emphasize what you think and say to yourself in your head.

The following pages review five physical techniques.

Physical Coping Technique 1: Instant Relaxation (The Bellybutton Technique)

Instant relaxation is one of the easiest and most effective techniques to use. It supports calm breathing and decreases the likelihood of hyperventilation, and you can use it any time, any place.

Here is how you do it: You put your thumb in your navel, and you rest your hand on your abdomen. You look down at your hand. Then you breathe deeply into your belly so that you can see your hand move with your inhalation. You observe that process, and you notice any feeling of calm or relaxation or anything else that you are aware of. Then, for the "advanced technique," if you like, you can move your hand away, and you breathe until your stomach moves. That's all there is to it. One of the special things about this advanced technique is that in addition to it being *instant,* it's *inconspicuous*. No one but you knows that you are doing it!

For many people, using this tool slows down their breathing, and a feeling of calm spreads through the body. It doesn't happen for everyone, because different things work for different people. And if this one doesn't work for you, that's perfectly okay. You'll choose something else.

If this technique does calm your breathing, you might be wondering: *Why* does this work? The answer comes from the fact that our brains need oxygen to function. When we are under stress and need oxygen the most, we often breathe shallowly, taking in *less* oxygen, at the very moment when we need it the most! Breathing so that you can feel your hand (or stomach) move assures that you will breathe deeply and take in the oxygen you need to deal with the stress at hand.

This process can prevent hyperventilation. You may have heard that you can also prevent hyperventilation by breathing into a brown paper bag. Maybe so, but most of us aren't very likely to use that tool at a job interview or a party! What's so elegant about this technique is that you've got this tool instantly available—any time, any place. Knowing that you have a tool that is with you everywhere you go, that works immediately, and that is completely inconspicuous can add to your sense of control. That's really powerful, since sometimes part of what seems so devastating about feeling anxious is that we may feel so *out* of control.

For some people, there may also be times when this belly button technique may *not* work. Those may be when a person is right in the middle of a panic attack. (The next tool described in this section *is* one that is often very effective during panic.) But this tool, this instant relaxation, is more something to do *before* a big panic attack happens, sort of as a "preventive" technique. In some ways, it's similar to the medicine people take for migraines when they first feel one coming on, or like medicine to prevent seasickness. It doesn't always stop the feelings once they're happening, but it can be really powerful when you use it ahead of time.

For most people, belly button breathing is a really good habit to get into doing regularly, regardless of your level of anxiety. Some people like to put a little sticky note on their computer monitor or refrigerator door that says "Breathe." You might discover another creative way to remind yourself to do it, something that fits in your life, something that no one but you could possibly have created!

An expert music teacher once commented that when her students are tense, they hold their breath and don't play as well. She tells her students, "Remember to breathe!" On one level, that's funny, because breathing is involuntary, and we're breathing all the time, whether or not we're conscious of it. On another level, though, it's really profound advice. When you're under stress, or overwhelmed, or panicking, or can't think of what else to do, sometimes a simple, straightforward direction is exactly what you need. So, to paraphrase that wise music teacher: If ever you don't know what to do, remember: *Breathe*.

Physical Coping Technique 2: Claire Weekes' Four Concepts (The Wave)[1]

The following method is one of the most powerful techniques you can use to ride through panic attacks.

It was described by Claire Weekes, an Australian psychiatrist. It has some words in it, but the words describe what you do with your body, so this program includes it with the physical coping techniques. Here are the words:

- *Face*: Don't run away.
- *Accept*: Don't fight.
- *Float*: Don't tense up.
- *Let time pass*: Don't be impatient with time.

As you say these words in your head, you might envision the shape of a wave on the ocean. It builds, it crests, and it falls.

Figure A.3 Shape of a wave.

The next wave is just the same. If you've ever surfed or swum in the ocean, or watched people do so, then you know that you can't fight a wave. People may *try* to "fight it," but they discover that the wave will always "win." It's bigger than we are.

Now you might visualize the shape of a wave of anxiety. Its shape is just the same. It builds, it crests, and it falls. And trying to fight *that* wave—like we do when we say, "Go *away*, stupid feeling"—also doesn't work well enough.

So, it has been said that the most powerful technique you can use with the wave of anxiety is learning to *ride* the wave, instead of fighting it. You let the sensations come, to crest, knowing, trusting, that they will diminish. You're like an expert surfer, riding the wave, going over that point of no return. Even at that moment when you feel temporarily out of control, you remember that you've been here before, that you will come down on the other side, and that you will be okay.

[1]See Weekes (1978) in References.

Here is another way you might think about the wave. Imagine that you are walking down the beach, and a really big wave washes over you. You might fall down or get the wind knocked out of you or scrape your knee. But you immediately get up and run a little bit back on the sand, away from the water. And the wave, being a wave and doing what waves do, goes back out to sea.

Figure A.4 Person on beach, briefly overwhelmed by wave, now recovering.

This is sort of like what happens when a wave of anxiety washes over you, and for a minute you feel overwhelmed. Again the wave (being a wave and doing what waves do) moves away, and even if you're a little shaken up, you're okay again.

Why is this concept so powerful? The answer is this: Once you learn to ride the wave, or let it wash over you, you know that when these sensations come, you have a *plan*. And you might notice that we say *when*, and not *if*, because if you're a *body reactor*, chances are that these sensations *will* come back. But rather than having to live in fear of it, like "Oh, no! What am I going to do if it happens again?" something has shifted. Something is different. What's different is that you now have this elegant skill, to remember, in your body, in your bones, at a kinesthetic, feeling level. And that can make a tremendous difference.

Physical Coping Technique 3: Autogenic Training[2]

Autogenic Training is a set of sentences that you say silently in your head, and if your body feels like doing what is in the sentences, it does so. Unlike some of the other tools, Autogenic Training is *not* an instant technique. It takes at least five minutes to do, and many people find it most helpful when they do it with their eyes closed. "Autogenic" means you do it yourself. (The "auto" part is like the "auto" in "automobile," meaning "self drive," and "genic" means "to do," so this is a good thing you do for yourself.)

Here are the sentences:

Breathing calm and regular.
My right arm is heavy.
My left arm is heavy.
My right leg is heavy.
My left leg is heavy.
My right arm is warm.
My left arm is warm.
My right leg is warm.
My left leg is warm.
My arms and legs are heavy and warm.
Heartbeat calm and regular.
My abdomen is calm, relaxed, and comfortable.
My forehead is comfortably cool.
I am calm, relaxed, and comfortable.

Then you take a deep breath. You might stretch like a cat waking up from a nap, and you might say to yourself something like this: "I am alert, refreshed, and energized, just like after a good night's sleep."

You can also do Autogenic Training at bedtime. Some people find it a comfortable and gentle way to get ready for sleep. If you do it then, it's suggested that you do it lying on your back, rather than on your stomach or your side. That lets the blood flow freely and comfortably through your whole body. Then, after you finish thinking the sentences, instead of saying anything about feeling as though you've had a good night's sleep, you might think something like this: "I am relaxed and comfortable and ready for sleep."

When you do Autogenic Training, your thoughts may drift away from the sentences. Or you may not consciously notice your body feeling any

[2]See Luthe & Schultze (1969) in References.

different while you are using this technique. That's okay. You don't need to force yourself to feel or think any particular thing. You can gently direct your thoughts back to the sentences if you like, or you can just let your mind wander. The sentences are a starting point from which you can move, if you like. You can add sentences about other parts of your body, like your shoulders, or the back of your neck: "My shoulders are relaxed and comfortable," or "My jaw is heavy and loose."

If you like visual images, you can add an image, too—anything you find beautiful and relaxing. One image that uses and deepens the sensations of "arms and legs warm, and forehead cool" is to visualize yourself outside, under a patio umbrella, overlooking the ocean or mountains or any other place that is special. You might be stretched out on a comfortable chaise lounge. You might imagine that your head is shaded by the umbrella and your arms and legs are in just the right amount of sun. Your arms and legs are warm, and your forehead is cool.

Sometimes it is said that Autogenic Training is good for most people to do regularly, even if they don't experience a lot of anxiety. And if you do have anxiety, and for some reason can't or don't want to take medicine, there is the perspective of viewing Autogenic Training as a "non-pharmacological prescription." Here is how one physician put it: Imagine that you have a "prescription" to do Autogenic Training twice daily for a month, doing it as faithfully as if you were taking a pill, and noticing how it makes a difference.

Physical Coping Technique 4: "Just Because"

"Just Because" is another "instant" technique, useful when we get irritated as well as when we feel anxious. It includes the following sentence for you to say to yourself any time it might be helpful:

> *"Just because...* (Insert whatever is going on, for instance, "So-and-so is being a pain in the neck"; "This bridge is high"; "I'm home alone"; etc.) *...doesn't mean I have to do this to my body. Now RELAX..."*

You make the word "relax" your cue to exhale. You take a deep breath and exhale again, and you immediately take your body into a state of relaxation, similar to what you have experienced through Autogenic Training, while lying on the beach, or in any other relaxing situation.

There are two different ways you can use this technique. Of course, you can use it in private, with your eyes closed if you wish, to soothe yourself. There is an additional and extremely valuable way you can use it: You can remember "Just Because" when you are "out there in the world," with people, with traffic—with all the "stuff" that sometimes gets us more anxious or irritated than we would like to be. This is a tool that may be especially useful on the many occasions when you need your eyes wide open and all your wits about you!

If you think about it, you might see that the sentence in "Just Because" is absolutely accurate. The fact that something unpleasant, stressful, or frightening is occurring doesn't mean that you have to tighten up your body. Your tightening up your body doesn't make you any better able to handle whatever is going on. In fact, it may have just the opposite effect. You may be raising your blood pressure and your heart rate and making yourself less able to handle whatever is going on.

Now, it makes perfect sense that we tighten up. It's sort of a conditioned response. It's like tightening your stomach as if you're bracing for a blow. But if we've learned to do that, we can also learn the opposite: to use these situations as "cues" to relax.

It also might be useful to consider that "Just Because" is a variation of a technique that sports psychologists and performance psychologists teach to athletes and performers so that they can transform that burst of adrenaline into a prepared readiness to perform. Some people like to remember that when they use this technique, they are probably in some rather well-paid company!

Physical Coping Technique 5: Mindfulness and 54321[3]

Mindfulness is a concept that comes from some Eastern philosophies. In recent times, it has also been embraced by Western medicine and psychology. Mindfulness is riding through whatever is going on, any sensation, any thought, any feeling. You don't judge it; you don't tell it to go away; you just let it be. You watch it change. It's like watching clouds in the sky: The whale becomes a bunny rabbit, and then the bunny's ears fall off, and it becomes a fish, and the fish turns into a little wisp of white fluff that just drifts away.

Mindfulness is sometimes taught by inviting people to take a single raisin. You hold it in your hand. You notice its little wrinkly surface, its color: Dark purple? Brown? Black? You sniff it. You put it on your tongue. You notice any taste: Tart? Sweet? You chew, swallow. You notice any thoughts, feelings, memories: "I hate raisins"; "This is so weird to eat just one raisin"; "I remember my grandmother's raisin cake"—whatever. You just watch one thought or image or feeling "morph" into another.

Then you are invited to notice other sensations. You might be aware of the chair against your back, or the pressure of your hand on your leg, or the sound of an airplane or a car outside. It's just there, it's not good or bad, it just is—and as you notice it, it turns into something else.

Recently, the January cover story of a news magazine[4] described 50 good things to do for yourself in the coming year. One of them was "learn to meditate." The writer was talking about trying to relax, meditate, use mindfulness, and she started thinking: "Did I take the garbage out? That gray sweater I saw on the Internet would go great with my new jeans." She said to herself: "Stop it! Here I am trying to relax, and I'm thinking about this stupid stuff!"

But the person who was helping her with this said something like this: "You let your mind go *wherever* it wants to go. And that includes the garbage and the sweater." That's precisely what mindfulness is about: letting your "monkey mind" climb and wander wherever it wants to go.

And when you get good at this, you can do this with any thought, any feeling, any sensation—including the ones that come with panic, such as your heart beating too fast. And when you can do that with those things, when breathing too quickly or the image of you losing it just morphs into something else, such as "My knee itches" or "Oh, someone's texting me," that changes it, and that can make a tremendous difference.

[3]See Holton (2000) in References.
[4]See Kotz (2007) in References.

54321

The 54321 technique uses a kind of guided mindfulness that can help you relax your body and your mind. This technique comes from Betty Alice Erickson, who is the daughter of psychiatrist and hypnotist Milton Erickson. This version has been adapted from those taught by Yvonne Dolan and Chuck Holton.[5]

Here is how it goes. In a relatively quiet (but not completely quiet) setting, with your eyes open, you pick a spot on the wall across from you. You focus your gaze on something. Moving your eyes around that spot, you say—and this can be aloud, softly, if you're in a place where it's appropriate to speak out loud, or, silently if you're not—five things that you *see*. For instance, you might say, "I see the window." "I see the chair in the corner." "I see the gray backpack on the floor."

You might not be sure when you get to five! Losing track of how many you have said is very common and perfectly okay.

Then you say, aloud or not, five things you *hear*. For instance, these could be some of them: "I hear the sound of the heat or air conditioning." "I hear a car outside." Again, you might not be sure when you've said five. And if it's fairly quiet, this might take a little longer. That's okay.

Then you say, aloud or not, five things you *feel* in your body, sensations or other things you may be aware of. "I feel my fingers on the paper." "I feel the chair against my legs." "I feel my glasses on my ears." If there is some sensation that is uncomfortable, including it is fine. It's just one of the five.

And then you go back and say *four* of each thing: four things I see, four things I hear, four things I feel. And then you do *three* of each, and then two, and then one. It's fine to repeat. And it's fine to get confused about where you are! And if you like, when you finish with one, you can go back to five again. You may find yourself repeating things, and that's just fine. And the process continues, as long as you like. At some point you might discover that instead of actively doing it, your awareness is just drifting. Again, that's just fine.

Sometimes people do a variation of 54321 silently before sleep. If your eyes are closed, you might not want to include five things you *see*. Instead, you might pick five things you're *thinking*. Here are some examples: "I wonder if it will rain tomorrow." "I hope my mom got home okay." "I have to charge my phone in the morning." Again, if there's something you're worried about, including it is fine. It's just one thought among many. Noticing five things that you hear may take a bit longer in a quiet room at night, and that's just fine.

During the day, or at night, or with any variation of it that you might create, 54321 is a tool for experiencing mindfulness.

[5]See Holton (2000) in References.

AN INTERESTING PERSPECTIVE

It might be noted that some professionals in the anxiety management world[6] *don't* always recommend using all the physical coping techniques included in this reading. You might ask: Why not? The answer is this: Sometimes people feel very relaxed, very comfortable, after using some of these methods. And consciously or unconsciously, they start thinking: I've found the cure for my anxiety. I'll just use my Autogenic Training, or whatever, and I won't be anxious any more. Without realizing it, they have just slipped into an "anxiety elimination" mindset. And then if the tool doesn't work, or it doesn't work well enough, they get critical of themselves, or of the program, and they just stop trying. This may be particularly likely to happen with people who are bright and highly motivated!

It is worth noting that this caution doesn't apply equally to all five of the methods included here. It may be a little *more* of a concern with belly button breathing, Autogenic Training, and "Just Because," and somewhat *less* of a concern with the wave and mindfulness. The reason is that with the wave and mindfulness, you're *expecting* that some discomfort may well be there, and that you will ride through it. With the others, there tends to be more of a hope that you will prevent discomfort from happening. In particular, with panic, worry, and some obsessive thoughts, sometimes unwanted reactions *do* happen, even when you use the physical coping tools. So, in the spirit of solution focused anxiety *management*, not anxiety elimination, that's something to keep in mind.

So, you now might be confused! Here we've been talking about and practicing these techniques, and now we are noting that some people don't recommend them!

Here is how we invite you to put all this together. Any tool that is included here was selected because it has been helpful to many, many people. The most important thing is to do what works for you. So it's absolutely appropriate to use these tools, and to notice what you discover. But if you try one, and it doesn't work, and you find yourself getting frustrated or critical of yourself, that's a signal that you might put that tool aside, at least for a while, and experiment with something different.

SUGGESTIONS FOR PRACTICE

Here are some ideas for experimenting with these ideas on your own. Please use *any* ideas or suggestions from this class or these readings in a way that works for you.

[6]See Wilson (2009) in References.

First, you are invited to sample any—or all—of the physical coping techniques presented here. Also please experiment with others you may have learned in the past. You might combine techniques or create a new variation! Be curious and discover what you like. Maybe different tools work better in different situations. Often learning about these coping techniques reminds people of other things they do, or used to do. There may be things that build feelings of calm or comfort, and there may be other things that help you to float through discomfort. Once you start noticing these things, you will probably discover more and more tools that are already in your life. Notice, share, and keep using what works for you.

The second suggestion is optional, because it involves having a panic attack—and this program will *never* "require" anyone to have a panic attack! So you might think about it like this: If you *do* have the "golden opportunity" to have a panic attack, you might notice how it feels different, and how you ride through it differently, as a result of learning this information, and as a result of being in a program with other people who sometimes have the same kinds of experiences you do!

SOLUTION FOCUSED ANXIETY MANAGEMENT

END OF SESSION FORM

Name ____________________________ Date____________________

When you first called for help with your anxiety	Your level of concern or caution is appropriate, not excessive. Anxiety is not so much a problem any more

0 1 2 3 4 5 6 7 8 9 10

What do you want to remember from today?

What helps you to cope with discomfort, uncertainty, worry, and stress?

What else do you want to continue, because you know it works for you?

APPENDIX B

Learner Readings for Topic Two: Behavioral Techniques

This reading covers the information presented in Topic Two. This may or may not be the first handout in this series that you are reading, and that is perfectly okay. You can begin any place in the series that you like.

In this series, you are learning to celebrate and build courage. You are discovering how to ride through sensations and discomfort in a way that works for you. You are learning that anxiety doesn't have to get in the way of the things you want to do, and you are learning that anxiety certainly isn't the most interesting thing about you. Please use, adapt, and share this material in any way that works for you. By reading this short handout, *right now* you are doing a good thing for yourself and taking a step in the right direction.

Topic Two covers behavioral techniques, which are tools that many experts encourage people to use for specific anxiety problems. The basic idea is this: As we get more familiar with something, the more comfortable we usually become with it. This is something you probably discovered on your own a long time ago!

EXPOSURE AND HABITUATION

There are two basic principles here: *exposure* and *habituation. Exposure* means you get yourself to experience the situation, place, sensations, thoughts, behavior, whatever, that's scary to you; and *habituation* means you stay there long enough for it to lose its power, so that it's not such a big deal anymore.

THE COMMONSENSE AND THE COUNTERINTUITIVE

Solution focused anxiety management is a fascinating combination of the commonsense and the counterintuitive. Commonsense is just what it says—common sense. Everyone knows what that means. Counterintuitive is the *opposite* of what you might expect. It's like putting salt in the cookies or sugar in the soup. It's like driving into a skid instead of away from it. It feels as though it doesn't make sense, as though it's going to make things worse instead of better, but it's actually a critical ingredient of the solution.

COURAGE LADDERS

Often, when we have a bad experience with something or are afraid of it for some other reason, we stay away from it. As a result, we never get a chance to learn that we can handle it, that it can be okay. So the way to learn it can be okay is to approach the experience a little at a time. This is definitely a commonsense approach. It's like learning to do anything else—playing an instrument, playing a sport, lifting weights (start light, go a little heavier).

Solution focused anxiety management calls this building a *courage ladder.* A courage ladder is a list of situations to enter, starting with the easiest and gradually making them more challenging.

In the class, we talk about using a series of note cards, one item on each card, because the most helpful way of doing this includes continually thinking of and adding new items, as shown here.

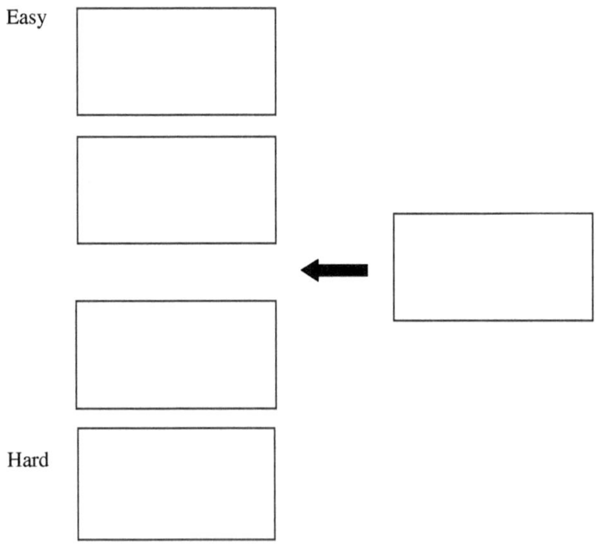

Figure B.1 Note cards for courage ladder.

Of course, you can also make a courage ladder by simply listing the steps on a piece of paper, "inserting" additional steps wherever they are needed.

And with a computer or iPad or other device, you can easily add to an ordinary list.

The steps in a courage ladder need to be small and very specific. For example, in the case of a person who is afraid to leave the house, "going to the grocery store" isn't an ideal courage ladder item. Why? The reason is that there is a big difference between going to the corner store for one item at 10:00 a.m. and going to a big supermarket for a week's groceries at rush hour.

Here is the beginning of a sample courage ladder (done as a computer document), with "baby steps" going from "easy" to "hard."

- Walk out on porch, husband home, when no one around, for two minutes.
- Walk to mailbox for mail, with no one around.
- Walk to mailbox for mail, when one neighbor is out. Say "Hi," even though it's hard.
- Walk around the block. If I see someone, I'll smile and say "Hi."

The following steps might be for a little later on:

- Go to a PTA meeting. It's a lecture, so not much pressure to socialize.
- Stop in at Mary's party for a few minutes (after telling her I can only stay briefly).
- Call my sister and suggest meeting for coffee. Expect that my heart will be pounding—and do it anyway.
- Remember something special about my sister, in preparation for getting together with her.
- Keep the date with her.
- That evening, reflect back on what I like best about how I handled it. Remember how brave I was!
- Walk around Community College with my sister.
- Sign up for a class at Community College.

And the process continues. Here are a few things to notice about the steps in this example. First, they include detail, specific names and places, and they include "setting things up" so that it will be easier to keep the steps small. Second, *expecting* the sensations is specifically mentioned. (For some people it's helpful to add this piece to *every* step on the courage ladder!) Third, savoring victories is part of the process, and it's worth including, as additional specific steps on your ladder.

It should be emphasized that the preceding courage ladder is just an example. There is absolutely no implication that all people who are growing their courage in the area of getting out of the house will have the same steps or do them in the same order. For someone else, going to a party might be more difficult than signing up for a class. Everything is individually tailored to the details in your life: people and places and, maybe most important, the things that are special about them and about you. So there are no "standard courage ladders" for driving, public speaking, or anything else. Every courage ladder is different, and it's custom designed *for* you and *by* you. Getting some ideas from this program, a therapist, or someone in your life sometimes helps to keep the steps small and specific, but no one knows the details that matter as well as you do. So if there is a "design team," you are its most important member!

And there is another thing. For some people, really important steps on the courage ladder might include planning how you'll acknowledge to someone in your life that you haven't reached out to him or her for a while. The courage ladder might include anticipating what that other person might say or do, and how you plan to respond, even if it's hard. It might include taking a little break and coming back to things later. Sometimes courage ladders include some steps on what to do when things don't go as you've planned, or when events bring something into your life before you've had a chance to take the steps that would ideally get you ready for it. As mentioned before, courage ladders definitely include both expecting things to be hard and reflecting back on your victories.

What do you do with a courage ladder once you have it? The most elegant thing is to *do* those things you just wrote down. You can do this fast or slowly, a little bit at a time. You might wait for a while and take many steps in quick succession. As with everything else, you have to take your steps in a way that works for you. But whatever your pace, experts on skill acquisition tell us that to grow your courage, *you do have to do the things on your courage ladder, and that there is really no good substitute for this.* Sometimes that means doing them even when you don't feel fully ready. Research on classes like this has shown that the people who do the things on their courage ladders are the ones who tend to get the best results.[1]

[1]See Quick (1983) in References.

TOOLS FOR PANIC ATTACKS

Can you make a courage ladder for panic attacks? Yes, this is an important variation. With panic attacks, many people benefit tremendously from "exposure" to two things. First, it can be helpful to spend time in the place or situation where panic happens. Second, and sometimes even more powerful and important, is exposing yourself to the *sensations* in your body that you fear and hate the most. The term "interoceptive exposure"[2] is sometimes used to describe deliberately bringing on the sensations.

So, how might you do this? To create the feeling of your heart pounding, you might run up the stairs. You could do that a little at a time by going up one flight, then two flights, and so on. Every time, you feel your heart pound, and you hate it, but you remember: "This is my practice. This is what the program said I would feel." And you notice that gradually your heart slows down, and the sensation subsides.

If the scariest thing for you is feeling dizzy, you might deliberately create that sensation, maybe by sitting in a swivel chair and spinning around a few times. You might feel dizzy or nauseous, but that's exactly what you want to reproduce. You stop, you wait, and gradually the feeling starts to go away.

To create a feeling that things are unreal (sometimes called "depersonalization"), you might stare real hard at something, just something like the back of your hand. Then you look away, look around you, see the familiar surroundings, and things start feeling real again. You can do the staring for gradually longer periods of time.

One very common sensation in anxiety is rapid breathing, or hyperventilation. You might think about how you could deliberately breathe faster. For some people, a really easy way to do that is to pant, like a dog. You feel your breathing speed up, you hate it, and then you just breathe normally, and you wait. And your breathing slows down again.

The next suggestion might sound totally bizarre: When you succeed in "bringing the sensations on," you *actively welcome* them and even try to *increase* them! You might be thinking that this is the strangest and most unpleasant thing you've ever heard. After all, you're reading this because you want to *get rid of* these feelings, and you're reading about deliberately *increasing* them! Yes, this can seem *so* weird. But you are invited to remember the perspective about the commonsense and the counterintuitive. As you probably have noticed, this interoceptive exposure part, deliberately

[2]See Craske et al. (1997) in References.

bringing on what you hate and fear most, is counterintuitive. It's the *opposite* of what you might expect. And even though it may feel so unnatural, some people find it one of the most useful things they can do to take the power away from panic.

TOOLS FOR "OBSESSIONS AND COMPULSIONS"

Next, we will consider how people sometimes use our exposure and habituation tools when they want to change the following two things: first, thinking too much about something, and second, doing too much of something (such as washing their hands or checking the locks all the time). Sometimes people call these their obsessions or compulsions. But you don't have to give these things "psychological labels" to be able to change them. Here, the first thing you might do is to pick the thought or behavior you want to decrease. You pick just one thing. Once you've selected it, then you *delay* or *postpone* doing it. You do this really briefly, maybe just for a couple of seconds. Then you postpone it just a little longer, and then a tiny bit longer. Maybe it feels weird to postpone it, but you discover that you can do it anyway. Or maybe it doesn't feel as hard as you thought it would! You let yourself be curious and just notice what you discover. And then maybe you start postponing it for increasingly longer intervals. The technical name for this is "exposure and response prevention," because you're "exposing" yourself to whatever is hard for you to tolerate, and you're "preventing" your typical response. And that helps you to become "habituated," to learn that you can tolerate longer and longer intervals without the thought or the behavior.

So, you experiment with this. And then, whenever you don't want to postpone it any more, you go ahead and think your thought or do your behavior. There is another thing you might try here: You go ahead and do your regular behavior, or you think your usual thought, but you change something about the *way* you do it. How might you do that? For a thought, you might *sing* it or say it in Pig Latin. For a behavior, when at any point you are done postponing it (for now), you might do it in slow motion, or you might decide to change some aspect of it. Some people who would like to wash their hands less often have discovered the trick of squeezing the soap pump with the hand that they don't usually use for that or picking up the cake of soap with the other hand. Some people discover wonderful and creative ways to "mess with" the habit they want to change.

TOOLS FOR SOCIAL SITUATIONS

For discomfort around other people, sometimes called social anxiety or social phobia, one of the most important tools is entering social situations a little at a time. You talk to people just a bit. You start with people who seem "safer" (and exactly who that might be depends on your interests and strengths). You might start by asking someone a question, maybe an open-ended one, so that the other person is likely to respond with more than "Yes" or "No."

Here is one little exercise that many people find useful when they are feeling shy about being in a place where people usually talk to each other. You imagine that you are an expert on shyness and are, in fact, the "second shyest" person in the room. Your mission is to see if you can discover the one person in the room who is shyer than you are. When you think you have figured out who that might be, you go over to that person and say something that will make him or her feel more comfortable. Some people discover that rather than trying to "hide" their shyness in that situation, they openly acknowledge it (for example, by saying "I'm *so* not good at small talk"). Again, this is somewhat counterintuitive—very different from trying to *hide* your anxiety or pretend you're super comfortable. Often, the other person says, "I'm not good at small talk either"!

Whatever method you use, it frequently helps to *expect* that the step might feel uncomfortable—and that you're going to do it anyway. And you might be surprised: It might be easier than you anticipated. It might be fun! Or it might be hard, and you might feel really proud that you did it anyway. You may never *love* big parties or giving talks or signing your name in public, but you learn that when you have to, you can do it. Accepting that you don't have to love it is actually another valuable ingredient of the solution!

TOOLS FOR "WORRY"

Worry is an extremely common experience. Some of us often expect that the worst is going to happen. We might feel anxious when something familiar is about to change. We might feel tension in our bodies a lot of the time. This is sometimes called "generalized anxiety." In response to our concerns, other people tell us "Don't worry," and we say that to ourselves, as well. Unfortunately, this commonsense suggestion often doesn't work well enough. So this program suggests some different ideas.

It has been said that people who get anxious "worship comfort" and "worship certainty." We may be "body reactors" and "mind reactors." (These are concepts introduced in Topic One. You may have already read about them; if not, you will be reading about them soon.) If your body or mind is "hard wired" to react really strongly to things, in a way it makes *no difference* what the particular *content* is of the worry (or the obsession, or the sensation). The specific content—the place you have to go next week, how cold it will be tomorrow, for example—just happened to "be there," and your mind "grabbed it," like little "Pac man guys" grabbing something, just because it was there.

So this program suggests this four-part idea:

1. Act *as if* the content were irrelevant.
2. Accept the worry, obsession, sensation (whatever it might be—this is useful for panic too) when it comes—like, "*Of course,* I'm having all these thoughts (sensations, doing this over and over); this is what my body (or mind) does!" Or, if it's helpful for you to give a name to what you're experiencing, you could say it like this: "*Of course,* I have these sensations, fears, thoughts—I have generalized anxiety disorder (OCD, panic disorder)!"
3. *Seek out* uncertainty.
4. *Seek out* discomfort.[3]

Again, this counterintuitive idea of deliberately seeking out what you most hate and fear might sound *totally weird*. But for many people, *grasping* this concept and then actually *doing this* results in decreased worry. "Getting this" may actually be more critical than the severity or duration of the anxiety, and that is good news for people who have felt worried for a long time or who have lots of anxiety.

Here is an interesting question you can ask yourself when you worry: Is the thing I'm worried about right now more *signal* or *noise*?

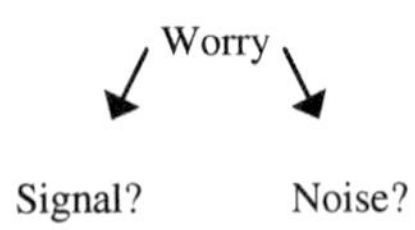

Figure B.2 Worry: signal or noise?

[3]See Wilson (2002a) in References.

This is like listening to music on the radio, where the music is the signal and the static is the noise. With anxiety, when your concern is more of a "signal," there really *is* something going on that is valid and legitimate to worry about. Once you recognize this, you can do some extremely useful and important things in preparation. You can problem solve. You can plan how you will cope if things are difficult. You can visualize the near future, when the hardest part of this is behind you. It is sometimes said that if you spend the afternoon worrying, what you have at the end of the afternoon is a headache. If you put a pen, pencil, phone, or computer mouse in your hand while you worry, what you have at the end of the afternoon is a plan. So you are invited to transform your worry into a plan.

If you decide that your anxiety is more "noise," you can use many of the tools introduced in some of the other readings, such as the physical coping techniques and thinking coping techniques. To use your "exposure" tools, you can "expose" yourself to uncertainty and discomfort in multiple ways. Here is one interesting and playful exercise to do in a restaurant: You are looking at a menu and are undecided about what to order: You might push yourself to make a decision in 20 seconds, and you actively look for the discomfort that comes with the possibility that you didn't pick the "best thing."[4]

Here is another thing to consider: If you ever can't decide whether your worry is "signal" or "noise," you might begin by assuming that there *is* something legitimate to be concerned about, and you plan for how you will cope with what might come up. Some people find it intriguing that a solution focused anxiety management class would suggest the more "cautious" stance as a "default position" approach to a situation!

There is some fascinating research that suggests that some people actually perform *better* on tasks if they take the time to anticipate what might go wrong and plan how they might handle the situation. If they *don't* take the time to do this, they actually feel worse and perform worse! Sometimes this is called "defensive pessimism," and there is a whole website on the topic (www.defensivepessimism.com).[5] Again, this is an example of a place where a counterintuitive approach works better for some people than the commonsense message of "Don't worry."

[4]See Wilson (2002b) in References.
[5]See Norem (2001) in References.

WRITE, READ, AND SHRED

Write, read, and shred is a much-loved technique for worry and obsessive thoughts. Here's how you do it. You get a pad of paper (lined paper is best) and pen or pencil, and you set a timer, like a kitchen timer, for 10 to 20 minutes. After you set your timer, you start writing what you're worried about—or anything at all. The only "rule" in this technique is that you are supposed to keep writing until the timer sounds. If you run out of things to write, you are supposed to just keep copying what you've already written, continuously writing until the timer sounds. Then you read it, silently, to yourself.

And then you shred it. If you don't have a shredder, you are supposed to take a pair of scissors and cross cut it in little tiny pieces and throw them away. This isn't a journal you keep to read later, or to bring to your therapist, or, heaven forbid, for your grandchildren to find some day. That's also why you never do this on your computer, and just delete it, because with modern technology, there is always a chance something could be retrieved. You are physically destroying what you've written. There seems to be something symbolic about cutting up and getting rid of your worry and doing it again the next day and the next day. This combination of writing your worry and getting rid of it becomes part of your routine. So that the things you think and write about don't interfere with sleep, many people find that it is best to use this method early in the day. Some people like to think of it being like "an emotional bowel movement," because when they "get it out," they feel much better!

TOOLS FOR ANXIETY ABOUT MEDICAL PROCEDURES

Here are some ideas for anxiety about medical procedures and appointments. Because many medical procedures can feel unpleasant and scary, it's really normal not to like those things. But when your anxiety interferes with taking good care of your health or getting care you need, growing your courage and coping are good and important things you can do for yourself. In many ways, exposure and habituation are applicable here, just as they are with any other fear. When people learn that they can tolerate a dental procedure, for instance, it might be easier to go to the dentist the next time. Sometimes it helps to openly acknowledge to the medical provider that you might get anxious, or wince, or make a noise (the counterintuitive perspective again). Some people find it helpful to have detailed information, from the doctor or dentist or lab tech, or from a handout, or from the Internet, about what will be done. Other people would rather not know the details. This is one of those situations in which the same thing doesn't work for everyone, and you need to discover what works for you. Some people like to distract themselves while a procedure is going on. You can count backward, find right angles in the room, or anything else. Whatever you do, it *definitely* helps to remember to breathe!

WHEN "PURE" EXPOSURE ISN'T APPLICABLE

As noted earlier, exposure and habituation are useful for medical procedures on many occasions. But there is another thing to consider here: the fact that there are some things—and some medical procedures fall into this category—that you *can't* (or wouldn't want to) do a little at a time. For example, no one would tell somebody to deliberately have five unnecessary minor surgeries in preparation for major surgery!

So, when exposure in "real life" is something you just wouldn't do, it can be helpful to *imagine* being in the situation. This may even include imagining the "worst case scenario." This may be easier to do than you might think, because people who experience anxiety tend to have *wonderful* imaginations! After all, they can imagine all kinds of terrible things! So, you are invited to use that excellent imagination to visualize yourself *coping* with whatever is going on. That absolutely doesn't mean that you have to like it! But you are doing it. You're getting through it. You're tapping strength and courage that are already solidly inside you. You already know how to do this. You have done it far more times than you may realize. You already know how to do boring, distasteful, and uncomfortable things. You might remember that you've taken out the garbage. You've probably paid taxes and insurance premiums. In school, you've studied for and taken tests. You may have kept an appointment with the urologist or the gynecologist. It wasn't something you loved, but you did it. You got it over with, and that was better for you, in some way, than avoiding it.

Sometimes, when we're imagining doing something that's really scary, and playing that "video in our mind," we consciously or unconsciously "stop the action" at the worst possible moment. This might be the moment when we're "freaking out" or can't possibly imagine it getting any worse. In this technique, you *don't* stop the action there. Instead, you force yourself to keep the video going. You play it out to the end: What happens next? And next? And next? *After* you have that horrible panic attack and they take you to the emergency room? *After* you get fired from your job? You finish the video, and you include the part where, even if your knee is bruised or your pride is bruised, someone else has created far more drama than you have, and you have picked up the pieces and moved on.

BEING ANXIOUS AND DOING IT ANYWAY

Sometimes when people read this, they have the following reaction: "Well, maybe I *should* do all that stuff—the imagining, the courage ladder, the bringing it on. But I'm not ready. I'm way too anxious right now. I need to wait till I'm ready." On one level, that's absolutely something to be aware of and to respect. After all, we all change at our own pace and in our own way. But, at the same time, you probably also know this: If you wait until you're 100% comfortable or "ready" to do something, you may be waiting forever! As a result, doing a *little* more than you feel "ready" to do can be useful. You might think of the situation like this: Being anxious and doing it anyway aren't mutually exclusive. It's sort of like walking and chewing gum: You can do both at the same time.

Here is an even more "physical" example: You might remember a time when you were in your car, either driving or riding, and you had to go to the bathroom. There was no place to stop, and you had to "hold it" for a while. You somehow drove, or were a passenger, safely, and appropriately, even though you "had to go." You already know *from your own experience* that it's possible for you to have both psychological and physical discomfort—and to do something safely and appropriately anyway.

DISCOVERING AND BUILDING ON HOW YOU LEARN

Now you are invited to discover how you best learn things. All of us, if you think about it, have an amazing amount of life experience. And we all have our individual ways of learning. So you are invited to think about a new skill you learned at some point—either recently or a while back, it doesn't matter—that was a significant piece of learning. Maybe it was something like learning to use a computer, or a cell phone, or a digital camera. Maybe it was learning to play a sport, or an instrument, or to speak a different language, or to do woodworking. Maybe it was learning to drive a car. Maybe it was learning how to take care of a baby. Maybe it was learning how to put in contact lenses. Whatever it was, allow yourself to remember what worked for you in learning that skill. What were the critical ingredients? Observing others? Practice, over and over again? Reading? Time alone, to make as many mistakes as you needed to make? What was the hardest part? The most fun? Did the learning happen gradually, a little at a time, or was there an "aha" experience, when suddenly you knew what to do? Allow yourself to enjoy remembering how that skill grew.

BUILDING YOUR COURAGE LADDER

Remembering how your learning grows will help you to build a courage ladder in whatever way feels right for you. So you are invited *right now* to create some little, tiny steps—the smaller, the better. You might remember that the courage ladder concept is one you can use to build all kinds of changes, from very behavioral ones to more internal or interpersonal ones. You can build a courage ladder for the sensations of panic, and you can use it to practice worrying and then doing something anyway.

Sometimes a good way to start your courage ladder is to write one really easy item, on one note card (or at the top of your list). Then you write a really difficult one on another card (or at the bottom of your list). Then you work forward and backward. Remember to add a card (or an item) where you *imagine* taking a step, before you actually do so. Then there is the step where you actually do it. Then you add the step where you tell yourself: "I did it!"

And if there is no particular thing in your life to increase right now, the courage ladder is a tool to keep in your toolbox, for whenever you need it later.

SUGGESTIONS FOR PRACTICE

Here are some ideas for experimenting with these ideas on your own. Please use *any* ideas or suggestions from this class or these readings in a way that works for you.

First, if you have already begun a courage ladder, as described earlier, you are invited to continue building and refining it. Once you start thinking of little steps, you will probably recognize more and more of them! Keep adding baby steps, and remember that the tinier and more specific they are, the better. Remember to include on your cards you visualizing yourself getting through the hard parts, and remember to include cards that remind you to celebrate what you've done.

Second, if you have a courage ladder, you are encouraged to take some steps on it. Not big ones—just little, tiny ones. You might notice how you use what you already know about how learning best happens for you. Notice how you learn, and change, even when it's hard, and celebrate your courage!

Finally, whether or not you currently have a courage ladder, you are invited to notice the times when you experience some discomfort, or distraction, of some kind, and somehow "do something anyway." An example might be: You're watching television, and you have a gas pain. It's not so bad that you have to get up and go to the bathroom, but you can feel it. You keep watching your program, and the feeling subsides. Or, you're walking across your bedroom, and you stub your toe. It hurts! You hop, and yelp, and maybe mutter your favorite four-letter word. But you continue wherever you were going. Or you're washing dishes. A song on the radio stirs a memory. Tears well in your eyes. And you keep washing the dishes through the tears. Or you go to your mailbox for the mail. You see a letter you are definitely not looking forward to opening. Your heart pounds. You have the urge to throw it away. But you carry it into the house and open it. Or your breathing starts getting short. You feel like a panic attack is coming. But you ride the wave, and your breathing calms down.

As you notice examples of this in your own life, you are likely to become increasingly aware of the amazing ability you already have, in so many areas, to "have discomfort and do something anyway." Pay attention to how you do that, and what that teaches you about "being anxious and doing it anyway."

SOLUTION FOCUSED ANXIETY MANAGEMENT

END OF SESSION FORM

Name ______________________________ Date______________________

When you first called for help with your anxiety	Your level of concern or caution is appropriate, not excessive. Anxiety is not so much a problem any more

0 1 2 3 4 5 6 7 8 9 10

What do you want to remember from today?

What helps you to cope with discomfort, uncertainty, worry, and stress?

What else do you want to continue, because you know it works for you?

APPENDIX C

Learner Readings for Topic Three: Thinking Techniques

This reading covers the information presented in Topic Three. This may or may not be the first handout in this series that you are reading, and that is perfectly okay. You can begin any place in the series that you like.

In this series, you are learning to celebrate and build courage. You are discovering how to ride through sensations and discomfort in a way that works for you. You are learning that anxiety doesn't have to get in the way of the things you want to do, and you are learning that anxiety certainly isn't the most interesting thing about you. Please use, adapt, and share this material in any way that works for you. By reading this short handout, *right now* you are doing a good thing for yourself and taking a step in the right direction.

Topic Three discusses how our thoughts support courage, coping, appropriate caution, and choice. It invites acceptance of feelings and reality, in combination with recognition of perspectives that make a difference. Like everything else in this class, please use this information in the way that works best for you!

THINKING TECHNIQUES

Sometimes when people have coped with a tough situation and you ask them how they did it, they say something like this: "I remembered that even though it feels like 'I can't stand it,' I *have* gotten through it before."

Sometimes a thought popping into your head soothes you. It reminds you of your strengths, or of a different perspective, and you feel better able to cope. If that has ever happened to you, you have discovered on your own something that modern psychology has written a whole lot about! Those are the thinking coping techniques, sometimes called "cognitive" techniques—another "tool in your toolbox" to experiment with and discover whether it fits for you.

So, *thinking* coping techniques are sentences or phrases you say to yourself in your head. Or they might be images you visualize, that support you as you approach a frightening situation. That's really important, because when we are feeling anxious or scared, we sometimes say things that *increase* rather than decrease our anxiety. For example, if a person keeps thinking, while on the way to a meeting, "I know I'm going to blow it; I won't have a thing to say; I'm going to feel like an absolute fool," he or she will probably feel *more* anxious by the time he or she gets there.

And we sometimes say things like that to ourselves in our heads without being fully aware that we are doing so. We may not realize at that moment that we can do something different. So learning about thinking coping techniques reminds us of something we probably already know: You can, and you probably already do, use your thoughts and images to support your courage and strength. This section invites noticing how you do that and doing more of it.

Here is the background for this. We sometimes assume that certain external events "cause" our feelings and our behavior. But the process is different from that. The exact same external thing—for example, a sunny day—can sometimes produce radically different reactions in different people. The reason is that external events—and internal reactions, too—have certain *meanings* to us. They trigger thoughts and images almost automatically. Sometimes these get called "automatic thoughts," and those reactions can have a lightning-fast impact on how we feel and what we do.

A	→	B	→	C
Event		Automatic Thoughts Meaning		Feelings Behavior

Figure C.1 Basic A – B – C diagram.

In our sunny day example, one person might be delighted that the sun is out, whereas another might feel internal pressure to be outdoors when she really wants to work on projects at home.

A	→	B	→	C
Sunny day		Oh, crap. Sun's out again. Have to go somewhere. Never get to do what I really want to do.		Irritable Sulks, snaps

Figure C.2 A – B – C diagram: Dislikes sunny day.

So, the challenge is this: If this person wants clouds and gets sun, is there anything she might say to herself in her head at Point B so that at Point C she might feel and do something different? Yes, there is: a powerful and amazingly useful two-part formula that helps you to make that crucial change at Point B.

The *first* step is to "accept" two things: first, the reality of the situation, and second, how you feel about it.

The *second* step is to say "But." And after the "But," you add something like this: "I'm going to be *stubborn* enough not to let that external thing stop me from what I really want to do." And that can make a *big difference* in how you feel and what you do.

So, in our example, "I wanted clouds, but got sun" is the "reality" of the situation. And "I don't like it!" is the feeling. Or, maybe the "feeling" is a mixed one, like this: "Part of me likes it and is actually tempted to go for a walk, and part of me doesn't like it because I *always* go for walks and never get to do quilting and inside stuff."

Now we will add Step Two: "But—I'm going to be stubborn enough not to let the weather stop me from what I really want to do. It's way easier to stay home when it's gray outside, but I really want to quilt today. I think I'll sit in this sunny window and work on my quilting."

A →	B →	C
Sunny day	1a. I wanted clouds and got sun.	Mixture of irritation, amusement, pride, satisfaction.
	1b. I don't like it. Actually, mixed feelings	
	But—stubborn, do quilting anyway	Quilting!

Figure C.3 A – B – C diagram: Using two-part formula for sunny day.

Here is an example involving anxiety. The external thing at Point A is an elevator. A person who doesn't mind elevators is probably thinking about the destination (friend or appointment upstairs) while waiting for the elevator (Point B). At Point C, that person's feelings are likely to be neutral, and the behavior is entering the elevator.

For the person who is afraid of elevators—and using our formula—the process might look like this. At Point B, there might be an intense focus on three things: how very dangerous it is, the high probability of something bad happening, and a feeling of helplessness, such as "There's nothing I can do to make it better."

But our courageous friend is about to use our formula. He or she might consider this "reality" of the situation: Elevators *do* sometimes get stuck. One *could* get trapped. Maybe part of the reality is that our friend actually *has* been stuck in an elevator in the past. And the "feeling" is "I'm scared!" Maybe it's also "I'm embarrassed about being scared," and "I really want to change this."

Next, our friend might use our step of saying, "But—I'm going to be stubborn enough to not let my fear control my life." And our friend might add something else. If fear *grows* by "turning up the volume" on the details of danger, on the probability of bad things happening, and on feeling helpless, then maybe fear *shrinks* by "turning down the volume" on those things. *Courage* grows when we "turn up the volume" on other things.

So our friend might remember things that help keep us safe and the likelihood of good things happening (or bad things ending). He or she might remember the many strengths that empower us and enable us to cope when things are tough. Our friend might remember, "I know that elevators really don't get stuck very often. And if this one does, I actually know some things I could do. I could call my friend on my cell phone. Sometimes phones work in elevators, so it's worth a try. Or I could push that little 'attendant call' button. I can remember to breathe. I can do this even if it's scary."

A →	B →	C
Elevator	1a. It could get stuck. b. I'm scared!	Fear (a little less) Get on anyway
	2. But—it probably won't. And if it does, I will use cell, call button, breathe, remember that I can do this!	

Figure C.4 A – B – C diagram: Using two-part formula for elevator.

In the next example, the scary thing at Point A is a *sensation*. This is incredibly valuable for anyone who gets *panic attacks*. In this example, at Point A, the person might be having chest pain. And the immediate thought at Point B is "Heart attack!" At Point C, the feeling is intense fear, and the behavior includes whatever we do when we feel very afraid.

Here is an example of how one might use Step One of the formula here. "The *reality* of the situation is that my chest is hurting. It *could be* a heart attack. It could also be one of those stupid panic attacks. When I was at the emergency room the last time this happened, they did an EKG and told me my heart is fine, and that this is panic. The *feeling* is that I'm scared. And I *hate* it when this happens. And I'm *confused*. I don't know if I should call an ambulance, or wait it out. Yuck!

Here is Step Two. "But—I need to remember that this probably is one of those 'expletive deleted' panic attacks I hate so much. Okay, breathe. I can still think. I can remember that they told me I'm a 'body reactor.' I can wait for it to pass. I can call my friend. I can use my brain. If I want some advice on what to do, I can call that emergency phone service that my healthcare offers and tell them what's going on. I've been through this before. I do know what to do."

And now, our friend may still feel scared, but it's very, very different from totally freaking out. There is empowerment, and soothing, and a plan.

A →	B →	C
Chest pain	1a. My chest hurts. It *could* be a heart attack. It could also be panic. The reality is that right now I don't know which it is. b. I'm scared! And more! 2. But—I need to remember: I'm a body reactor. It probably will pass. I'm not helpless. Breathe! Use your brain. Call healthcare provider if you need to.	Fear (a little less) Sense of control

Figure C.5 A – B – C diagram: Using two-part formula for chest pain.

This is so incredibly important because we may not always be able to change certain things that happen out in the world. We also may not be able to control our first, immediate reaction, or certain sensations in our bodies. But we *can* learn to see things in a different way. You probably already do so, maybe more often than you realize. And that can make a tremendous difference in how you feel and in what you do.

Another way of writing this is shown in the following chart.

Thoughts Now (might increase anxiety)	Alternate Thoughts (might decrease anxiety)

Figure C.6 Thoughts and alternatives basic chart.

On the following pages, the second column of the chart includes things that people sometimes say to themselves in their heads that end up making them more anxious than they want to be. In the next column, for each one of these thoughts, there are several alternatives, things that you might say instead. These are alternatives that could empower you or give you a different "take" on the situation.

The way to use this chart is to read a thought on the left. If it "sounds like you," you might want to put a mark next to it, in the first column. Next, you read the suggested alternatives on the right. If any of these seem like they might be useful to experiment with instead, you might put a mark next to those, in the right margin. Better yet, if there is a thought that you are already using or can think of, you might add it (under "What else?"), because the very best thoughts are the ones that come from you!

Worksheet C.1

SOLUTION FOCUSED ANXIETY MANAGEMENT
AUTOMATIC THOUGHTS AND ALTERNATE PERSPECTIVES WORKSHEET

Check here if this one sounds like you	Common Automatic Thoughts	Alternate Perspectives	Check here if this one might be useful
	I. Weird physical symptoms again. I bet I'm going to lose it.	1. I need to remember: I'm a body reactor. 2. These feelings will build and crest and then come down on their own, just like they always do. 3. The fact that they're here right now doesn't mean I'm going to lose it. 4. These feelings don't always turn into a full panic attack. 5. Now that I know what they are, they aren't as scary as they used to be. 6. (If taking medicine) Now that I have this medicine in me, the sensations don't scare me as much. The medicine helps them just drift away. 7. What else?	
	II. I'm getting anxious. I'm not going to be able to function (speak, drive, take this exam, stay in this room, ______________).	1. Yes, I will. I've done it before. 2. It's like "walking and chewing gum at the same time." 3. The discomfort I feel at first will subside. 4. Hang in there. You can do it. 5. What else?	
	III. I can't go. I'll fall apart.	1. That's how I feel right this minute. I can allow that to be there, and get ready to go, even with my feelings, and watch the feelings change. 2. What do I need to do to nurture myself right now? 3. What will be more helpful: a "push" to go, even in the presence of my anxiety, or "permission," to take my time—or both? 4. What else?	

	IV. I take pride in my high standards, and I'm not measuring up.	1. Yes, it's hard for me when I don't do as well as I'd like. I need to be really gentle and nurturing to myself right now. 2. I can ask myself: What is the single most important thing I can do to right now to feel proud of how I handled this? 3. If I've made an error, I can acknowledge it, with self-respect and dignity, and get things back on track. 4. "What do they call the person who graduated at the bottom of the class in medical school? Doctor." 5. What else?	
	V. If I can't do it perfectly, I'd rather not do it at all.	1. It's uncomfortable for me when I'm imperfect, but I can remember that I don't have to be perfect in order to do a good job. 2. Pushing myself to be perfect sometimes becomes counterproductive, because so much energy goes into worrying that it can detract from my performance. 3. When something goes imperfectly, I can get back on track. 4. Being able to recover seamlessly may be an even more important skill than doing it perfectly in the first place. 5. Requiring perfection contradicts everything we know about skill acquisition and climbing courage ladders. 6. Elbert Hubbard: "The greatest mistake you can make in life is to be continually fearing you will make one." 7. Do two things imperfectly every day. 8. What else?	

	VI. I can't help it that I have a short fuse when I get anxious. After all, I have a chemical imbalance!	1. Yes, I get irritable. But that doesn't give me license to lash out at other people. 2. Lashing out usually doesn't get other people to change much anyway. 3. People just start telling me that I have an "anger problem," and the focus shifts away from whatever I wanted to express. Instead, I look like the bad guy! 4. It's *not* completely true that "I can't help it": If someone said, "Hey, you get a hundred thousand dollars if you can keep from lashing out," I bet I could do it—even if I do have a chemical imbalance. 5. What else?	
	VII. I've always been a sensitive person. I can't handle rejection or criticism or people being mad at me.	1. Yes, criticism and conflict are hard, but I *can* cope with them. 2. I've done it before, and I can do it again. 3. I need to remember that people may not approve because of *their* issues. It isn't always because something's wrong with me. 4. Relationships are resilient, and even though it might be hard to remember right now, sometimes disagreement and working it through make relationships stronger. 5. Sometimes I'm sensitive, but I have more strength inside than other people realize—and maybe more than I realize, too. 6. What else?	
	VIII. There's something very wrong with me.	1. It sure feels like that when these reactions happen! 2. I need to remember that experts tell us that anxiety can manifest itself in lots of different ways. 3. I can get checked out medically if I have concerns that there's something medical going on that I don't know about.	

		4. I can remember that if I've been diagnosed with an "anxiety disorder," the thing that is "wrong with me" has a formal name ("anxiety disorder"). 5. I'm here: I'm doing something about it; I'm getting treatment for it. 6. What else?	
	IX. Calm down. Don't worry about it.	1. That's *way* easier to say than to do! 2. Given my style, and how I'm "hard wired," I probably *will* worry sometimes, and maybe more than other people do. 3. If my worry helps me to prepare, or to handle it when things are hard, then I'm using it in a productive way. 4. I think about *many* different things—some of them are things I worry about, but lots of them have nothing to do with my worries. 5. Some of my thoughts are actually pretty creative! 6. What else?	
	X. I can't handle it if things don't go the way I want them to. (Someone once said we all have a little two-year-old inside, and that little person has a temper tantrum when he or she doesn't get his or her own way! I sure know that little person inside me!)	1. I can treat myself the way I would lovingly nurture a two-year-old: I would hold that frustrated little person tight and say "I know how you feel." 2. I can remind myself, "You don't have to like it, and it's okay to fuss a little if you need to. And after you fuss, you *will* get through this." 3. What else?	
	XI. I need things to be just a certain way, and I lose it when things are different.	1. Yes, structure and order and routine support me a lot, and it *is* harder for me when things are different. But I understand that about myself, and that insight helps me to cope. 2. It helps me so I *don't* "lose it." 3. I'm practicing strengthening my "flexibility muscles." 4. What else?	

	XII. I can't handle uncertainty or change or when things go wrong.	1. I don't like those things, but I actually have more capacity to tolerate them than I may give myself credit for. 2. After my initial reaction subsides, I will use the resources, internal and external, that support me. 3. I can remember my sense of humor. 4. Elbert Hubbard: "Life is one damned thing after another." 5. John Lennon: "Life is what happens to you while you're busy making other plans." 6. What else?	
	XIII. I'm socially inept.	1. If social interactions are difficult for me, I can grow my skills with practice. 2. I can smile. 3. I can ask questions. 4. I can ask other people about themselves. 5. I can listen. 6. I can remember that being quieter is okay. 7. What else?	
	XIV. After what happened to me before, I can't do it (go there, try that) again.	1. Of course, I'm apprehensive. But I care too much about doing this *not* to go back. 2. It *will* be hard at first. 3. It's important to me to do this, so I'm going to tolerate the discomfort. 4. What else?	
	XV. I'm too anxious to practice.	1. Although it absolutely feels that way, practicing is actually one of the very best ways of growing my skills and comfort and confidence. 2. The more I do it, even with my discomfort, the better I will get, and the less anxious I will be. 3. There is the counterintuitive again! 4. What else?	

	XVI. The worst possible thing is going to happen. I just know it will.	1. It *feels* that way, but I need to remember that *feeling* that something bad will happen doesn't mean that the bad thing *will* happen. 2. The reality is that I absolutely don't know at this moment what the future is going to bring. Whether for better or worse, I cannot predict the future! 3. It's true that the worst *could* happen, even if the probability of it is low. But the *possibility* of something bad happening doesn't mean that there is a high *probability* that it will. 4. The best could happen, too, and there could be an outcome that is in between. 5. I need to remember that I've tolerated uncertainty before, and I can do it again. 6. I have more ability to tolerate "not knowing" than I sometimes give myself credit for. 7. What else?	
	XVII. If there is something bad that might happen, I can't stop obsessing and thinking about it.	1. It may *feel* like worrying prevents bad things from happening, but it actually doesn't. 2. What *does* help is planning and problem solving and anticipating how I might avoid trouble—and planning how I'll cope with it and support myself if something bad does happen. 3. When worry visits me, I need to use it as a reminder to start problem solving as soon as possible. 4. If this isn't the best time to do problem solving, I can allow the thoughts to "just be" and then allow them to drift elsewhere. 5. I can distract and soothe myself. 6. I can write my worries or worst fears, or share them with a trusted person if that helps me. 7. I can decide what I need right now and do what works for me. 8. What else?	

	XVIII. I can't stand being alone. I have to have someone with me.	1. I may not *like* being left alone. It's lonely and sometimes I worry, but I *can* stand it. 2. Sometimes being alone is actually fun. I can do exactly what I want and don't have to worry about anyone else! 3. What else?	
	XIX. My anxiety is a result of very real past trauma, so it's going to be with me forever.	1. Reality now is different from reality then: Something may have been necessary for survival once, but *not* now. 2. I learned that old response; in the same way, I can learn a new response now. 3. The past is not an excuse. 4. A trauma may leave a scar forever, but an arm or leg with a scar can still work and play—and so can I. 5. What else?	
	XX. Avoiding is better than facing it. If I don't put myself out there, at least nothing bad is going to happen.	1. On one level, it may be true that nothing bad will happen, but on another level, if something truly needs to get done eventually, avoidance only postpones the inevitable. 2. It's still hanging over me. I will feel better when I get it over with. 3. If this is something I really *do* want to do, or maybe part of me wants to do, I'm going to feel frustrated and disappointed in myself. 4. For some situations, choosing not to do something is absolutely a legitimate option. 5. I can choose *not* to do something for now and change my mind later. 6. I can—and I don't have to. 7. What else?	

	XXI. My anxiety is going to show. People are going to be able to tell how anxious I am. I'll be humiliated.	1. Telling others about my situation, in self-respect and dignity, when *I* choose to do so, is a way of taking control and creating a safe environment for myself. 2. Self-disclosure usually enhances relationships, while concealing detracts from them. 3. Self-disclosure frequently results in others acknowledging their own fears, which may be more like mine than I realized. 4. What else?	
	XXII. I *have* to be in control. I can't stand it when I'm *not* in control.	1. There are people, and situations, and sensations in my body that sometimes I just can't control, however much I wish I could. 2. To accept these moments when I temporarily feel out of control is really the ultimate control (a pretty powerful existential statement). 3. What else?	

Now that you have read the ideas in the worksheet, you are invited to reflect on the ones that resonate for you. You might also want to consider which of these things you would be most likely to say to a child or a dear friend. You probably already say some wonderful and supportive things to the people in your life! It is also possible that, like many of us, you may have a bit of a "double standard": Sometimes we are so nurturing to other people—and so "mean" to ourselves. So, if you ever can't think of what you might say to yourself at Point B, or on the right side of the chart, you might consider what you might say to a child. People sometimes talk about having an "inner child," and you can nurture the "child" within you.

How might you use all this information? One way is to experiment with "catching yourself in the act" of having the thoughts or images that get you more anxious than you would like to be. When you notice one, you might experiment with saying an alternative in its place. Doing so may well feel awkward, and it probably won't eliminate discomfort entirely.

But gently reminding yourself of the alternate perspective is worth the effort. That's true even if you do this experiment awkwardly or self-consciously, and even if you don't fully believe the alternate view. The process still can decrease the intensity of your distress. And as this happens, you might notice other thoughts and feelings. You might notice your capacity to tolerate discomfort. You might feel empowered. Or there might be something else, something that we haven't thought of yet. So, you are invited to play with this on your own, with curiosity about what you discover.

Now you are invited to practice this process, using a chart like the one in the following example. Notice that the Alternatives column has been divided into two parts, one for accepting the reality and the feelings, and one for the "But—," just like in our two-part formula. In this example, a man is worried about a job interview. His thoughts snowball, and he begins to imagine catastrophic consequences. For each thought, he has accepted the reality (that the things he fears *could* happen) and how he feels about it (he is scared). The acceptance allows him to take the next step: considering how he would cope, even in the most difficult of circumstances.

Thoughts now	Alternatives	
	Accept a. Reality b. Feeling	But…
I won't be able to answer their questions.	True. Uptight, maybe defensive.	I might be okay. Will review PowerPoint, say "That's a good question."
I'll have a panic attack during the presentation	I might. Embarrassing.	Sweating doesn't always mean full panic. Politicians sweat! Not always noticeable. It will pass.
They'll laugh at me.	Yes, they might. Humiliating.	They probably won't. I wouldn't! I can ignore, laugh too.
We won't get the bid.	Possible. Bummed, obsess.	I'll do my best. Okay to lick wounds; then—next project.
I'll be fired.	Could happen. Devastating.	Probably not. Suck it up, look for new job, go on.
My wife will leave me.	Possible. Devastating.	Probably not (me going overboard…) we'll talk, plan. If worst happens, mourn, go on.
I'll be homeless.	Could happen. Dreadful	Not likely. But if so, after pain, write next chapter. Start with big box!

Figure C.7 Thoughts and alternatives worksheet, worry about interview example.

There is no implication here that the man is actually about to become homeless! Rather, this is a metaphor. Whatever your worst fear may be, the message is this: If it happens, take a small step. (Here, it is finding a big box, like the ones refrigerators come in, and moving it to a safe, sheltered place.) This is the first step in his solution.

Now that you have reviewed this example, you are invited to complete the *Thoughts and Alternatives Worksheet* with an example from your own life.

Worksheet C.2

SOLUTION FOCUSED ANXIETY MANAGEMENT
THOUGHTS AND ALTERNATIVES WORKSHEET

Thoughts now	Alternatives	
	Accept a. Reality b. Feeling	But…

Now that you have completed this worksheet, you might notice how this perspective differs from how you have thought about the situation before. Many people notice that the active invitation to consider—and accept—the possibility of the very worst of the worst is *very* different from past messages we have received. Over and over again, most of us have been told *not* to worry. But that often doesn't remove our fears. Too often, if someone *only* tells us—or we say to ourselves—"Chill out" or "Don't make such a big deal about it," it doesn't silence that worry inside. We *do* worry: "But what if it *does* happen?" Our secret fears tell us that the "bad stuff" absolutely *could* happen, even if it's not very likely. And that possibility scares us. Taking a moment to recognize and accept that fact helps us to see that we're not weird or crazy for wondering about it. Once we do that, in a way we're better able to consider the alternative: a scenario in which even if the worst happens, we find a way to mourn, cope, and go on.

It has been said that in behavior therapy, the first "wave" said: Change your behavior. Then there was a second "wave" that said: Change your thoughts. That was the "cognitive" part. And now there is a "third wave" that says this: It's not just about changing your thoughts. It's also about changing your *relationship* to your thoughts. This is the acceptance part, or the mindfulness part. So we talk about changing our behavior *and* our thoughts *and* our relationship to our thoughts. And we might add to all of that: You have to discover the unique things that work for *you*. In solution focused anxiety management, all of these things are ingredients of the solution.

SUGGESTIONS FOR PRACTICE

Here are some ideas for experimenting with these ideas on your own. Please use *any* ideas or suggestions from this class or these readings in a way that works for you.

The basic suggestion for this section is an invitation to notice your thoughts. As you do so, you are invited to be curious about the ones that support your courage, coping, appropriate caution, and choice. You are invited to remember where you learned these thoughts. If there was a caring person in your life, either in the past or in the present, who said supportive things to you, you might imagine that that person is with you now. That person might be cheering you on and reminding you of how you got through before. And if you discover thoughts that make you more fearful than you would like to be, you might consider what you would like to say to yourself instead. Or you might consider what you would say to a little child who was scared and say that to yourself. And as you do that, you are invited to notice how that makes a difference.

SOLUTION FOCUSED ANXIETY MANAGEMENT

END OF SESSION FORM

Name ____________________________ Date_____________________

When you first called for help with your anxiety									Your level of concern or caution is appropriate, not excessive. Anxiety is not so much a problem any more	
0	1	2	3	4	5	6	7	8	9	10

What do you want to remember from today?

What helps you to cope with discomfort, uncertainty, worry, and stress?

What else do you want to continue, because you know it works for you?

APPENDIX D

Learner Readings for Topic Four: Life Issues and Anxiety

This reading covers the information presented in Topic Four. This may or may not be the first handout in this series that you are reading, and that is perfectly okay. You can begin any place in the series that you like.

In this series, you are learning to celebrate and build courage. You are discovering how to ride through sensations and discomfort in a way that works for you. You are learning that anxiety doesn't have to get in the way of the things you want to do, and you are learning that anxiety certainly isn't the most interesting thing about you. Please use, adapt, and share this material in any way that works for you. By reading this short handout, *right now* you are doing a good thing for yourself and taking a step in the right direction.

Topic Four discusses some issues that many people find useful while, or after, they are growing courage, coping, appropriate caution, and choice in their lives. It is possible, of course, that some of the information may not seem relevant to you. Like everything else in this class, please use this information in whatever way you like!

THE PROS AND CONS OF MANAGING YOUR ANXIETY

The first topic is the pros and cons of managing your anxiety. The reason is that a really important step in growing courage is making the active decision to do it. Of course, you *already* know a lot about courage, even *before* you deliberately decide to increase it. But even when courage is already present, making the decision to increase it can be a powerful and important step, and it's worth talking about.

Now, it often helps to make and support a decision to change if, around the time you are contemplating the change, you anticipate the pros and cons of making that change. This is the same kind of thing that lots of us do, either deliberately or without fully realizing it, in everyday decisions. You might even make a little chart, like this one.

Pros	Cons

Figure D.1 Pros and cons.

Here is an example of a sample pros and cons worksheet for a decision about whether or not to get a dog.

Pros	Cons
Companionship	Cost of dog
Protection	$ - food
I really want one!	$ - vet, shots
Special in childhood	Plan for vacation, cost
For my child (grandma, etc.)	Time, responsibility, for walks
Ice breaker to meet people	Kids might not feed him even though they say they will
Walking the dog will give me exercise!	I might be sorry I got him and feel guilty
	Would have to face pain when I lose him some day

Figure D.2 Pros and cons of getting a dog.

The more specific you can be, the better, for both the pros and the cons. When you complete your chart, you might think of it as being like a balance scale. You probably notice that it's not just the "number" of items on a side that makes a difference. Some items just simply are more important! And if the "weight" of the pros is greater than the "weight" of the cons, you get the dog. You know that there will be costs, financial and otherwise, but if that's the decision that feels right for you, somehow you will find some ways to deal with them.

The same process applies to managing anxiety. For example, for the very common concern of "anxiety driving on the freeway," there are pros, the good things it will bring into your life when you grow braver there, and there may be cons as well. One might ask: How can there be cons for getting braver? Isn't getting braver a "good" thing? Of course, it is! At the same time, even good things sometimes bring challenges to our lives. It's like the saying "You'd better not wish for something; you just might get it." The implication is that once you've "got it," you have to deal with it. Cons are worth considering, because being solution-focused absolutely doesn't mean that we can't talk about concerns or problems. Talking openly about them helps us to discover solutions.

Here is a sample chart for "building your courage so you can drive on freeways."

Pros **(of building courage for freeways)**	**Cons** **(of building courage for freeways)**
Get to work—keep my job	Might panic
Get to school	Could get in an accident
Water park!	Money for gas
Be able to drive my mom to the hospital if there's an emergency (or anyone, if they need it)	And tolls
Independence	And parking...
Share driving on trips	I might get in the wrong lane and get lost
Feel normal	Deal with traffic, gridlock
Proud that I'm not letting this stop me!	Lose my reason not to go to those family things

Figure D.3 Pros and cons of driving on freeway.

The con of "losing your reason not to go" might benefit from a little explanation. Suppose that you are regularly invited to family get-togethers in a city that is about two hours away by freeway. Everyone understands that you usually don't go because you don't drive on freeways and need to find a ride. You actually don't like the gatherings much anyway. So once your relatives discover that you are driving more now, you can't as easily say "I can't drive there." Maybe you'll go, and maybe you won't—an example of our "You can—and you don't have to" perspective—but regardless of which you choose, your driving has led to a dilemma you (mostly) didn't have before. As someone once said about a situation like this, "It was so easy when I just didn't do freeways!"

If you are a friend or relative of someone who experiences anxiety, you can make a chart of the pros and cons for *you* of *that person* becoming more courageous. Many of the things would be exactly the same as they were on the previous chart. Others might have an additional "twist" to them."There might be "good selfish" pros, things that might be good for *you,* apart from or in addition to any good things they bring to the other person. For the cons, too, some would be exactly the same as on the first chart. In addition, from the "good selfish" perspective, there could also be cons or concerns as your friend or relative grows braver.

The additional thoughts on a significant other's chart might include these.

Pros for me (of my significant other building courage for freeways)	**Cons for me (of my significant other building courage for freeways)**
If significant other gets a job, less pressure on me	Significant other might spend more $
My significant other will be able to do more errands	I might miss my role as the "needed driver" and our time in the car together
More time for me—don't have to go along on all my significant other's trips	My significant other might get too independent!

Figure D.4 Pros and cons of my significant other driving on freeway.

The reader is now invited to use (or reproduce) the grid on the following page to create a personal chart, for some area in your life where you want to grow your courage. If you are a support person, you can do your chart either for pros and cons of more courage in some area of your own, or you might consider the perspective described previously.

Worksheet D.1

SOLUTION FOCUSED ANXIETY MANAGEMENT

WORKSHEET: PROS AND CONS

Pros	Cons

Sometimes people wonder: What if there aren't any cons? What if there is absolutely nothing "bad" that you can think of? Someone who wants to feel less panicky might say: "What could possibly be 'bad' about not having panic attacks any more?"

If there are no cons, there are no cons! Please don't feel as though you have to create them! However, you might want to consider whether there is anything like this one that sometimes comes up for the "panic attack situation": What if I get overconfident, and then a panic attack comes on when I'm not expecting it? Would that feel really horrible?

As you do this exercise, don't be afraid to anticipate the cons, because identifying them in advance will make you better able to deal with them. To evaluate the pros, you might reflect on some of these questions: What might I gain in my personal life? In social situations? At work? In how I feel about myself? In how I view other people? In little details of my world that will make so much of a difference?

Once your list is complete, you might think of it as being like a balance scale, with the pros on one side and the cons on the other. As you imagine it that way, notice which side tilts down because it is heavier. You may not have very many cons, or you may have some fairly substantial ones. If the latter is the case for you, that's quite valuable to be aware of, because it gives you a head start on discovering some creative ways of dealing with them. Meanwhile, remind yourself of your pros! Reminding yourself of your pros is a powerful way to sustain your commitment to change.

There is another thing you can do with this chart. You can add a third column: "How I might deal with each con."

Pros	Cons	How I might deal with each con

Figure D.5 Pros, cons, and how I might cope with each con.

Here, you don't pay much attention to the pros. They're still there, of course, and they're wonderfully important in so many ways, but here, you focus on the cons and ways of coping with them. Here is an example of how the third column might be completed for the freeway example described earlier.

Pros (of building courage for freeways)	Cons (of building courage for freeways)	How I might deal with each con
Get to work—keep my job	Might panic	Might not! Ride the wave. I can feel sensations and still drive safely.
Get to school	Could get in an accident	True. Anyone could. But those other drivers want to get there safely, too. If something happens, I will do what I need to do to get through it.
Water park!	Money for gas	I'll have to plan where I'll go and how much I'll need for gas. If I need to cut back elsewhere, I can figure out how or drive less.
Be able to drive my mom to the hospital if there's an emergency (or anyone, if they need it)	And tolls	Same as above
Independence	And parking…	Same as above
Share driving on trips	I might get in the wrong lane and get lost	I will plan, and I will get off when I can. I have my phone and my GPS.
Feel normal	Deal with traffic, gridlock	Anticipate it, acceptance, and some music on the sound system.
Proud that I'm not letting this stop me!	Lose my reason not to go to those family things	I can talk to them directly and let them know that I won't always be there. I can do this, and our relationship will survive and maybe even grow stronger.

Figure D.6 Pros, cons, and coping with cons for driving on freeway.

You can use the following blank chart when you want to add "How I might deal with each con" to this exercise.

Worksheet D.2

SOLUTION FOCUSED ANXIETY MANAGEMENT
WORKSHEET: PROS, CONS, AND DEALING WITH CONS

Pros	Cons	How I might deal with each con

Here is another variation that can be especially helpful with decisions. This one is called "the cons and the cons" because it doesn't address the pros at all.

Cons of X	Cons of Y

Figure D.7 Cons of X and cons of Y.

Here is an example done by someone who is considering quitting a job that feels stressful and wants to use this tool to support making a decision.

Cons of quitting job	Cons of staying at job
No salary or benefits!	Have to deal with boss
Feel bad about myself	Feel unfulfilled
Might regret it later	Always tense

Figure D.8 Cons of X and cons of Y for job example.

You might notice there is some space between the two columns. In that space, you add another column: "How I would deal with each con," for each side. The completed chart looks like this.

Cons of quitting job	**How I might deal with each con**	**Cons of staying at job**	**How I might deal with each con**
No salary or benefits!	Look for a job, use savings	Have to deal with boss	Reflect on what has helped before
Feel bad about myself	Reach out to people, do something there wasn't time for when I was working	Feel unfulfilled	Imagine that work has suddenly become more fun
Might regret it later	Allow mourning, be gentle with myself, find other good road to go down	Always tense	Use tools from this class

Figure D.9 Cons of X and cons of Y for job example, completed chart.

The message is that either choice has a downside—that's the cons column—but each one also has some ways of coping, taking care of yourself, getting through. Whichever fork in the road you take, there are ways you can take care of you.

The following blank chart is for your use in decision making, either now or as a tool for the future.

Worksheet D.3

SOLUTION FOCUSED ANXIETY MANAGEMENT

WORKSHEET: "THE CONS AND THE CONS"

Complete the two cons columns first. Then go back and complete the two "How I might deal with each con" columns.

Cons of X	How I might deal with each con	Cons of Y	How I might deal with each con

I CAN'T VERSUS I DON'T WANT TO

Suppose you woke up tomorrow and, for some reason, you didn't have your fears or anxiety any more. Once you figured that out, you certainly would be delighted. There would probably be some things that you couldn't wait to start doing, or places you'd like to go. And there would probably be other things that you still wouldn't be eagerly anticipating. For example, most of us don't actively look forward to doing our income tax or getting blood drawn.

So there might well be situations, or maybe certain interactions, that you avoid now "because of your anxiety" that you still would like to avoid. That's the most normal thing in the world! But you may not have had much practice recently thinking about what and whom you would *prefer* to avoid. After all, if you're in a panic, who has the luxury of contemplating "Hmm, I'm not sure I want to do this"? When you're in high anxiety mode, whether you *want* to or not is irrelevant. Instead, it's more like this: "Get me out of here! I *can't*!"

This section suggests that sometimes it is helpful to start thinking about how you would, or *could*, get out of situations if you chose to do so. You may choose *not* to avoid them 99% of the time—you may be delighted to finally enter those situations—but it's important to remember that you have the *right* not to want to do certain things—sometimes or at all—even if you're not afraid of them. It's like our perspective of "You can—and you don't have to," that emerges repeatedly in this program.

This means transforming "I can't..." to "I don't want to." Or "I'd rather not." Or sometimes, the more accurate feeling is mixed, sort of like this: "Part of me wants to, and part of me doesn't want to, and the part that doesn't want to feels stronger right now."

I can't...	I don't want to...
	I'd rather not...
	Part of me wants to, and part of me doesn't want to, and the part of me that doesn't want to feels stronger right now.

Figure D.10 I can versus I don't want to.

Notice the *right now* in that last one. Notice how it leaves open the possibility that the other side, the one that "wants to" may feel stronger later on!

And you might notice which way you feel stronger, emotionally: saying "I can't" or "I'd rather not." For many people, the "I don't want to" option feels better, more like a personal choice.

So here is an idea for an experiment: When the immediate thought about something is "I can't do that! I would lose it if I did that," you might want to experiment with substituting something like this: "Part of me wants to, and part of me doesn't want to, and the part of me that doesn't want to feels stronger right now"—in preparation for a time when you truly will feel less afraid.

Think how interesting it would be if our society taught a class called "Ambivalence 101" at every level of the educational system. Ambivalence means mixed feelings. The overarching theme of "Ambivalence 101" would be this: Mixed feelings are normal.

Ambivalence = Mixed feelings
Ambivalence 101 = Mixed feelings are normal!!

In preschool, we would teach our kids: It's perfectly normal to *love* to go to school because they have cool toys and to *hate* to go to school because they make me lie on my rug at nap time. Or in fourth grade: I love soccer because the meets are in neat places, and I hate it when Coach yells at me. Or in high school: I want to go to the dance, but I have a zit and am afraid no one will want to dance with me.

No one teaches us that mixed feelings are normal, but they are. They are *so* very normal, and they are everywhere. So that leads to a little experiment you can do with mixed feelings. You can notice them in all kinds of everyday places—most of which, by the way, may be totally separate from anxiety—and you can be curious about how many you can discover. You might notice examples like these: "I want to eat that, but I don't want to get fat," or "I want that new gadget, but I don't want to spend the money." Exercising your "mixed feeling muscles" is wonderful practice for identifying and coping with the mixed feelings that so often accompany anxiety.

ASSERTION

The next topic is *assertiveness* and how it interfaces with solution focused anxiety management. Assertiveness (or assertion) may be a concept with which you are already familiar. The process described earlier, saying "I'd rather not..." or "I don't want to..." (and I *do* want to...., maybe even more important!) often is supported by assertiveness.

Assertiveness means expressing, or *asserting*, what you want, what you are feeling, or what you plan to do. Without violating the rights of anyone else, you value your own. You say what you want directly and kindly. Assertion is different from *passivity*, where you allow others to choose for you. It's also different from *aggression*, where you protect your rights but might put other people down in the process. And it's different from a *passive aggressive* position, where on the surface you go along with other people but find a way to get back at them in some way later.

So here is an example of passive, assertive, aggressive, and passive aggressive handling of the same situation: A friend is asking for a ride to the airport at a time that is really inconvenient for you.

A *passive* response might be to agree to do it. You might be aware of sensations in your body, maybe your chest tightening or your breathing speeding up, and there might be a flash of emotional arousal, but mostly you are aware of "not wanting to make waves." You don't want to risk having this person mad at you.

An *assertive* response might grow from awareness of all those mixed feelings and sensations. You might be conscious of being torn, but on the "balance scale" of "Do I risk having someone mad at me?" versus "Do I need to pay more attention to my own needs right now?" the need to take good care of yourself is heavier. So you might say something like this: "I'm afraid that isn't going to work for me. I know it's a hassle to get to the airport, but this time I'm not going to be able to help out." You may say it in a way that conveys empathy and kindness—and that at the same time is clear. Your attitude and tone communicate that your decision about the airport trip is absolutely not a rejection of your friend. You recognize that there may be some "pushback," and that if it comes, you can tolerate it and maintain what you need to do to take good care of you. You may feel some pride that you did this, even though it wasn't totally comfortable.

An *aggressive* response might sound something like this: "Are you crazy? You know I can't do it then! You just expect me to drop everything because you suddenly need something. You have a hell of a lot of nerve!"

Here is a *passive aggressive* stance. When you're passive aggressive, you do what's being requested, but you also somehow "get back at" the other person. So in this example, you might say "Yes" and then show up a little late for the airport ride, or you might roll your eyes or say something sarcastic or hurtful. We may or may not be consciously aware that we're doing these things.

Can you hear and feel the difference between the assertive and aggressive responses? It's a crucial difference, because sometimes people feel as though the only alternative to being passive is to be aggressive or abrasive. Some people grew up in families where it felt as though people alternated between never expressing their wishes, on one hand, and exploding in anger, on the other. Or maybe we saw role models being passive aggressive. If we haven't seen people in our lives do a lot of assertive responding, and if we haven't yet discovered that assertiveness eventually strengthens relationships, it naturally is going to take a little more practice to grow our assertiveness now.

You may have heard of assertiveness before. And you may be thinking that, as a concept, it certainly makes sense. But you may be wondering: What does assertiveness have to do with anxiety management?

The answer to that question is this: As people grow braver, and as they can do things they didn't do in the past, they may realize that there is something they *can* do but don't *want* to do. Here is an example: a woman who has been afraid of elevators for a very long time, but who is riding them now. Her co-workers go to lunch every Friday at an upscale restaurant on the 15th floor of a nearby office building. She has never gone along, and everyone has always understood that the reason was that she "didn't do elevators." But now, it's only a matter of time until someone sees her on an elevator and says, "You're doing elevators now. Now you can do our Friday lunches!"

She recognizes that she has a dilemma. She doesn't really *want* to eat out on a weekly basis. She thinks, "Yuck. That place is expensive. It's a lot of calories that I don't need right before the weekend, and these people are not exactly my best friends. But I have to work with them, and I don't want to seem weird or not social. Yuck. You know, it was way easier when I just didn't do elevators!"

So, she has some choices. She could be passive and just start going, even though she doesn't want to. She could be assertive and say something like this: "I'm not really up for going every week. But I'd love to be able to join you when there's a birthday or special occasion." She recognizes that there is a "risk" here that they won't want her occasionally if she isn't a member of "the every week gang," but she knows she can tolerate that possibility and say what feels right for her. She could also be aggressive and retort, "Just because you all take two-hour lunches on company time doesn't mean I'm going to start doing that!" Or she could be passive aggressive by going along and regularly "forgetting" to bring money or a credit card. This situation illustrates how sometimes, as we grow braver, we face choices and decisions that may not have come up for us before.

Here are some additional thoughts about assertiveness. Being assertive involves an attitude: truly believing that assertion, rather than manipulation, submission, or hostility, ultimately leads to more satisfying personal relationships. You absolutely do not have to become unaware of, or insensitive to, the other person's feelings to be able to express your own. Just the opposite is the case, because the process is enhanced when you hear and appreciate the other person's perspective.

Sometimes people do fine with assertion when first bringing something up, but when given some "pushback," they either back off into passivity or explode into aggression. Once you have said what you want to say and perhaps repeated it, doing something different from "being assertive" for a while may be more helpful. (*What* you do actually may not matter a lot, as long as you do something different!)

And just because you *know how* to be assertive doesn't mean you will *choose* to do so on every possible occasion. You can ask yourself: How important is this situation? Will this make a difference later? (Remember again the wonderful concept of "I can—and I don't have to....")

In addition to the times that saying "No" supports us, there are many, many times when assertion reminds us to say "Yes": "Yes" to the things we want to do, to our dreams and goals (which may be different from the other person's, but not necessarily incompatible with them). Maybe we can say "Yes" to everyone's needs, if we think creatively, "outside the box." We can say "Yes" to doing things that are important to us even when anxiety has been there. Sometimes saying "Yes" might include saying "Yes" to caution, welcoming it into our lives, as one ingredient of the solution—not the entire solution, but one component of it.

Here is one additional thing about assertion. Although assertion is always available for expression of *your* feelings, it doesn't always succeed in changing the other person's feelings or getting the results you want. Sometimes, no matter how assertive you are, no matter *what* you say or do, a situation or person may not respond the way you want. When that happens, you can still take really good care of yourself by recognizing that you have options. You might decide to use acceptance. You might be curious about creative ways you can make things work for you. And you can eventually decide to change a job or living situation or relationship that isn't good for you. You can take whatever amount of time you need to decide. Again, "you can—and you don't have to." Knowing how to be assertive isn't the only tool you use in your life in making decisions, but it's another "tool in the toolbox" for expressing your feelings and taking care of you.

So if assertiveness is a useful concept for your life, you can notice yourself in a whole range of different situations. Where are you already being assertive? You might be curious about instances of good assertion and ability to tolerate "pushback" that are already there, even if you haven't been paying attention to them. Noticing your good assertion will help you to continue it. Again, you certainly don't have to be assertive all the time! Sometimes, it feels right to make a different choice.

And, if at some point you notice that you haven't made the assertive choice, and you think you might like to do so in the future, you might let yourself think about what the assertive choice would look and sound like. Like any other skill, assertiveness grows with baby steps and repeated practice, even in the presence of discomfort.

DEVELOPMENTAL TASKS

The next topic addresses how life issues interface with anxiety. Sometimes people are so focused on their anxiety concerns that they lose sight of what issues they would be facing at this point in their lives if they just had a "normal" amount of anxiety. You might notice here that "normal anxiety" does *not* mean *no* anxiety, because, as this program emphasizes in so many ways, *some* anxiety is absolutely normal!

Consider how children go through developmental stages: weaning, toilet training, separating from their parents. As adults, we go through developmental stages as well, regardless of whether we feel a lot of anxiety or don't feel very much anxiety. It can be helpful to reflect on what those stages are, and which one or ones you and the people in your life are "in," and what the tasks and issues of those stages are. It also may be useful to think about how you are facing these things. There are multiple ways of dealing with issues, *even if* you have some fear. And when you are less anxious, or put a different spin on things, you may be able to deal with these tasks even more creatively than you are now.

The following chart summarizes some of the things people often think about and face at different times of life, in a framework adapted from Erik Erikson.[1] It includes common tasks and Erikson's view of the "core issues" at each stage.

[1] See Erikson (1959) in References.

Phase of Adulthood	Core Issues	Tasks and topics people address during this time of life
Adolescence (emerging adulthood)	Identity vs. Identity diffusion	We establish what kind of person we are going to be as adults, separate from family of origin while still connected to it. We may shift values in the process of establishing career, relationships, lifestyle. We find a way to balance dependence and independence.
Young adulthood	Intimacy (commitment) vs. Isolation (lack of commitment)	We consider and often make commitments to relationships, work/career/education, values. We "put down roots" or get "on the road" to a goal. We may have increasing financial responsibility.
Middle adulthood	Generativity vs. Stagnation	We reconsider earlier choices and may reaffirm them or make changes in work, relationships, and other activities. There may be multiple financial demands on us. We may be more aware of health concerns, aging, and mortality, and that awareness helps us to make choices that enhance life now.
Older adulthood	Wisdom vs. Despair	We may face retirement transitions and choices about use of leisure time. There may be losses of health, strength. Our housing needs may change. We have connections with, and get support from, the younger generation. Widowhood and bereavement bring appropriate mourning. We may be more patient. We may have a larger sense of "the bigger picture."

Figure D.11 Phases of adulthood, issues, and tasks.

Again, you may be wondering: All of this may be very profound, but what does it have to do with solution focused anxiety management? The answer is this: If you think of life as a journey down "the road of life," sometimes we hit "bumps in the road." And if you are a body reactor, guess what your body and mind are going to do when it hits those bumps: It's going to do its thing, whatever that may be. You can recognize that and ride through it and use your tools to get back on track. That process can make a tremendous difference.

So, you are invited to reflect on these three questions:

1. What issues am I facing in my life these days?
2. How would I be dealing with those things if I just had a normal level of anxiety (not "no" anxiety)?
3. What does that tell me about how I might deal with those things even with my level of anxiety?

When we start talking about "a normal level of anxiety," people sometimes ask: What "counts" as a normal level of anxiety? In the same class, we might have someone who is afraid of driving but flies in airplanes without difficulty. Someone else may be afraid of shots but drives just fine. If you think about the short list of things that some people are afraid of—shots, public speaking, sweating, eating, sex, swimming, losing one's job, foreclosure, having enough money to retire in times of unprecedented financial meltdown, staying at home alone, getting a haircut, crossing the street, earthquakes, hurricanes, wildfires—you probably will recognize some places where you already have a completely appropriate degree of caution.

So, you are invited to reflect for a moment on this question: What is an area where you feel as though your degree of anxiety or caution is *appropriate*? Not excessive, but fully appropriate. Maybe it's one of the ones mentioned earlier. Or maybe it's something different.

Now you are invited to consider how you take appropriate precautions in that area and what that tells you about your capacity for healthy, appropriate anxiety.

SUGGESTIONS FOR PRACTICE

Here are some ideas for experimenting with these things on your own. Please use *any* ideas or suggestions from this class or these readings in a way that works for you.

One suggestion is to continue to reflect on our three questions. Again, they are: What issues am I facing these days? How would I be dealing with them with a normal level of anxiety (not "no" anxiety)? What does that tell me about how I might deal with those things even *with* my level of anxiety? And you might consider how you already know how to take appropriate precautions, probably in so many ways, and what that tells you about your capacity for healthy, appropriate caution.

Here are a few other things to experiment with:

You might continue to think and/or write about the pros and cons of making changes—and that really interesting idea of "how I would deal with each con," or our variation about "the cons and the cons."

You might want to experiment with changing "I can't..." to "I don't want to...," or "Part of me wants to, and part of me doesn't want to, and the part that doesn't is stronger right now."

You might decide to strengthen your "mixed feelings noticing muscles"—this sort of goes along with the previous one. As with any other skill, your awareness of mixed feelings and your comfort with them will grow with practice.

And if assertiveness is something you want to grow, you might want to notice times when it is already present in your life. You might notice the times you use it to say "Yes" as well as "No," because those choices might be especially important. You might decide to play with assertiveness or to experiment with it, maybe at first in tiny ways, and you can be curious about what you discover.

If you have not already done so, please see the following End of Session Form.

SOLUTION FOCUSED ANXIETY MANAGEMENT

END OF SESSION FORM

Name ____________________________ Date____________________

When you first called for help with your anxiety	Your level of concern or caution is appropriate, not excessive. Anxiety is not so much a problem any more

0 1 2 3 4 5 6 7 8 9 10

What do you want to remember from today?

What helps you to cope with discomfort, uncertainty, worry, and stress?

What else do you want to continue, because you know it works for you?

REFERENCES

Beck, A. (1993). Cognitive therapy: Past, present, and future. *Journal of Consulting and Clinical Psychology, 61*(2), 194–198.

Bliss, V. (2010). Extreme listening. In T. Nelson (Ed.), *Doing something different: Solution-focused brief therapy practices* (pp. 109–116). New York: Routledge.

Connie, E. & Metcalf, L. (Eds.) (2008). *The Art of Solution Focused Therapy*. New York: Springer.

Craske, M., Rowe, M., Lewin, M., & Noriega-Dimitri, R. (1997). Interoceptive exposure versus breathing retraining within cognitive-behavioural therapy for panic disorder with agoraphobia. *British Journal of Clinical Psychology, 36*(1), 85–99.

De Jong, P., & Bavelas, J. (2010, November). *What is different about SFBT?* Plenary, Solution Focused Brief Therapy Association 2010 Conference, Banff, Alberta, Canada.

de Shazer, S. (1985). *Keys to solution in brief therapy*. New York: Norton.

de Shazer, S. (1988). *Clues: Investigating solutions in brief therapy*. New York: Norton.

de Shazer, S., Dolan, Y., Korman, H., Trepper, T., McCollum, E., & Berg, I. (2007). *More than miracles: The state of the art of solution-focused brief therapy*. New York: Haworth.

Dolan, Y. (2009, November). *Advanced solution-focused listening*. Albany, New York: Workshop, Solution Focused Brief Therapy Association Conference.

Dolan, Y. (2011, November). *SFBT: Practice that makes a difference to the client*. Bakersfield, CA: Keynote address, Solution Focused Brief Therapy Association Conference.

Duclos-Robinson, A. (2009, June). *Diagnosis and treatment planning*. San Diego, CA: Workshop, Kaiser Permanente Educational Meeting.

Duncan, B. (2010). *On becoming a better therapist*. Washington, DC: American Psychological Association.

Duncan, B., Hubble, M., & Miller, S. (1997). *Psychotherapy with "impossible" cases: The efficient treatment of therapy veterans*. New York: Norton.

Eifert, G., & Forsyth, J. (2005). *Acceptance & commitment therapy for anxiety disorders: A practitioner's treatment guide to using mindfulness, acceptance, and values-based behavior change strategies*. Oakland, CA: New Harbingers.

Ellis, A. (2003). Early theories and practices of rational emotive behavior theory and how they have been augmented and revised during the last three decades. *Journal of Rational-Emotive & Cognitive-Behavior Therapy, 21*(3/4).

Erikson, E. (1959). Identity and the life cycle. *Psychological Issues, 1*, 1.

Fisch, R., Weakland, J., & Segal, L. (1982). *The tactics of change*. San Francisco: John Wiley & Sons, Inc.

Fiske, H. (2005). Five small-group exercises for experiential learning of SFBT. *Journal of Family Psychotherapy, 16*(1/2), 155–158.

Fiske, H. (2008). *Hope in action: Solution-focused conversations about suicide*. New York: Routledge.

Fiske, H., & Moon, H. (2011, November). *Solution focused training for trainers*. Bakersfield, CA. Solution Focused Brief Therapy Association Conference.

Fraser, J., & Solovey, A. (2007). *Second-order change in psychotherapy: The golden thread that unites effective treatments*. Washington, DC: American Psychological Association.

George, E., Iveson, C., Ratner, H., & Shennan, G. (2009). *BRIEFER: A solution-focused practice manual*. London: BRIEF.

Gilligan, C. (1982). *In a different voice: Psychological theory and women's development*. Cambridge, MA: Harvard University Press.

Hayes, S. (2006, October). *Confronting avoidance*. San Francisco, CA: Presentation, Psychotherapy Networker Symposium West.

Hayes, S., Follette, V., & Linehan, M. (2004). *Mindfulness and acceptance: Expanding the cognitive behavioral tradition*. New York: Guilford.

Hernández, P., Gangsei, D., & Engstrom, D. (2007). Vicarious resilience: A new concept in work with those who survive trauma. *Family Process, 46*(2), 229–241.

Holton, C. (2000). *The 5-4-3-2-1 technique: Charles Holton, LCSW.* Retrieved from http://www.quotationspage.com/subjects/life/.

Hubbard, E. (2012, May 30). *The quotations page.* Retrieved from http://www.quotationspage.com/quote/101.html.

Hubbard, E. (2012, May 30). *Tivate.* Retrieved from http://tivate.com/quotes/greatest-mistake-quote-elbert-hubbard.

Huppert, J., & Roth, D. (2003). Treating obsessive-compulsive disorder with exposure and response prevention. *The Behavior Analyst Today, 4*(1), 66–70.

Kotz, D. (2007). Get happy and live longer. *U.S. News and World Report, 141*(24), 48–49.

Lambert, M. (1992). Psychotherapy outcome research: Implications for integrative and eclectic therapists. In J. Norcross, & M. Goldfried (Eds.), *Handbook of psychotherapy integration* (pp. 94–129). New York: Basic Books.

Lebow, J. (2007). A look at the evidence. *Psychotherapy Networker, 31*(2), 44–47.

Lennon, J. (1980). *Beautiful boy.* On Double Fantasy [vinyl], Los Angeles: Geffen Records.

Luthe, W., & Schultz, J. (1969). *Autogenic therapy.* New York: Grune and Stratton.

Miller, W., & Rollick, S. (2002). *Motivational interviewing: Preparing people for change.* New York: Guilford.

Norcross, J. (2005, April). *Tailoring the therapeutic relationship to the individual patient: Evidence-based practices.* San Diego, CA: Workshop presented at Kaiser Permanente Educational Meeting.

Norem, J. (2001). *The positive power of negative thinking.* New York: Basic Books.

Nylund, D., & Corsiglia, V. (1994). Becoming solution-forced in brief therapy: Remembering something important we already know. *Journal of Systemic Therapies, 13*, 5–11.

O'Hanlon, B. (2003). *A guide to inclusive therapy: 26 methods of respectful resistance-dissolving therapy.* New York: Norton.

Prochaska, J., & DiClemente, C. (1992). *The transtheoretical approach.* New York: Basic Books.

Quick, E. (1983, Spring). *Brief integrative phobia treatment.* Paper presentation, White Plains, New York: Fourth National Phobia Conference.

Quick, E. (1996, December). *Anxiety scores before and after Anxiety II Class.* Unpublished document, San Diego, CA: Kaiser Permanente.

Quick, E. (2001). Strategic solution focused therapy. In R. Corsini (Ed.), *Handbook of innovative psychotherapies* (2nd ed., pp. 660–669). New York: John Wiley & Sons, Inc.

Quick, E. (2008). *Doing what works in brief therapy: A strategic solution focused approach* (2nd ed.). San Diego, CA: Elsevier.

Quick, E. (2010, February). *The doing what works approach to solution focused therapy.* Amsterdam, The Netherlands: Mastercourse.

Quick, E. (2012). *Core competencies in the solution-focused and strategic therapies: Becoming a highly competent solution-focused and strategic therapist.* New York: Routledge.

Quick, E., & Gizzo, D. (2007). The doing what works group: A quantitative and qualitative analysis of solution focused group therapy. *Journal of Family Psychotherapy, 18*(3), 65–85.

Rosen, S. (Ed.), (1991). *My voice will go with you: The teaching tales of Milton H. Erickson, M.D.* New York: Norton.

Saavedra, J. (2006, February 14). *The first effective unified protocol for anxiety disorders.* http://www.amazon.com/Acceptance-Commitment-Therapy-Anxiety-Disorders/dp/1572244275#_.

Segal, J., Williams, J., & Teasdale, J. (2002). *Mindfulness-based cognitive therapy for depression.* New York: Guilford.

Seligman, M., Rashid, T., & Parks, A. (2006). Positive psychotherapy. *American Psychologist, 61*(8), 774–788.

Sharry, J., Madden, B., & Darmody, M. (2003). *Becoming a solution detective: Identifying your clients' strengths in practical, brief therapy.* New York: Haworth.

Simon, J., & Nelson, T. (Eds.), (2007). *Solution-focused brief practice with long-term clients in mental health services: I am more than my label*. New York: Haworth.

Sperry, L. (2010). *Core competencies in counseling and psychotherapy: Becoming a highly competent and effective therapist*. New York: Routledge.

Trepper, T., McCollum, E., De Jong, P., Korman, H., Gingerich, W., & Franklin, C. (2010, April 10). *Solution focused therapy treatment manual for working with individuals*. Retrieved from thesfbta.org. website: http://www.sfbta.org/researchDownloads.html.

Trepper, T., Treyger, S., & Yalowitzh, J. (2007, November). *Solution focused sex therapy. Workshop, Solution Focused Brief Therapy Association Conference*. Toronto: Canada.

Walser, R. (2011, June). *Introduction to acceptance and commitment therapy*. San Diego, CA: Workshop, Kaiser Permanente Educational Meeting.

Walter, J., & Peller, J. (1992). *Becoming solution-focused in brief therapy*. New York: Bruner Mazel.

Watzlawick, P., Weakland, J., & Fisch, R. (1974). *Change: Principles of problem formation and problem resolution*. New York: Norton.

Weekes, C. (1978). *Peace from nervous suffering*. New York: Bantam Books.

Wilson, R. (2002, December). *Treatment of obsessive compulsive disorder*. Orlando, FL: Milton Erickson Foundation Brief Therapy Conference.

Wilson, R. (2002, December). *Treatment of worry and generalized anxiety disorder*. Orlando, FL: Milton Erickson Foundation Brief Therapy Conference.

Wilson, R. (2009). *Don't panic* (3rd ed.). New York: Harper Collins.

Wolpe, J., & Lazarus, A. (1966). *Behavior therapy techniques: A guide to the treatment of neuroses*. Oxford: Pergamon Press.

Yapko, M. (2011, September 24). *Interview with Reid Wilson*. Retrieved from http://www.socwel.ku.edu/jimk/810handouts/AdvancedClinician.htm.

SUBJECT INDEX

Note: Page numbers followed by "f", "t" and "b" indicate figures, tables and boxes respectively.

A

FSC
www.fsc.org
MIX
Papier | Fördert gute Waldnutzung
FSC® C083411

Kolibri 360 GmbH
Ferdinand-Jühlke-Straße 7
99095 Erfurt, Deutschland
produktsicherheit@kolibri360.de